Effective Group Communication

How to Get Action by Working in Groups

Effective Group Communication

How to Get Action by Working in Groups

Ernest Stech & Sharon A. Ratliffe

NTC NATIONAL TEXTBOOK COMPANY • Lincolnwood, Illinois U.S.A.

1987 Printing

Copyright © 1985 by National Textbook Company
4255 West Touhy Avenue
Lincolnwood (Chicago), Illinois 60646-1975 U.S.A.
All rights reserved. No part of this book may
be reproduced, stored in a retrieval system, or
transmitted in any form or by any means, electronic,
mechanical, photocopying, recording or otherwise,
without the prior permission of National Textbook Company.
Manufactured in the United States of America
Library of Congress Catalog Number: 84-60546

6789 ML 98765432

APR 88

We appreciate the learning and success we have experienced while working in groups with many people. We dedicate this book to all of those people.

CONTENTS

SECTION 5 GROUP PROCESS

SECTION 6 FUNCTIONS AND MESSAGES

SECTION 7 PROCEDURES AND LEADERSHIP

SECTION 8 SETTINGS

FOREWORD

We very well may be living in the age of the group. In business, education, labor, religion, government, and most other aspects of life, plans are discussed and decisions are made by people working in groups. A large number of books exist on such topics as small groups, group discussion, group dynamics, and quality circles. Many books focus on research. Most of the books are quite technical and are not particularly helpful in practice. On the other hand, books do exist on how to lead or be a member of a small group. Unfortunately, many of these books are not based on theory or research.

This book covers the important issues in group work as defined by people who have studied groups in depth. This book approaches these important issues in a way that makes sense to people who must work in such groups. The book is divided into eight major sections:

1. Background

2. Foundations

3. Formal and Informal Structures

4. People and Their Relationships

5. Group Process

6. Functions and Messages

7. Procedures and Leadership

8. Settings

Each of the first seven sections has three chapters. A common format is used for all sections: The first two chapters present concepts and principles illustrated with case studies and examples. The third chapter in each section is devoted to practical applications of the concepts. We will describe the content of each section more closely.

Section One: Background

As the section title suggests, these three chapters provide you with background material for the remaining chapters in the book. Chapter 1 discusses the variety of groups that exist and provides a way of classifying them in terms of organizations, communities, and professional associations. In Chapter 2, the focus is the communication process as it occurs in groups. Chapter 3 provides an analysis of the impact of ethics (values) on group work. The chapter includes a review of four key values in American society: democracy, individuality, honesty, and loyalty.

Section Two: Foundations

This section provides the basic foundation you will need to understand how groups function. In Chapter 4, you will become familiar with the factors outside of the group itself which affect how the group functions internally. Next, Chapter 5 focuses on the distinction between formal and informal ways of functioning. Chapter 6 will help you understand how to match groups to the demands put on them by external forces in the environment.

Section Three: Formal and Informal Structures

In Chapter 7, you will become aware of the formal structure of groups. Chapter 8 focuses on the informal structure, the relationships people form with one another. In Chapter 9 you will learn how to put your knowledge of group structure to practical use in order to better understand and complete group tasks.

Section Four: People and Their Relationships

The structure of a group consists of people connected to each other through lines of communication. Each line or link represents a relationship. Chapter 10 is a discussion of people and their motivations and needs. Chapter 11 focuses on the relationships among people. In Chapter 12, you will learn specific skills needed to develop and maintain effective relationships in group work.

Section Five: Group Process

As people form structure and relate to each other in groups, they interact. We refer to this group interaction as *process*. Changes occur over time in what is said, how it is said, and who says it. Group process is dynamic. Chapter 13 focuses on group process within meetings. In Chapter 14, the process that occurs between meetings is explored. Chapter 14 also discusses group process throughout the life of a group. Chapter 15 presents methods you can use to intervene in group process for the purpose of helping the group progress toward common goals and objectives.

Section Six: Functions and Messages

Every group has tasks. They set goals and objectives. Chapter 16 focuses on the group functions that must be performed for a group to accomplish its goals and tasks. Chapter 17 discusses the ways in which language can be used and misused in group discussions. Chapter 18 presents strategies that you can use to persuade groups to accept ideas.

Section Seven: Procedures and Leadership

There are a wide range of group procedures, from standard parliamentary procedure, problem solving, and planning, to more recently developed methods such as brainstorming, the nominal group technique, and the delphi method. Chapter 19 presents parliamentary procedure, problem solving, and planning. Brainstorming, the nominal group technique, and the delphi method are discussed in Chapter 20. Chapter 21 focuses on leadership. It provides practical methods for managing a group meeting. These methods involve membership and attendance, tasks and goals, time and length of meetings, and location and facilities.

Section Eight: Settings

This section includes five chapters, each of which focuses on a specific setting and the type of group you will find in it. In Chapter 22, you will learn about the features of work units. Work units are groups whose members do their jobs with other workers. The committee may well be the building block of modern corporations and communities. The committee is the focus of Chapter 23. The contemporary topic of negotiating and bargaining teams is presented in Chapter 24. Groups that set policy are discussed in Chapter 25. These include governing boards and commissions. The latest development in group work, teleconferencing, is the subject of Chapter 26.

This book can serve many uses. Obviously, it can be used as a textbook in such places as community colleges, professional schools, and in other settings where people need to learn the practical fundamentals of group work. This book also can be used as a text for professionals involved in continuing education, adult learning, or advanced-credit programs offered by professional associations or industry. However, the book also is intended for personal use as a practical handbook. For example, the chapter on leadership will provide a systematic checklist for planning meetings and for creating new groups. If you are going to join a group, the chapters in Section 2 on assessing the group situation and the functioning of a group can be extremely helpful.

Being an effective leader or member of a group is not an easy task. It does not come naturally. Perhaps it is because so many committees have been so poorly managed that people take seriously the saying that a camel is a horse designed by a committee. It is our hope that this book will contribute to fruitful and enjoyable group experiences for you, both now and in the future.

ELS
SAR

BACKGROUND

CHAPTER 1

THE VARIETIES OF GROUPS

Palo Alto, California, Friday morning. The Board of Directors of a local high technology company are meeting to discuss recent developments in the company and the industry:

CHIEF EXECUTIVE OFFICER: I want you all to know that we are going to need more capital to fund our developmental projects—and to keep up with our competition. Sales are going well. You can see this from the April sales report. However, we are not going to have enough surplus cash to carry on the developmental projects—particularly the one for the new high-speed printer head.

BOARD MEMBER: Harry, how do you propose to create this capital? Another stock offering? Seems a bad time to me.

CHAIRMAN OF THE BOARD: Well, that's one option. I think we have some others. Tell them, Harry.

CHIEF EXECUTIVE OFFICER: One possibility is a merger. We have just been approached by CMS Industries. They have put out feelers. And one attractive feature is that CMS has a surplus of cash right now— but not great growth potential. We have the growth potential but need the cash.

Flint, Michigan, afternoon of the same Friday. A quality of work life (QWL) group is meeting at a local automobile parts plant:

STEVE (Chairperson): Okay, Sheryl checked our ideas with the Tool Crib Department. They said it probably would work, but they would need to have about six weeks warning.

SHERYL: Yes. They really wanted to know about it ahead of time because our idea means they have some more record keeping.

SALLY: Why?

SHERYL: I don't know. Something to do with usage records.

PERRY: We better check that out some more. Management could come back and reject our idea if it means more record keeping.

STEVE: That's right. Sheryl, why don't you and Sally find out what kind of records they keep and how our change would affect their record keeping. I would like to see us make the change without more paper-work.

SHERYL: Okay.

Lubbock, Texas, early evening of the same Friday. A small group of neighbors are meeting during an outdoor barbecue:

BOB: What's the word on the zoning? Where do we stand?

CARL: Well, seems like the developer has got an inside track. Looks to me like the board is going to approve the apartments.

MILLY: We can't let that happen! You know how much traffic there is going to be down these streets if they put in those apartments? They are going to have another 300 to 500 cars a day going down each of our streets—it's the only way to get to the apartment buildings.

MARK: Why don't they create new access to the apartments on the north side?

BOB: Money. City doesn't have it. Developer won't put it up.

MARK: Then I say we fight!

Seattle, Washington, that Friday evening. Five members of a small local congregation are meeting in the living room of one member:

BETTY: Now our job is to put together a worship service for the Sunday after this one. Bob will be out of town and can't do the sermon. He thought it would be nice to have one Sunday worship service done completely by lay people.

EARL: Do you have any ideas, Betty?

BETTY: I wanted to hear from each of you.

DEL: We know from experience that Earl can get together a fine sermon. We could build a service around that.

EARL: I appreciate your confidence, Del, but I'm swamped with work right now. I just don't have the time. It takes me three or four evenings to write a sermon—with all the background study I need to do.

DEL: What else can we do?

SUSAN: Why not do a dialogical sermon?

DEL: What's that?

SUSAN: Well, two people talk to each other. One asks questions. The other answers. That sort of thing.

DEL: Who can do that?

EARL: Since Susan suggested it, she ought to do it!

On one Friday, a Board of Directors meets in Palo Alto to plan business strategy, a QWL group gets together to devise a better way to get work done, neighbors discuss the possible impact of a proposed new apartment complex, and several church members plan a worship service. Each situation involves people working together in groups to get something done.

On any given day in the United States, hundreds of thousands of small groups meet to get work done. Groups meet in schools, hospitals, churches, homes, businesses. Groups meet over lunch, early in the morning, late into the evening, during the work day, and on weekends. Corporate managers consult with one another and with subordinates. Doctors, nurses, and therapists function in patient care teams. City governments depend on citizen commissions and boards. Everywhere we turn, groups have become a part of our modern world.

Types of Groups

Groups exist in many variations. The basic features of groups and meetings, however, are fairly consistent. Variations that do occur make differences in the ways groups function. In this chapter, we will introduce you to different kinds of groups. The chapter will provide information about the types of groups most common in the lives of workers, professionals, and citizens. The varieties of groups are like a tree with three main branches. The three principal settings in which groups exist are discussed in the three sections of this chapter:

1. Groups in organizations

2. Groups in communities

3. Groups in professional associations and unions

Once we have examined the types of groups, we will explore what occurs when people work in groups. You will learn about ways of assessing groups to determine how to work effectively within typical groups. You also will begin to understand ways in which some groups are different. You will learn how to use those differences to work successfully with these groups. We will examine groups in terms of their structure, their members, their process, their internal messages, and their leadership. We will look at ethics as it applies to group work. Then we will return to the kinds of groups by

The Varieties of Groups

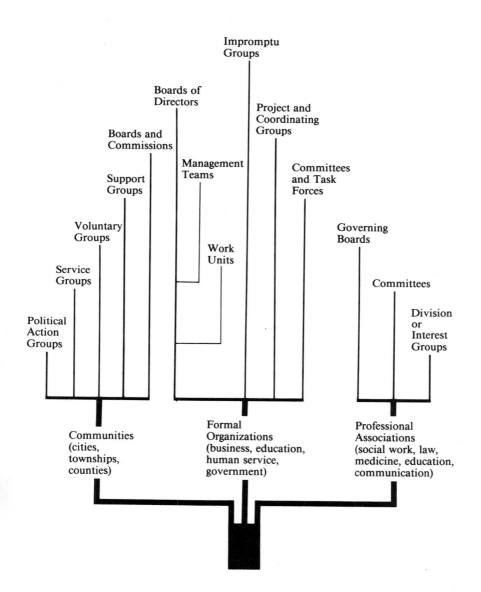

Impromptu
Groups

Boards of
Directors

Project and
Coordinating
Groups

Boards and
Commissions

Management
Teams

Committees
and Task
Forces

Support
Groups

Voluntary
Groups

Governing
Boards

Work
Units

Service
Groups

Committees

Political
Action
Groups

Division
or
Interest
Groups

Communities
(cities,
townships,
counties)

Formal
Organizations
(business, education,
human service,
government)

Professional
Associations
(social work, law,
medicine, education,
communication)

looking at the various settings in which groups exist. We will begin our discussion of types of groups by exploring groups found in organizations.

Groups in Organizations

An organization is a large collection of people who hold positions arranged in levels. Some employees are subordinate to others. At the lowest level of authority are workers. Above the workers are supervisors or managers. Usually a few managers, often vice-presidents, directors, or division heads, have authority over supervisors and managers. A diagram of the relationships between the positions at various levels within an organization is called an *organizational chart*. Such charts reflect the formal structure of a group. The formal structures of groups will be the focus of Chapter 7.

Organizations usually are large. They include thirty or more people who, because of the size of the group, are anonymous to some extent. It is not possible to know everyone in a large organization. Organizations seem to have a life of their own. They survive in spite of the death, retirement, transfer, or resignation of individual workers or managers. Organizations include many different kinds of groups. We will discuss six of these:

1. Work units

2. Management teams

3. Committees and task forces

4. Coordinating and project groups

5. Boards of directors

6. Impromptu groups

Work Units

By far the most common formal group in an organization is the work unit. This is a group of people who function under a single supervisor and either work on a single task or have a specific area of expertise. The specific task of a work unit may be to inspect parts and assemblies or to sell clothes to people in a mall. If a work unit is staffed by people who have a common area of expertise, it may consist of accountants, philosophers, teachers, nurses, or social workers. All those assigned to a work unit know where they belong. Examples of work units include an accounting department, a quality-control department, a retail store's clerks, a ward of a hospital, a small university, or the counseling staff of a human-service agency. Work units represent the fundamental level of an organization.

Management Teams

Other higher-level organizational groups are composed of individuals who function in more than one work unit. These are the managers who supervise the work units and are at the same time members of a management team. The management team may be a group made up of the supervisors of several departments. Industrial plants, for example, often include such departments as production, quality control, purchasing, transportation, maintenance, and industrial engineering. The heads of these departments constitute the plant's management team. A human-service agency may be organized by program: adoption, family counseling, marriage counseling, and counseling for persons with disabilities. One social worker will direct each program. These program directors constitute the agency's management team.

The work of the management team is to coordinate the activities of the departments or programs within a division. If the organization is large enough to have several divisions, there will be a management team for each division. If the industrial plant, agency, university, or hospital is too small to have divisions, there will be a single management team. If an organization such as General Motors is large enough to have a great many divisions, management teams may exist at more than one level within the organization. In this case, there will be a management team for each division. Another management team, consisting of representatives from the several divisions, will exist at a higher level. The General Motors Corporation is an example of a large organization with many divisions.

Committees and Task Forces

When a group is drawn from different departments but is given a specific responsibility or project that cuts across departmental lines, it is called a *committee* or *task force*. For example, a hospital committee might include representatives from nursing, accounting, and records. Their task might be to evaluate the procedures used in discharging patients. Nursing examines discharge procedures to make sure that only patients who are medically prepared to leave are discharged. Accounting examines the procedures for paying hospital personnel for their services to the patient. Records reviews the procedures for the paperwork for patient release.

Task forces are created to oversee specific projects. The installation of a new computer in a school system often calls for a task force. It may consist of teachers, counselors, principals, and accountants. Such a task force might be created prior to the purchase of the computer. It would remain in existence through the installation process. Once the computer is on line, the task force is discharged. Most organizations have committees and task forces.

Coordinating and Project Groups

A very specialized version of a committee is called a *coordination* or *project group*. These typically exist in an organization where the project method of management is common. Aircraft and defense companies are examples. These companies often take on special projects. When they do, a project group is formed. If the project is designing airplane X or airplane Y, engineers currently employed will do the work. The engineering department already employs engineers who are experts in areas such as power plants, airfoils, and structures. Airplane X, however, will have its own project group to coordinate the design and construction efforts for that aircraft. Airplane Y will have another project group.

Some project groups exist for the life of a project and then are discharged. Standing, or permanent, coordinating groups also exist. One large organization has a standing coordinating group whose responsibility is information processing. A representative of each major division and department attends coordinating group meetings. The agenda consists of problems experienced in the organization that need expertise or cooperation across division or department lines. Once a problem is identified and listed as an agenda item, representatives of the departments affected report at the group meeting. They describe progress in solving the problem. Most organizations have coordinating and project groups. Some organizations have given permanent status to these groups by calling them *standing project groups.*

Boards of Directors

At the top level of an organization there often is a board of directors or board of trustees. Members are elected or selected and assigned the responsibility of setting company policy. They direct the organization through both high and low economic periods. A board may have from three members to as many as twenty.

Usually the board of directors or trustees represents the stockholders of a corporation, or the citizens in a public or community organization. The members of the board are expected to make decisions that are for the good of the whole organization. Often they set overall strategies for a company. These strategies may include such diverse activities as competing with or merging with other organizations.

Impromptu Groups

Boards, project groups, committees, task forces, management teams, and work units are formal groups. They appear on an organizational chart or they have a specific purpose or mission statement. They schedule regular meetings, have agendas or work schedules, issue minutes or progress reports, and their membership is well defined. But the most common kind of group in most organizations functions very differently. This group is called an *impromptu group.*

An impromptu group exists whenever two or more people meet to discuss a problem, exchange information, or reach a decision. Such groups have a shifting membership depending on who is interested and needed. They have meetings when a problem or issue arises. They are not recognized officially. Because they have no official status, impromptu groups often are overlooked in books about groups. We will focus on them in Chapter 8 when we consider the informal structures of groups. Here are two examples:

1. An impromptu group may gather in the plant manager's office to discuss a problem with the finishing equipment on one line. The plant manager, the finishing supervisor, an engineer with expertise in finishes, and the production manager are present. These people are on different levels within the organization. They meet to solve the problem in finishing equipment and then the group disperses. There probably will be no record of the meeting. A discussion occurs, decisions are reached, and then the individuals concerned are responsible for correcting the problem.

2. A clinical psychologist in a social service agency returns from a conference with information about a new treatment method. She begins to tell one of her co-workers. Other people overhear the conversation and come over to listen. The new method sounds very effective. Someone suggests that she should bring up the method at the next staff meeting. The people around the psychologist are part of a work unit. They have no formal standing. However, they made a decision that could have a far-reaching impact on the agency.

People who work in organizations may engage in many impromptu meetings in a single day. Even though these groups are not formally a part of the organization, their meetings are a vital part of a healthy company or community group.

Groups in Communities

Just as organizations have several types of groups, so do communities. We will describe five types of community groups. These include:

1. The political action group

2. The voluntary group

3. The service group

4. The support group

5. Boards and Commissions

Community groups differ from groups within organizations in one important way: there are no levels within community groups. A community group usually consists of residents or citizens each having a more or less equal voice. However, since communities consist mainly of either residential or commercial neighborhoods, residents and citizens may have very different points of view. We will describe the five types of groups in which those views most often are expressed. Let's begin with the political action group.

The Political Action Group

Political action groups are more or less permanent organizations that stay abreast of civic decision-making. They attempt to influence community decisions. A homeowners' association might be considered a relatively permanent political action group. A homeowners' asociation not only maintains the standard of life within a complex of homes, it usually observes the events in the community at large to determine how those events affect the persons living in the complex. New buildings, safe street crossings, waste disposal, new industry, and the support of a political candidate are some community-wide concerns that might receive the attention of a homeowners' association.

Political action groups may have a life span that corresponds with the life of an issue. Parents Concerned for Child Safety at the Intersection of Main and Oak Streets might be such a temporary group. This group exists only as long as it takes to have a traffic light installed. Political action groups exist both to observe and influence the decision-making process in community, state, and national affairs.

The Voluntary Group

The voluntary group is characterized by the willingness of members to volunteer time and resources to assist in the work of a formal organization. Parent–Teacher–Student Associations, Gray Ladies, Candystripers, Friends of the Library, Big Brothers, and many other volunteer groups help improve the quality of service and life in formal organizations.

The Service Group

The Lions, Optimists, Jaycees, Future Farmers of America, Boy Scouts, and Girl Scouts are service organizations. These groups attempt to provide a better quality of life for their members and the communities in which they live. Service groups often organize fund-raising campaigns for the good of the community. They may work to add a new wing to a hospital, for example, or to provide emergency shelter and clothing for flood victims.

The Support Group

The support group exists for the mutual support of its members. These groups are common in urban, suburban, and even rural areas. The focus of such a group may be substance abuse, such as alcoholism. The members of the group may be alcoholics or the families of alcoholics. The group may or may not be associated with larger parent organizations such as Alcoholics Anonymous or Alanon. Other support groups may focus on parents without partners, single adults, persons with chronic pain, or terminal illnesses. A support group may focus on any collection of individuals who have needs in common. Support groups permit people to exchange feelings as well as ideas about coping with life. They provide a place to find out that others share similar problems and a place to talk about and share ways of coping with their problems.

Boards and Commissions

In many communities, citizens are asked to serve in a voluntary capacity on boards and commissions. These may include such groups as planning commissions, mental health boards, commissions on aging, or airport boards. The people who serve on boards and commissions usually are appointed by elected officials such as a mayor or by an elected commission. Service is voluntary, however. The board or commission may have a formal status in the local government with a written mission or goal statement and bylaws. The board or commission may be required to hold public meetings and vote on issues. Yet the members are neither elected by the citizens nor are they employees of the government.

Groups in Professional Associations and Unions

Professional associations and unions fall between formal organizations which exist in industry, education, and health care, and local, voluntary community groups. In a professional association, people come together to exchange knowledge and expertise. They attempt to provide a unified position to legislators and other political and professional groups. A union is a professional group composed of people who have specific common interests in pay, fringe benefits, and other working conditions.

In almost every type of work, there is either a professional association or a union. Sometimes the two overlap. For example, the National Education Association is both a professional association for teachers and a national teachers' union. The Hospital Financial Management Association is the national association for persons who work in the financial departments of hospitals. The United Auto Workers is the national union for production-line personnel in the automobile industry.

We will discuss three types of groups common to professional associations and unions:

1. Governing boards

2. Committees

3. Divisions and interest groups

All three types of groups are found in both professional associations and unions. In a union, divisions exist on the basis of the type of labor, by geographical location, or by manufacturer. We will examine each of the three types of groups.

Governing Boards

Governing boards typically are elected. In a union setting, the representatives are elected at the local level to attend regional and national conventions. The professional association usually has a nominating procedure. Members can make nominations and be nominated for local, regional, and national offices. Sometimes national officers come directly from the regional sections of an association. In both professional associations and unions, governing boards are expected to be representative of and responsive to the wishes of the members of the organization.

Committees

Committees may be formed to manage ongoing issues, functions, or problems facing an organization. A professional association often creates committees on dues, membership, publications, and programs for conventions. A union may have committees on the working conditions to be negotiated in a contract. Like governing boards, the committees are supposed to be representative of the membership. In this way, members' views can be heard and are reflected in programs and positions. Because they are representative, the committees in associations and unions tend to be quite large. They may include as many as twenty or thirty members.

Division and Interest Groups

The membership in a professional association or union can be very diverse. For example, the American Psychological Association includes, among others, persons interested in clinical psychology, people who study how human beings think, and industrial psychologists who specialize in testing methods and job design. In such an association, people with similar specific interests join together to form a division. Each division elects officers who are responsible for representing the views of the division in meetings with representatives of other divisions. In a union, the interest groups may be organized by manufacturer. For example, United Auto Workers is organized in three departments: Ford, General Motors, and Chrysler. A union might also be organized geographically: the northeastern division, the midwestern division, and the southern division.

Summary

The variety of groups has been explored in this chapter. Groups exist within organizations, communities, professional associations, and unions. In each setting, the types of groups and their names differ.

Groups within organizations include boards of directors or trustees, management teams, and work units. All three are a part of the formal structure of authority and responsibility. There also are committees and project (coordinating) groups which cut across departments and divisions. The most common groups in an organization are the impromptu gatherings of people who talk over problems and issues on an informal basis.

A community may have political action, service, voluntary, and support groups. These groups bring together people with similar backgrounds and interests for their common good. There also are boards and commissions on which citizens serve. These are not a part of the formally elected government and members are not employed by the government.

Many people also belong to local, regional, or national professional associations and unions. Governing boards, committees, and interest groups or divisions are the types of groups which exist in associations and unions.

The principles of group life cut across all of these groups to some extent. In the chapters which follow, characteristics of group life will be explained. We will explore the practical implications of these characteristics.

REFLECTING/EXPLORING

1. List by name the groups in which you are a member. Then identify each group as an organizational or community group, or a professional association or union. Finally, identify each group by specific type within the three general divisions. Reread the descriptions of each type of group you have listed. How well do the descriptions fit your groups?

2. Visit the chamber of commerce in your community. Ask for a listing of various groups within your community. Identify those groups which are organizational, community, and professional associations or unions. How would you describe group life within your community?

3. If you work with an organization, use your experience. If you do not, then interview a friend who does. Identify specific examples of the six types of groups listed on page 7. What relationships exist between these types of groups in the organization? How does each group contribute to completing the work of the organization?

4. What types of groups within your community affect your life as an

individual even though you may not be a member of them? In what ways might community groups be helpful to you in your work or home life? How do these groups contribute to the quality of life in your community?

5. If you are a member of a professional association or a union, use your experience. If you are not, interview a friend who is a member. Identify examples of the three types of groups identified on page 13. How do each of these types of groups contribute to the work of the association or union?

CHAPTER 2

GROUP COMMUNICATION

We can begin our exploration of communication within groups by looking in on Alice who is attending a planning meeting for a local arts guild. She hears the issue of judges being discussed. There have been problems in the past with judges being too severe or too lenient. Alice thinks to herself, "Someone needs to come up with a new way of selecting judges." This thought is vague in the sense that it focuses only generally on the topic. While the discussion continues, Alice continues to think: "I can't just say a need for a new way . . . what work? . . . how solve? . . . need study? . . . use committee. . . ." Alice does not formulate thoughts into complete sentences.

Thinking occurs in fragments. What work? translated from an inner thought fragment to external communication to group members might be, "We need to focus on the issue of the criteria for selecting judges and determine once and for all how to achieve consistency among judges' ratings." The translation represents the end result of a member's mental reaction to an issue or problem before the group. The problem first stimulates fragmentary thoughts within the member. That member then communicates outwardly to the other members her ideas on the issue before the group. Group communication begins with the willingness of individual members to direct their energies to common concern. It is this multiple focusing of individual energies on the group cause that is the primary advantage of working in groups.

Success in group work usually depends on how well group members communicate with each other. Your success as a group member will depend primarily on how well you understand and use the communication process. This chapter will be focused on that process. We will divide it into four sections. These include:

1. Basic elements of the communication process

2. Content and relationship levels of message

3. Feedback: creating a two-way process out of a one-way process

4. Complexity of communication in groups

We will begin with the basic communication elements to demonstrate the process of communication and how it works in groups.

The Communication Process

We will use a series of diagrams to explain communication. Let's go back to Alice, who has decided that the planning group should appoint a committee to study judging, to get information from other art guilds, and to provide options from which the larger group may choose. She puts her original thought fragments (the intended message) into words. This part of the communication process is called *encoding.* The choice Alice (Person A) makes in encoding her thought fragments as a message intended for a listener is shown in the following diagram:

Encoding the Message

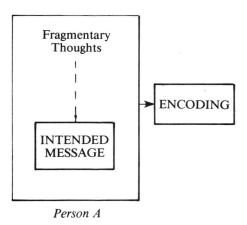

Person A

Messages communicated between group members consist of two parts: the verbal code and the nonverbal code. The nonverbal code is often referred to as *nonverbal cues.*

Both verbal and nonverbal codes may be represented visually (they can be seen) or auditorily (they can be heard). Words, numbers, graphs, sketches, charts, pictures, signs, written reports, and minutes are examples of verbal codes. Nonverbal codes include gestures, facial expressions, posture, seating arrangements, and clothing.

Virtually everything in the immediate environment, except the verbal codes themselves, that may have an effect on understanding is thus a nonverbal code.

After encoding, the next logical step is sending the message. In our example, Alice (Person A) *encodes* her message, puts her thought fragments into full sentences. She sends her message, sitting forward in her chair (nonverbal code), stating the words so that others can hear them (verbal code) and using a tone of voice that suggests a genuine concern (nonverbal code). Alice's message, with its verbal and nonverbal parts, has been added to the diagram to complete her initial role in this interaction.

The group member (Person B) listening to Alice attempts to make sense out of her message. Making sense out of a message adds three new parts to our diagram of the communication process. Now the diagram includes *receiving, decoding,* and the *received message.* In order to receive the message, Person B must be able to see or hear the message as sent by Person A. Once Person A's message is received by Person B, Person B may choose to decode it.

The term *decoding* represents a complex part of the process. When a person uses Morse code, decoding is a simple process of matching symbols to symbols. Dots and dashes are matched to letters of the alphabet. Decoding in human communication does not involve matching meanings to

Sending the Message

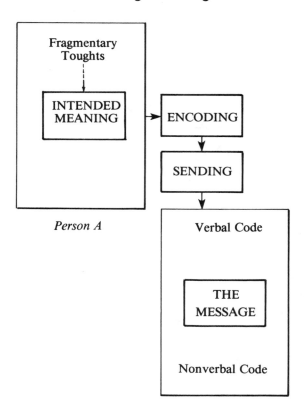

Receiving and Decoding Messages

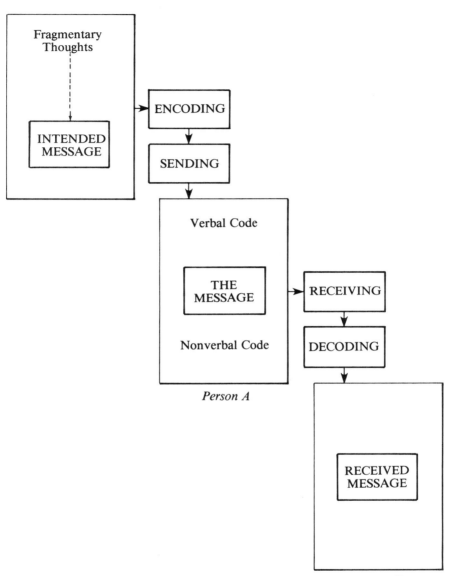

words or numbers. If it did, communication would work much better than it does. In human communication, Person B takes the message as heard and seen and assigns a meaning to it. Person B's meaning for the message may or may not match the meaning intended by Person A. In fact, the listener may go far beyond the intended meaning, or, conversely, may put very little meaning into a message that was rich in possibilities. We will refer, then, to Person B's meaning for the message as the *message received* to distinguish it from Person A's intended message. This is one way of remembering a basic communication principle: the meaning is *not* in the message; the meaning is in the persons who are communicating.

Content and Relationship Levels of a Message

The complexity of communication between Preson A and Person B is compounded by the nature of a message. Every message has two levels: content and relationship. The content level consists of what is actually said and is made up primarily of the verbal code. Within Person A and Person B, content meanings are assigned to the message. Bill says, "Let's move on to something else. I'm getting bored talking about the budget. We aren't getting anywhere." The content consists of "move on, budget, not getting anywhere."

Now consider the impact of Bill's statement on other members of the group. This is the relationship level of the message which, consisting of nonverbal code or cues, becomes the relational meaning for the message when interpreted by sender and receiver. Let's suppose the budget was a vital item to Shirley. Bill's statement then becomes a challenge. Shirley's internal reaction might be one of anger. She might make a sarcastic comment about Bill's lack of knowledge on money matters. She might try to gain support from other members of the group for continuing the budget discussion. In either case, Bill's statement has an effect on his relationship with Shirley; there is conflict and hostility now where there might have been neutrality or even friendship before. As you might have assumed by now, the relationship level of a message often is established more by *how* a statement is made (nonverbal cues) than by *what* is said (verbal cues).

What we say and how we say it affects other people and their feelings. It indicates who has power and who does not. It establishes who will team up with whom. It creates and defines the ways people treat each other. This is an absolutely vital point. You cannot understand what is going on in a group meeting without knowing about the relationships between the members. Who likes whom? Who cannot get along with whom? Who is considered competent? Who is seen as caring and considerate? Who belongs to cliques or coalitions? These factors often have a far greater bearing on the outcome of a group meeting than the more rational matters of information and deduction and decision-making. On page 21, we have provided you with an expanded diagram of the basic elements in the communication process. We have added content and relationship levels to the message itself

Relational Communication

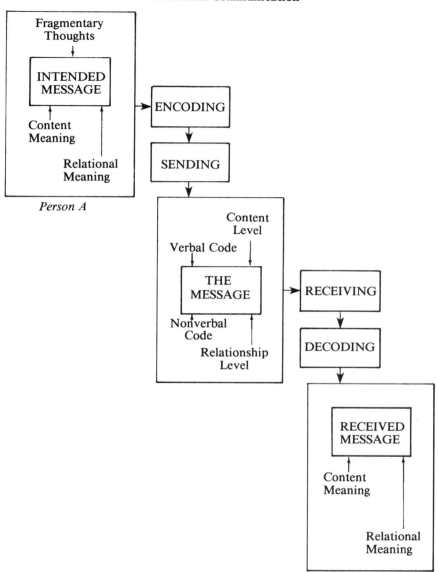

as well as adding content and relational meanings for Person A and Person B.

Relational communication is important because relationships between people may result in the content of a message not being heard or being heard but misunderstood. Even if the content is understood by Person B precisely as intended by Person A, the message as sent may result in defensiveness or hostility or competition on the part of the receiver and the message may not be used. When messages are not used, the group process and group work is impeded.

Feedback: Creating a Two-Way Process Out of a One-Way Process

Even as revised, our diagram shows only the basic elements for one-way communication from Person A to Person B. Communication is usually not one-way—certainly not in groups! Members react to messages. They respond to each other. The response is called *feedback*.

When Person A talks, Person B may establish eye contact, nod, or smile. These are nonverbal feedback cues that indicate Person B is probably alive and awake—nothing more. We know that we can pretend attention by nodding and smiling while not hearing a word of what the other person is saying. However, Person A at least knows that Person B is there, physically. Person B is probably *receiving*. If this kind of minimum feedback is not observed, Person A may wait for it or request Person B to pay attention.

To find out if Person B is trying to decode the message, Person A uses other cues. If Person B asks questions for clarification or summarizes the received message, Person A can assume Person B is trying to make sense out of the message. If Person B's version suggests that a different message has been received than the one intended by Person A, Person A can reword or rephrase and try again to get the intended meaning across.

As you may have already guessed, feedback is just as complex as sending the message. Feedback also has content and relationship levels. What we have said about the content and relationship levels of the message applies equally to feedback. In a sense, when Person B gives feedback to Person A, that feedback is actually Person B's intended message. In a continuing interaction, Person B and Person A continue to shift roles as sender and receiver, alternately providing each other with messages and feedback.

On page 23, we have added feedback to our communication diagram. The diagram of the communication process is now complete. Ideally, the interaction process would look like the diagram at the top of page 24.

The Communication Process

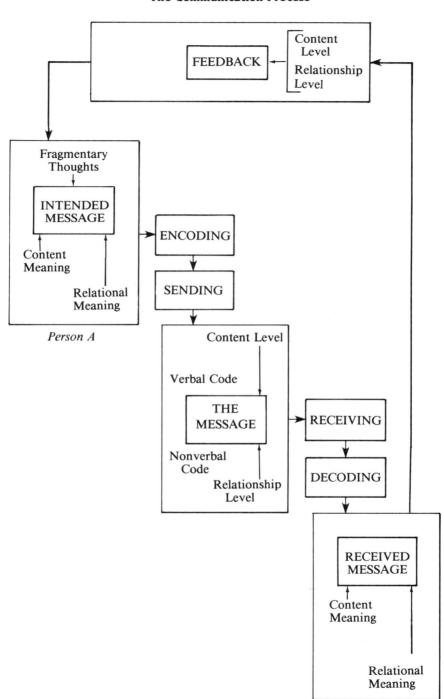

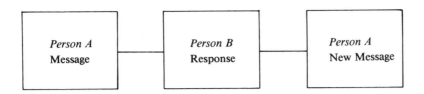

By *response* we mean that Person B hears what A says and comments on it. The message at both content and relationship levels is received as intended. Here is an example:

PHIL: I think we need to develop a more complete plan than the one we have here.

WILL: What do you mean by a "more complete plan," Phil?

PHIL: Well, I think we need more detail. You know, who is going to handle the various tasks? What are the deadlines? How will the tasks be coordinated?

WILL: I see. You want to have more specifics in our plan. I agree. I think that's a good idea.

In each case, Will responds directly to Phil. This does not happen in real conversations very often.

A second version of a conversation could look like the following diagram.

Instead of responding to Person A, Person B injects his or her own message. This is nonresponsive. Not having feedback from Person B, Person A repeats the initial message, trying to get a direct response from Person B. An example, using Phil and Will again, might look like this:

PHIL: I think we need to develop a more complete plan than the one we have here.

WILL: Our problem is the budget. We just aren't anywhere near close to being right on this budget. It is unrealistic. We'll never get this done for that amount of money.

PHIL: We need more detail in our plan. We need names and dates and responsibilities.

WILL: Okay. But the real problem is the budget.

Here Will is pushing his own idea, the budget problem, and not responding to Phil. This kind of exchange is common in groups.

Complexity of Communication in Groups

Very complex communication usually occurs when Persons A and B are joined in a group by others. One individual may express an idea. Another will pick up on that idea, extend it, and then introduce a totally new idea. The next person must decide whether to continue the original idea or follow up on the most recent idea.

Group interaction may involve ten or more people. Patterns of response become intricate. In what order do people speak? Who responds to whom? What kinds of responses occur? Is a comment really a response or an introduction of new material? As members or the leader of a group become more sophisticated, as their skills in observing and using communication in groups become fine-tuned, these kinds of questions occur to them.

The complexity of group communication results not only from the number of people involved but also from that group's history. Meetings do not occur in a vacuum. Most groups hold a series of meetings. They occur in a *context*. Meetings exist in a setting: a culture with norms, taboos, and certain rituals. Meetings occur in a larger social system with roles and expectations about how people in roles will behave. The culture and the social system constitute the context of a meeting. It therefore becomes important to specify that a group is from XYZ Corporation in Atlanta, Georgia, or from the Weaver Street neighborhood in Altoona, Pennsylvania. In addition, we need to know the history of these two groups: what sorts of events have occurred in their immediate pasts, and what happened in their distant pasts.

A meeting is preceded by communication events. Often there are premeeting discussions. The members of the group meet with one another or exchange memos or phone calls before a scheduled meeting. They might talk about items on the agenda or how to approach a particular issue. Some members may try to gain support for a particular position or to create a coalition. Others may simply speculate on what will happen at the meeting. Therefore, events in a scheduled meeting grow out of premeeting discussions as well as out of prior meetings.

Groups do not cease to exist when a meeting ends. Members tend to discuss meetings, particularly emotionally charged meetings. This is called *processing*. One feature of processing is that members mutually attempt to assign meanings to what happened. They share perceptions. They describe

Group Elements That Affect Meetings

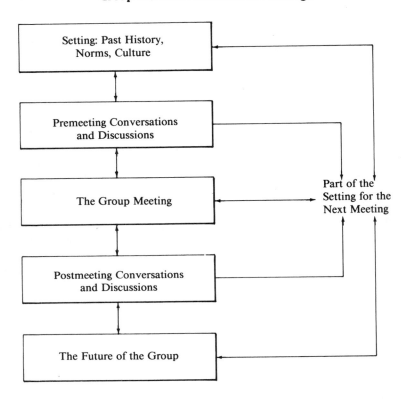

their reactions. These processes literally *give* meaning to the events of the meeting. Together with the formal outcomes, decisions, plans, and solutions, they become part of the setting or context for the next meeting. We have diagrammed the elements within the life span of a group that affect a scheduled meeting.

These elements exist within the psychological and sociological context for the group meeting. If others were to ask what Carmen meant in the meeting this morning when she demanded to know what was going on in the executive committee, they would have to be able to answer the following questions:

1. What was the agenda for this meeting? What was being discussed?

2. What was Carmen's role in this group?

3. What was Carmen's relationship to other members of the group?

4. What kind of norms are there about expressing anger in groups in this setting?

5. What happened in the last meeting of this group? Had Carmen attended? Was she part of some important event?

6. What had been said about Carmen before this meeting or after the last meeting?

7. To whom had Carmen talked after the last meeting or before this one?

8. What is likely to happen at a later meeting of the group? Is there something coming up that Carmen wants to see happen—or not happen?

Answers to questions such as these assist an individual in reaching an overall understanding, even though it may not be possible to get an answer to every question. Simply asking the questions serves as a reminder that communication in groups is a complex process and usually involves more than first meets the eye. That reminder, in itself, promotes understanding.

Summary

People who work in groups complete tasks mainly by communicating with each other in face-to-face situations. In fact, the success of group work usually can be determined by how effectively group members communicate. This chapter described the communication process. The basic elements of the communication process involve the encoding of ideas and feelings by one person who creates and sends a message to another person. The second person decodes the message and may or may not receive the message as it was intended by the person who sent it. A message includes both content and relationship levels and may be created from both verbal and nonverbal codes. When the people who receive the message respond, they provide *feedback* to the sender of the message. Feedback may include questions for clarification and a summary of what was received. Feedback creates a two-way communication process. It provides the sender with information about how the message was received.

Communication in groups is complex because of the number of people involved and the history and expectations members have for each other and for the group. Premeeting and postmeeting discussions also become a part of group meetings and of the group's past and future. It is important to understand and become skillful at communicating in groups because groups are an important part of everyday life.

REFLECTING/EXPLORING

1. Listen to your conversations this week at work or in your community groups. Listen to the choices you make when you decide to speak. Listen to how you put your fragmentary thoughts into complete sentences. Do the sentences you put together differ depending on the person you are talking with? Are you aware of making choices during this encoding process to provide clarity in either the content or relational meaning you want to communicate? Select a minimum of three communication situations and jot down some notes about your encoding behavior.

2. Observe others in your groups. Notice the nonverbal and verbal codes within their messages. What content and relational meanings do you assign to the information you receive from each code? Do the meanings you assign seem consistent between the verbal and nonverbal levels? If you are getting one message from the verbal level and another from the nonverbal level, to which message do you give your strongest attention? Jot down some notes on a minimum of three communication situations in which you are particularly aware of the content and relational meanings you assign to the verbal and nonverbal codes within messages.

3. Observe others in groups as they provide feedback to you or to each other. Notice whether the feedback given to the speaker seems to suggest how accurately receiving and decoding have occurred on the part of the listener. Make note of at least three observations about feedback during the week that you would like to discuss. Jot down your observations.

4. Observe a group in action. Before the group meeting begins, assign a letter to each person and draw a chart that represents where each individual is sitting. As the interaction occurs, draw a line between two individuals each time communication occurs between them. Note the times a person addresses the group as a whole rather than a specific group member. Keep a record of the number of times this occurs for each person. When the group meeting is finished, study your chart. What have you learned about the complexity of communication within groups? Write down your observations.

5. Choose one of the groups you used in activities 1 through 4. List several specific statements you might share with the group for purposes of helping members understand and improve the ways they communicate. How and when might you explain this information to the group?

CHAPTER 3

ETHICAL DECISIONS IN GROUPS

It should come as no surprise to you that working in groups involves decisions. When group members take part in making decisions, their values come into play. Most decisions require compromises among values such as loyalty, honesty, and fairness. The ways in which group members exercise their values in making decisions brings us to the area of ethics. Let's examine two case studies.

Case Study 1. Alex is a member of a committee whose task it is to develop a program for improving the quality of customer service. There are members on the committee from seven departments in the main office of a large chain of department stores. In a conversation over lunch, Alex learned from his friend, Harry, that the credit department deliberately is not following through on services to customers. Harry is a member of that department. He is upset by the situation. At the same time, Harry is afraid for his job and for the jobs of his co-workers if information about the lax service becomes known beyond the department.

Values are involved in this situation. Alex has value conflicts. The knowledge he has gained should be reported to the committee if he is loyal to the company. Yet he also feels loyal to his friend, Harry. Alex's loyalties are divided. By speaking out, Alex could jeopardize Harry's job. By not speaking out, Alex takes part in covering up a situation that conflicts with the interests of the company and with the task of the committee. Harry also has value conflicts. Loyalty to co-workers dictates that he remain silent. Fairness to the company requires speaking out.

Case Study 2. Barb teaches at Roosevelt Junior High School in Marysville. She is a member of a group whose task is to review the performance of co-workers. Members of the teaching staff work closely together. They see themselves as a "family" more than as co-workers. The performance of three teachers will be reviewed this year. Two of the teachers, Marilyn and Barb, are close friends. Marilyn has become a problem on the staff because her attitude, "teaching is just a job to be done," has hurt her work. She no longer contributes to staff meetings or even to casual professional conversations in the lunchroom. Her attention is on her own children rather than on the children she teaches. Other teachers talk about Marilyn's attitude and her behavior. They have mixed feelings.

Barb is caught in a common ethical dilemma. She believes in the individual rights of each human being. She values family life and parents who are concerned with their children. However, Barb questions how fair Marilyn's new behavior is to the students she teaches, and, indeed, to everyone on the teaching staff. What if all teachers ceased to practice their profession? Teaching effectiveness would suffer.

Ethical decisions invariably imply a conflict between two or more sets of values. This chapter focuses on values common in group work. We have divided the chapter into three sections.

Four basic values affect group work in the United States. These include:

1. Democracy

2. Individuality

3. Openness

4. Loyalty

Conflicts affect basic values in group work. Conflicts exist:

1. Among the four basic values

2. Between the four basic values and four opposing values

Three criteria are useful for groups making ethical choices.
These include determining the degree of concern for:

1. Selves

2. Clients and customers

3. Other groups

The information in this chapter will help you make the difficult decisions. We will begin with the four basic values involved in group work.

Four Basic Values Affect Group Work

In American culture, four values seem to have the greatest impact on groups and on the people who work in them: democracy, individuality, openness, and loyalty. We will examine each of these values in terms of its effect on group life.

Democracy

A central value in the United States is democracy. It is commonly recognized as the one person, one vote principle. Ideally each person has an equal chance of affecting an election or a decision. (Most of the procedures to be discussed in Chapters 19 and 20 stem from this ideal.) Parliamentary procedure especially has been an expression of democratic ideals.

There are two kinds of democracy: representative and participatory. In a *representative democracy,* voters elect someone to represent them in a legislative body or on a council or commission. Sometimes work groups or community groups are also based on equal representation of departments or neighborhoods. Representatives are expected to use their best judgment even when it is not consistent with the short-term best interests of the people who elected them. Raising taxes may be unpopular but necessary for national defense or for maintaining schools.

In *Megatrends,* John Naisbitt suggested that a trend may be emerging in the direction of *participatory democracy.* Actually, this is closer to the original meaning of the term *democracy.* In participatory democracy, the people who are affected by a decision vote on it directly. The use of referendums and recall elections are examples of people voting directly on issues close to their hearts, pocketbooks, and values.

In group work, the idea of democracy is basic. Each person on a committee or in a work unit expects to have an equal voice in the policies and procedures that affect the group. If such participation is denied, people often organize to ensure that their voices are heard. Historically, participation and voting have been deeply ingrained in the American spirit. This value is held by virtually all groups. The democratic ideal is the reason most groups are formed and continue to exist.

Individuality

There are a number of nations in which democracy is a high ideal. The United States is somewhat unusual in its emphasis on individuality. We prize the idea of the silent, solitary cowboy riding the plains. Men and women who start and succeed in their own businesses are interviewed, written about, and admired. Conformity is often looked down upon. To be a member of the crowd is considered degrading. Good people stand up and stand out. Sometimes they even stand alone.

The emphasis on individuality runs counter to working in a group situation. Almost by definition, groups do not permit individuals to stand alone. Consensus or a majority vote results in a decision. The person who refuses to vote or who has a minority opinion may not like the decision. However, his or her opinion is not the one reported out of committee. Power is exerted indirectly and directly by the members of the group against the loner. However, successful group members and leaders remain sensitive to the value of individuality. Sometimes the greatest wisdom for the group comes from the single, less popular voice. The time and energy required to hear each person's views usually increases the effectiveness of the group's choice, decision, or proposal.

Openness

In his major study of values in American society, Milton Rokeach found that the single most highly ranked value was honesty. In a group, honesty translates into openness. People want to know the truth. They want to be treated openly and directly. They do not want to be lied to and manipulated.

Some values conflict with openness. For example, most people want to be sensitive to the feelings and needs of others. Individuals have a right to privacy and confidentiality. Therefore, it is not workable or wise to be totally open or frank at all times. Yet most people would prefer to know if they were doing something that is considered wrong or displeasing to others.

In group work, every person has a right to information others have that is relevant to the task. The more open the communication in a group, the greater the chance that each person will make a reasoned and effective decision when the group votes or attempts to reach consensus. It is important that each group member know what other members have agreed to informally. Agreements made between some members prior to a meeting and unknown to other group members tend to undermine trust and teamwork.

Loyalty

The final value central to American life at work and in communities is loyalty. Members of groups are expected to be loyal to those groups. Loyalties can become confusing when a person has been assigned to a group to represent a department or a neighborhood. The individual may agree more strongly with the coordinating committee position than with the ideas of the group he or she represents. How to vote becomes an issue for this person. Loyalty is an important factor.

The expectation that group members will be loyal to the group leader seems to be particularly high. Some leaders demand total loyalty from group members. One example is the presidency of Richard Nixon. He apparently expected his advisors and staff to be totally loyal, loyal to the extent of committing perjury in order to protect him from political harm. In some industries, employees are expected to use the products manufactured by the firms in which they are employed. City workers are often expected to live within the city in which they work. Members of athletic teams are expected to speak well of each other, the coach, and the team even when personal and team problems exist. The effective team member must achieve a balance between the values of loyalty, honesty, individuality, and democracy. This means understanding and managing conflicts between values.

Conflicts Affect Group Work

Ethics involves making choices when values conflict. The popular basic values of our society do not exist in isolation. Conflicts often exist among them. Conflicts also exist between them and other values. We will examine both types of value conflict.

Democracy Conflicts with Individuality

Conflict often exists between democracy and individuality. In a democracy, decisions are made either by consensus or by a majority vote. Group members are expected to support the decision. Some groups find that they have arrived at a false consensus. Everyone agreed in the meeting but some people had reservations when they voted. Other groups use voting procedures but the minority does not accept the majority vote. The usual expectation is that everyone should support the decision arrived at through the democratic process until there is another opportunity to discuss, debate, and vote. Sometimes this expectation becomes an issue of loyalty.

Many people do not want to support the majority decision. They are individualists. Some of these people choose to leave the group. They may create their own group or try to function without a group. Also there are cases where the individualist sabotages the group decision by simply not carrying it out in practice even though agreeing to it in discussion.

Group decisions may violate an individual's strongly held personal principle. For example, a community group may vote to support Medicaid-funded abortions. One member is strongly against abortions of any kind. In another instance, a board of directors agrees with management to pursue the development of a new drug, but one member of the board thinks that the drug is a potential problem for society and a liability for the corporation. In such cases, individuality struggles against democracy. The majority wins, but the individual still has options.

Openness Conflicts with Loyalty

Another example of conflicting values occurs between the norm of openness and the need for loyalty to a group. On a professional athletic team, several players may be known to be using drugs. One player acts as a dealer. The question becomes whether or not other team players should disclose the names of the team members involved with drugs. Loyalty to the individuals dictates silence. Openness dictates that the names should be disclosed.

This conflict exists in government and industry, too. A product has a defect in design that could cause injury or death to users. A government agency has let contracts that are being misused by the vendors. Should an employee who knows of these practices be open and disclose them? Loyalty to the organization say no. Honesty says yes. Decisions made daily by individual group members and by the group as a whole affect choices between competing values.

Value Conflicts

Another kind of value conflict exists. There are values other than democracy, individuality, openness, and loyalty which can come into conflict with four basic values.

The Basic Values	*The Opposing Values*
Democracy	Efficiency
Individuality	Good of the whole
Openness	Sensitivity
Loyalty	Rationality

Each of the opposing values implies a potential problem for its opposite basic value. We will describe these problems.

Democracy and efficiency. Democracy is not efficient. Discussion which continues until each member has spoken and consensus is reached often takes hours, or even several meetings. People who want to reach decisions quickly often view the time spent in reaching consensus as wasted.

Committees and task forces sometimes are criticized for inefficiency. In business and industry, decisions must often be made quickly. If they exist, committees may be bypassed. Whenever organizations and communities are faced with crises, groups can expect to be ignored. The tension created by the conflicting desires, to use democratic procedures and to be efficient, is a very real factor in communities and organizations. Groups must cope with both demands.

Individuality and the good of the whole. While Americans prize the rugged individualist and the entrepreneur, another value exists that requires seeking the greatest good for the largest number of people. Group decisions often conflict with the choices or beliefs of one or two members. Yet the group decision is based on whatever is viewed as the best choice for the common good. Social systems are based on the concept of limiting individual freedom for the good of the whole. Prisons are an extreme example of this value in practice.

A group is more than a collection of individuals. The decisions resulting from group deliberations are the result of combining and integrating the views and concerns of all members. Group decisions can be powerful tools because nearly all members support them. The rugged individualist who ignores the wishes of the group may face criticism and isolation. The group may reject the individual or the individual may resign from the group. In any event, this conflict can be stressful. The stress felt by group members who attempt to balance the good of the whole with the need for individuality exists in most groups.

Openness and sensitivity. Common courtesy is primarily based on the value of sensitivity for the feelings of other people. Laws that preserve the confidentiality of personal records also stem from the value of sensitivity. Most people have personal histories that include failures and other incidents they prefer to forget or keep private. Absolute frankness would require disclosing such information. Sensitivity suggests that individuals have a right to personal privacy and confidentiality.

Group members must constantly balance the desire to be open and frank with the need to be alert and sensitive to the feelings of others. In some groups the balance tips so far toward sensitivity that honesty is completely dropped. Interactions in such a group become superficial and meetings consist of hollow rituals. People do not confront one another about issues. Instead they play games in which they pretend to get along. At the other extreme, groups exist in which people are expected to bare their souls. Individuals disclose differences of opinion and displeasures with other members even over minor concerns. Somewhere between these two extremes lies an appropriate balance between openness and sensitivity. The members of every group must find that balance.

Loyalty and rationality. Blind loyalty to the goals and work of a group can result in problems. Decisions may not represent the wishes of individuals whom the group represents. Solutions may not work when attempts are made to implement them.

Rationality is used here in the sense of reality testing. In this kind of rationality people are aware of the changing factors in their environment. They are alert to new information about problems and issues. They assess and analyze information to come to an understanding that is as current, accurate, and realistic as possible. They base their decisions on this reality.

The opposite condition is described in Irving Janis's term, groupthink. Groupthink results when relatively little input about the current situation exists and the group begins to filter out information that does not conform to the group view of reality. Loyalty to the group is considered more important than collecting and analyzing practical information.

If you refer to case study 1, you can probably imagine how quickly the credit department for the department store chain could fall into the trap of groupthink. If Alex decides to be loyal to his friend, Harry, the members of the credit department could continue to serve clients poorly. They might begin blaming customers and really come to believe that it is the customers' fault that service has deteriorated. Eventually, customers would turn to other stores and members of the credit department might lose their jobs.

Every group faces ethical decisions. Basic values such as democracy and individuality or openness and loyalty are often in conflict. The basic values conflict with other values such as efficiency, the good of the whole, sensitivity to persons, and rationality. Making ethical decisions in groups requires making choices among these values. We recommend three criteria that you may wish to use in arriving at ethical decisions.

Ethical Choices in Groups

Group members can use three criteria to assess their individual contributions to the group, the statements made by others, and the group's decision. These criteria can be phrased as questions.

1. To what extent do my ideas and the discussion of the group reflect a concern for ourselves?

2. To what extent do my ideas and the discussion of the group reflect a concern for the clients or customers this group serves?

3. To what extent do my ideas and the discussion of the group reflect a concern for other groups within the community or organization?

These three concerns surface during group discussions. We will examine each concern.

Concern for Ourselves

Vince Lombardi, the former coach of the Green Bay Packers, is reported to have said "I love all of my players, even the ones I don't like." The use of the word "love" may seem unusual in a very aggressive and physical sport such as football. Yet what Lombardi probably meant was that he cared about and was concerned for all of the players on his team.

Unfortunately, group members may display a great deal of love for themselves at the expense of others. As with all matters of value, there is the possibility of going to extremes. Some groups are very self-serving. They exist in order to support and preserve themselves and their members at all costs. This is especially true of groups who have power over others. Boards, commissions, councils, management teams, and groups of people elected to public office often have an overriding concern for the continuation of their own influence.

A group may go to the opposite extreme, however. Groups of social workers, teachers, or nurses may be so devoted to their clients that the result is a great deal of stress and even sickness among group members. A more balanced stance is important. People must take care of themselves, even be concerned for and love themselves, in order to remain healthy and sane. Extreme devotion to a group goal and to the work of the group can have the opposite effect.

Concern for the Clients or Customers

Almost all groups exist in order to serve. Their goals are to create products, provide services, represent others, or influence citizens, purchasers, and users. Sometimes concerns for clients and customers are forgotten.

In their popular examination of high-achievement corporations,

In Search of Excellence, Thomas Peters and Robert Waterman point out that the most successful corporations are highly oriented toward their customers. Some large companies actually request customers to come to their headquarters to make suggestions for new products or for product improvements. This concern for the client or customer is a mark of distinction and success.

Concern for Other Groups

Most groups exist in order to serve but also to serve in the midst of a structure consisting of related groups: committees, task forces, work units, and boards. In their deliberations, groups must consider the impact of their actions on these other groups.

If one group strives for dominance and control in an organization, their goal may result in reduced effectiveness for the total organization. The organization provides a structure in which the individual divisions and departments can contribute to each other and to the overall goals of the organization. The total integration of the organization may be destroyed if one group begins to take control. Successful groups see beyond their particular goals and tasks to the total purpose of the whole organization.

Answering these questions about ethical choices in groups is not easy. Most people struggle with their values and their concerns for the group members, for the clients, and for other groups. Perfect decisions are not possible when ethical choices are involved. The best decision probably will be the one that meets all three criteria to the greatest extent.

Summary

Ethics in group work is a matter of deciding among and balancing competing values. There are no absolute guides for ethical behavior in groups.

Four basic values affect group work in the United States. These values are democracy, individuality, openness, and loyalty. Democracy implies that all members have a voice in decisions. Individuality works against group decisions since pure individuality would result in each group member making a separate decision whenever common agreement is lacking. Openness is highly prized and suggests that groups should function as frankly and directly as possible. Finally, loyalty to a group involves support of other group members and of group decisions.

Conflict may occur among these four values. In addition, these basic values may conflict with other values which tend to be opposites. These include efficiency, the good of the whole, sensitivity to others, and rationality.

In assessing the ethics of personal participation in groups, three questions can be raised: Is there a concern for selves? Is there a concern for clients and customers? Is there a concern for other groups? Usually there are no perfect answers to ethical questions. The best decision typically is the one that satisfies all three criteria to the greatest extent.

REFLECTING/EXPLORING

1. With a group of friends, discuss the two case studies presented in this chapter. As you make decisions about what Alex or Harry and Barb should do, what values seem to be in conflict?

2. Observe or participate in a problem-solving discussion. When criteria are listed by which each possible solution is to be evaluated, identify the values that either are directly stated or implicit in each criteria. What do you learn about yourself and this group as a result of this activity?

3. Observe a city commission meeting. Make a list of the procedures used and the ways in which the meeting is conducted that reflect the values of democracy, individuality, openness, and loyalty. To what degree do you believe your list is typical of public meetings within the United States?

4. Reflect upon a decision recently made by a group of which you are a member that involved ethical considerations. What values were in conflict? Using the three ethical questions as a guide, how effectively do you believe the decision was made?

5. Observe your own behavior in groups over a period of a week. Include family, work, and community groups. Also include groups whose decisions have an effect on you even though you may not be a part of the group. Keep a record of the values implicit in that group's work and decisions. Which of your own values seem to agree with those made by your groups and by groups that affect you? Which of your values seem in conflict?

Section One: Reading List

Information on small group research and theory:

Luft, J. *Group Process: An Introduction to Group Dynamics.* Palo Alto, CA: National Press Book, 1970.

Payne, R. and C. L. Cooper. *Groups at Work.* New York: John Wiley and Sons, 1981.

Shaw, M. E. *Group Dynamics: The Psychology of Small Group Behavior.* New York: McGraw-Hill, 1971.

Information on ethics:

Janis, Irving L. *Victims of Groupthink.* Boston: Houghton Mifflin, 1972.

Naisbitt, J. *Megatrends: Ten New Directions Transforming Our Lives.* New York: Warner Books, 1982.

Peters, T. J., and R. H. Waterman, Jr. *In Search of Excellence: Lessons from America's Best-Run Companies.* New York: Harper and Row, 1982.

Rokeach, M. "Authority, Authoritarianism, and Conformity." In *Conformity and Deviation,* edited by I. Berg and B. M. Bass, pp. 230-57. New York: Harper and Row, 1961.

FOUNDATIONS

CHAPTER 4

THE GROUP
ENVIRONMENT

Factors that exist outside a group affect the group's internal functioning. In this chapter, we will show you how to assess the outside factors for any group of which you are a member. Let's first look at these factors and their effects in a real life situation:

In Bloomingdale, there are two restaurants across the Mohican Highway from each other. On the north side of the street is a fast food restaurant, Hamburger Heaven. The parking lot is large and a drive-through lane circles the building. Inside Hamburger Heaven there are blue and brown plastic booths and seats. The customers walk up to a shiny stainless steel counter to order and to wait for their food.

Le Michelin is an exclusive French restaurant on the south side of the street. A formally dressed maitre d' approaches customers when they enter and asks if they have reservations. After they have been seated, the customers are handed a large, six-page menu featuring a wide variety of selections. Le Michelin is a restaurant with a four-star rating. The restaurant caters to people who are willing to spend quite a lot of money to eat a professionally prepared meal cooked to their taste.

The people who work in Hamburger Heaven and Le Michelin are work groups. Their situations illustrate the effects of outside factors on the internal operations of a group. The outside factors that affect these two restaurants result in two very different approaches.

At Hamburger Heaven, the competition consists of the other fast food restaurants in town as well as those in the state and country. There are three criteria for success at Hamburger Heaven:

1. Serve the food fast so that no one has to wait very long.

2. Keep the food inexpensive but tasty.

3. Make sure the food looks and tastes exactly like the food at any other Hamburger Heaven in the United States.

The people who started the Hamburger Heaven chain used a business strategy that works for a large national chain:

1. Hire unskilled but trainable employees who are willing to work for minimum wages.

2. Hire intelligent supervisors who push the employees.

3. Institute weekly or monthly inspections by district and regional franchise managers.

This business strategy is one that is used in groups in a wide variety of settings. Rules and procedures govern all activities. Deviations are not permitted. Leaders have power and are instructed to use it. Everyone is accountable. Managers live with the hope of promotion to district supervisor. The output of the group must be consistent in terms of both quality and cost. This type of strategy is also used in the offices of the clerk and treasurer in local government, as well as in hospitals, clinics, and some school systems.

Le Michelin represents the opposite extreme. The competition includes a few other high-quality restaurants in the area. However, there is no need for the food at Le Michelin to be consistent with food served at any other restaurant. In fact, people come to Le Michelin precisely because items on the menu are unique. The criteria for success at Le Michelin are different from those at Hamburger Heaven:

1. Every guest must leave the restaurant feeling positive about the food and about herself or himself.

2. Meals are prepared to the individual tastes of each customer.

3. New menu items are developed occasionally to pique interest.

The business strategy at Le Michelin is entirely different from that at Hamburger Heaven. It is typical of a group that strives for originality and individuality:

1. Hire very experienced chefs, sous chefs, salad chefs, waiters, waitresses, bartenders, cocktail waitresses, and greeters.

2. Pay employees well and ensure that they receive large tips.

3. Create a team feeling by using an informal style of leadership so that people will be motivated to work as professionals under their own direction.

The owner of Le Michelin has her office on the premises. It is an interesting office. There is no desk or file cabinet. The office contains comfortable furniture. It is a place people can gather to discuss problems and solutions. An easel with paper provides a means for lists and diagrams. During restaurant hours, the owner mingles with customers. She serves drinks and clears tables.

The procedures used at Hamburger Heaven and Le Michelin are not restricted to restaurants. Many groups, committees, task forces, and boards have similar operating procedures. There are five factors that seem to create the difference between the work groups at Hamburger Heaven and at Le Michelin. These factors are related to the degree of formality in group communication. In this chapter, we will help you identify and effectively manage the factors outside the group that affect the degree of formality inside the group. In the next chapter, we will examine the degrees of formality inside the group. In chapter 6, you will learn how to match groups to their situations.

Five Major Factors Affect Group Functioning

People who study behavior have identified five outside factors that influence group communication. This chapter describes these factors and the ways they can be used to determine how formally a group might work in order to achieve high levels of efficiency and effectiveness. The five factors are:

1. The nature of the environment. This includes all of the outside forces which may affect the group—any person or social or political institution that may influence either the group members or the group process. The environment may be (a) Stable and simple, in which case the group functions most effectively using formal, fixed procedures; (b) Dynamic, changing, and complex, in which case the group functions most effectively in informal ways.

2. The accountability of the group to a larger unit or higher authority. The supervisors, committees, boards, and officials to which the group must answer and from which the group receives directions.

3. The professionalization of group members. The amount of education and training of group members. A group whose members have and require a large amount of education related to their jobs is highly professionalized. This group usually works most effectively in informal ways. A group whose members have and require little education and training to do their work has a low degree of professionalization. This group functions most effectively in formal ways.

4. The type and amount of power exerted by the group leader. Leaders have formal (coercive) power when they are in a position to reward employees (with raises, promotions, and time off) or to punish them. Leaders who have informal (persuasive) power rely on personal expertise and personal characteristics for their influence in the group.

5. The nature of the task. The work of the group may require high levels of technology and be referred to as structured. Tasks requiring little technology are called unstructured.

The five major environmental factors are shown in the following diagram. They not only influence the way the group functions, but affect each other as well.

Factors That Influence Group Functions

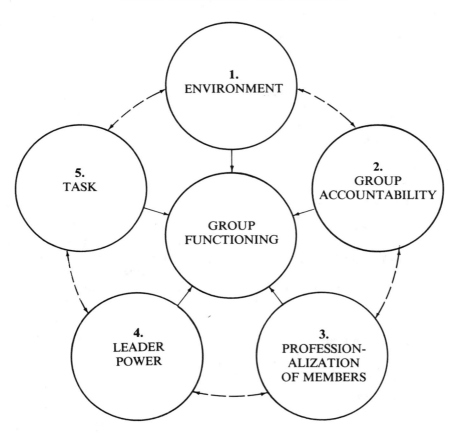

We will look at each factor separately and then examine their impact as a whole. It is important to remember that these are not the only factors that affect the ways groups function. We believe they are the major ones.

The Environment

All groups exist in a context or setting. Groups don't operate in a vacuum. Even the most private family unit is influenced by the neighborhood community, the organizations that supply food, clothing and other necessities, and the outside lifestyles of family members. Most groups are affected by environmental factors such as:

1. Other groups around them

2. The nature of the organization of which they are a part

3. Political, legal, and ethical expectations

In a college classroom, the environment consists of the instructor, the students, the norms of college classes, the expectations of students and faculty, the learning process, the regulations of the school, and the physical setting. These clearly are not the same as the factors that might influence a group in an industrial organization, or a group trying to get the zoning changed in a small town, or in the family group mentioned earlier. The setting for the Harvest Festival Committee is a local community. Sally, Joe, and Frank hold a meeting of sister and brothers in the kitchen to decide who will do which weekly household chores.

The environment includes all of the outside forces which affect a group— the competition, various governmental units, clients and customers, and all of the other people and social institutions which might have an impact. The environment for a group may range from mostly *stable and simple* to quite *dynamic and complex.* Generally, stable and simple environments permit groups to operate in formal, fixed, and procedural ways. Stability characterizes an environment that does not change rapidly. There is no urgent need to collect and process information about what is happening outside the group. Information can be collected slowly.

Decisions on what to do next can be made in a calm manner over a matter of weeks or months. Various agencies in the judicial and legislative arms of government function in a relatively stable, simple environment. Contrast this way of functioning with that of a group which must face many rapid changes. Rapid changes occur when the environment includes many competing groups. Competing groups must constantly modify what they do in order to succeed. They must get information repeatedly and quickly. They must make decisions often to keep up with the competition. Football teams, for example, live in a dynamic, complex environment.

A group that is competing with directly with other groups is one that faces a complex, dynamic environment. Athletic teams are a prime example. Teams must adapt constantly to what their opponents are doing. Neither team has advance knowledge about what will happen. A retail store competing with other similar stores is another example. Store managers typically do not tell their competitors when their next sale will be or when they are going to introduce a new line of merchandise.

Some groups function in much more stable and simple environments. In the stable, simple setting:

1. There is less need for lots of information.

2. The information is easy to get.

3. The information does not change rapidly.

4. Changes in information are always announced.

5. The group has control over any changes in information.

These are groups which go by the book. For example, in an IRS office, the basic information consists of the various laws and regulations on income taxes. If there is going to be a change, everyone is notified, sometimes as much as a year in advance. Laws, regulations, and court decisions are widely disseminated. Consequently, the environment of an IRS office is relatively more stable than that of a small ice cream store trying to compete with several other stores in a small community.

Types of Environments

The complex, dynamic environment is one in which:

1. The group must obtain a great deal of information from other groups or individuals in order to make decisions.

2. Information changes rapidly.

3. Information is hard to obtain.

4. Information may change unexpectedly.

5. There is a lack of control by the group over the matters which affect it.

To make the difference between the simple, stable environment and the complex, dynamic environment clearer, look over the items in the following checklist.

A Checklist for Assessing the Environmental Factors Affecting a Group

All groups operate within a larger environment—a community or organization. Read over the statements below and decide whether they apply to the group you are assessing.

YES   NO

☐   ☐   1. The group must obtain information from other groups or individuals in order to make decisions, solve problems, or get work done.

☐   ☐   2. The information obtained from outside changes more rapidly than the group meets, works together, or makes decisions. The group constantly seems to be out of date with current information unless someone briefs the members between meetings.

☐   ☐   3. The information is hard to obtain, is complex, or requires much preparation.

☐   ☐   4. The information obtained from outside may change unexpectedly either in amount, direction, or quality. It must be reviewed frequently and carefully.

☐   ☐   5. The information obtained from outside deals with matters that are not under the control of the group.

If you marked *yes* three or more times, the group faces a fairly unstable, dynamic information environment and probably has to function somewhat informally. If you marked *no* three or more times, the environment is stable and predictable, permitting a more formal mode of functioning.

By using the checklist, you can assess the environment of a particular group. If three or more of the items apply to a group, the environment tends to be dynamic and complex. This tendency is greater if four or five items are answered yes. If three or more no answers apply, the environment is more stable and simple.

Group Accountability

One important factor in a group's environment is the accountability of the group to a larger unit or a higher authority. The supervisor of a work unit in an organization reports to a division, department, or district manager. The supervisor is thus accountable to the higher authority. A planning commission in a municipality reports to a city commission or trustees. Groups that are carefully controlled by a larger unit or higher authority use more formal procedures. Groups that are not closely supervised (less accountable) use more informal methods of operation.

High versus low accountability. Accountability is highest when:

1. Reports must be provided frequently.

2. There are many comprehensive rules.

3. Reporting includes detailed statistics.

4. There are many detailed criteria to meet.

5. There are numerous regulations or rules covering the performance of the group.

Again, groups may differ on these items. Every bank has a department where employees sort the checks written by customers and enter them on data processing equipment. This procedure allows the bank to issue monthly statements on checking accounts and keep track of the money taken in and issued. Such a department must meet two strict requirements: accuracy and speed. The manager of the work unit can collect statistics quickly and easily on the number of checks processed per day or per week. The number of customer complaints that result in corrections are known. These are measures of efficiency and accuracy. Such a group is highly accountable. Frequent reports can be made, while one is usually required at the end of each day. The rules governing the work are tight. Detailed statistics can be kept on performance. It is easy to set criteria on how many checks per day should be processed and the permissible error rate. Finally, there are banking regulations and state and federal laws covering the group's work. Such a group has high accountability.

In contrast, a booster club for local high school athletics is much less accountable. A report may be submitted to members and the school district once every semester or school year. There are no comprehensive rules on how the group should function. Very few state or local laws apply to the club. Detailed statistics are hard to get other than total dollars collected. It would be difficult to put into numbers the degree of enthusiasm shown by the members or their effect on the morale or the team members. As a result, no fixed and simple criteria can be set up for judging the club's performance. Such a club is not free to do anything at all. Yet within very broad limits, the club can do a lot of different things without getting into trouble or causing problems. Such a group has low accountability.

The relationship between environment and accountability. High accountability is more likely when the environment is fairly stable and simple. It is easier to hold a manufacturing department accountable for units produced, scrap rate, and costs than it is to do the same for a research department, where results are always somewhat uncertain. Sometimes environmental factors can be changed to increase or decrease the accountability of groups to higher levels of authority. You may want to think about your groups in terms of this possibility.

The following checklist includes these factors: (1) the frequency of reporting, (2) the comprehensiveness of rules, (3) the use of detailed statistics, (4) the existence of fixed criteria, and (5) the existence of laws or regulations.

A Checklist for Assessing a Group's Accountability

Many groups report to a higher authority in a community or organization. Read over each statement below and decide whether it applies to the group you are assessing. If the group does not report to any higher authority, simply answer no to all of the items below.

YES   NO
☐   ☐   1. Reviews are conducted of the group's performance or output on a daily or weekly basis.

☐   ☐   2. There are fairly comprehensive rules available to the group on procedures and operations.

☐   ☐   3. Reviews of the group's performance are based on detailed statistics.

☐   ☐   4. There are formal evaluations of the group's performance or output based on fixed criteria.

☐   ☐   5. There are local, state, or federal laws or regulations which govern the functioning of the group.

If you checked three or more items *yes,* the accountability of the group is fairly high and the group is likely to be run in a formal manner. If you checked three or more items *no,* the group is more apt to be run in an informal manner.

Group Member Professionalization

Doctors, lawyers, professors, and other professionals learn to work without much supervision. In the process of being educated and trained, professionals learn to work on their own. They find out what is expected of them. They follow rules on their own. If anything goes wrong, it is up to a professional body or association to discipline the person. On the other hand, nonprofessionals work under a set of rules and regulations set up by a company, government department, or other organization. There are managers and supervisors to see that the rules are followed. The factor of professionalization of group members strongly influences group function.

A group of professionals see themselves as equals, able to interact and make decisions based on their professional expertise. They are more likely to function in informal ways. A group of nonprofessionals will probably function in more formal ways. A leader usually sets up procedures and directs group members in their work.

Consider the classroom teachers in a school. Clearly they have specialized training and education, including certification in their specialties. Many of them attend local, regional, and national conventions on teaching methods, curriculum, and other professional concerns. They read magazines and journals on teaching or in their particular interest or subject area. They attempt to adapt their teaching methods to particular groups of students and to devise new and better ways to teach.

Contrast these teachers with a typical production group in a factory. This work group functions differently. When a new assembly procedure or new product is introduced to the assembly line, the workers are instructed how to do their tasks. There is little or no formal education or training involved. There are no journals or books on the subject. There are no seminars or conferences to attend. The workers are expected to do their tasks exactly as taught. They are not expected to innovate.

The differences between the ways the teachers and the factory workers function is due to the accepted social rules (norms) related to teaching and industrial production. The differences are not related necessarily to the actual abilities of the two groups. In fact, some industries are attempting to professionalize their workers by involving them in decisions about production methods. These workers function in groups called quality circles, quality of work-life groups, job enrichment groups, or employee involvement groups.

The more professionalized employees tend to work in organizations with less stable and more complex environments and with less direct accountability. The professional is expected to be able to adapt to varying conditions and live up to the standards of the profession. There also are differences in how a supervisor, manager, or leader of a group functions with professional and nonprofessional personnel. We'll examine these more closely in Chapter 21.

High versus low professionalization. Once you have determined where your group falls on the scale of professionalization, you will find it useful to use the communication skills that fit the level. You also may want to consider changing the level of professionalization through increased or decreased employee involvement in decision making.

You can assess the degree of professionalization in a group by using the following checklist.

A Checklist for Assessing Group Member Professionalization

Read over each statement below and decide whether it applies to the members of the group you are assessing.

YES   NO

☐   ☐   1. The members of the group attend conferences, seminars, conventions, training sessions, and college courses dealing with their group tasks.

☐   ☐   2. The members of the group write or call persons in other parts of the state or nation to obtain needed information on how to complete tasks or do work.

☐   ☐   3. The members of the group regularly read journals, books, magazines, and other printed material dealing with the mission and work of the group.

☐   ☐   4. The members of the group have specialized education, training, or apprenticeship experience which permits them to adapt to the changing demands of group tasks.

☐   ☐   5. The members of the group attempt to innovate, create, or change the ways of doing tasks in the group on their own in order to improve efficiency and effectiveness.

If you checked three or more items *no,* the group members are relatively nonprofessional. The group would probably run best in a fairly formal manner. If you checked three or more items *yes,* the members are relatively professional and will probably desire or demand more involvement and less formality.

Leader Power

There are several kinds of leader power in a group situation. Some power is based solely on the individual's position and role as a formal leader.

Formal (coercive) power. With formal leadership comes the power to reward through raises, promotions, and time off, and the power to punish through demotions, suspensions, and lack of raises. The leader's title alone carries some power. It's called legitimate power. The formal leader may also have access to other powerful people. This is sometimes called connection power. The leader who has a great deal of reward, punishment, connection, and legitimate power can easily persuade or force employees to do what is expected. This works most effectively with relatively nonprofessional employees in organizations that function in a stable, simple environment with high accountability.

Informal (persuasive) power. Situations with professional employees, complex environments, and low accountability call for another kind of power. For example, leaders have expert power when they are better at doing tasks or have greater experience and knowledge than group members. Such a leader has greater expertise. Another kind of power is information power. A manager may have access to information that others do not have. In other cases, the leader is someone who is liked and respected and has power derived from personal characteristics. These kinds of power imply that the leader and subordinates are relatively equal in terms of motivation. The leader relies on persuasion, logic, and personal influence.

    The following checklist is intended to identify the type of leader power in a group. Answering three or more of these items yes indicates fairly high coercive power while three or more no answers suggest greater reliance on persuasive power.

A Checklist for Assessing the Power of a Group's Leader

Read over each statement below and decide whether it applies to the leader of the group you are assessing. Please note that you should evaluate whether the leader is likely to do the action described.

YES   **NO**

☐   ☐   1. The leader punishes members of the group through criticism, taking over tasks from them, giving low evaluations, demotions, or holding back pay raises.

☐   ☐   2. The leader has an official title or position which gives that person power and prestige over the other members of the group.

☐   ☐   3. The leader rewards members of the group through praise, high evaluations, promotions, pay raises, and more responsibility.

☐   ☐   4. The leader knows other persons in the organization or community who are important and can use these connections to get things done.

☐   ☐   5. The leader is admired and respected by the other people in the group. People will go along with the leader's ideas for this reason.

If you checked three or more items *yes,* the leader power is coercive and the group is likely to be run in a formal manner. If you checked three or more items *no,* the group is more likely to be run in an informal manner.

The Task of the Group

A basic feature of work is the degree of technology involved. Some kinds of tasks involve a high level of technology. Very efficient, effective, and well-known ways are used to get the work done. A common word used for this is *automation.* We immediately think of machines and robots.

The common fast-food restaurant is an example of high technology in the restaurant business. In the "good old days," workers created and invented as they went along. Hamburgers were made by people who formed some ground beef into a patty, put it on the grill, flipped it once or twice, put it on a bun, and served it. You could order a hamburger well done or rare and with any combination of condiments and spices in the kitchen. There were oliveburgers, pickleburgers, and even peanut-butterburgers. The problem was that you could not be sure what was going to happen. How big would the patty be? What kind of meat would be used? How well cooked might it be?

In today's fast food restaurants, the hamburger is standardized. Machines weigh the meat, shape it, and package it. There are strict instructions on how long to cook the patty, when to flip it, and what goes on it. As a result, employees do not have to be as thoroughly trained in cooking. The customer gets a very consistent product even though it might not be of the highest quality.

Structured versus unstructured tasks. Group tasks range from those with relatively high levels of technology to those with little technology. When a great deal of technology is used, the task is termed *structured.* When less technology is involved, tasks are *unstructured.* Specific tasks undertaken by a group can be analyzed from this standpoint. It is useful to think of all the tasks the group has completed in the last weeks or months. How structured or unstructured are they?

Normally, structured tasks are associated with a stable environment, high accountability, low professionalism, and formal leader power (coercion). When there is a standard technology and the task is structured, there will probably be little change in environmental demands. (If there were many changes in environmental demands, the task would involve more thinking time and variety.) Accountability can be high because there is a standard, predictable way to get things done. The leader can enforce the standards. The workers are not encouraged to be professionals but simply to produce as much and as quickly as possible.

Five characteristics exist when tasks are structured:

1. There is a great deal of knowledge available on how to do the tasks.

2. There is little thinking time involved.

3. The long-term results are very predictable.

4. Success can be seen quickly when tasks are done.

5. There is little variety in the kinds of tasks.

The following checklist shows the items to use in assessing the degree of structure.

A Checklist for Assessing the Degree of Structure in the Group Task

Groups have tasks to perform, work to do. The nature of these tasks influences the way the group functions. Read over each statement below and decide whether it applies to the group you are assessing.

YES NO

☐   ☐ 1. There is a clearly defined body of knowledge or guidelines which direct the group members in their work.

☐   ☐ 2. The group members are able to handle problems or situations without having to spend time thinking about them or doing research.

☐   ☐   3. As decisions are made or work efforts completed, the long-term results are generally predictable ahead of time.

☐   ☐   4. When tasks are completed, people are generally aware in a short time (from a day or less to a week or so) if their efforts have been successful.

☐   ☐   5. The kinds of tasks the group must deal with in a meeting or in a typical week are mostly of the same type; there is little variety.

If you marked *yes* three or more times, the group deals with fairly structured tasks and probably has to function somewhat formally. If you marked *no* three or more times, the tasks are fairly unstructured, permitting more informal functioning.

The Influence of Outside Factors

It should be clear that formal ways of functioning work best in groups that have a stable and simple environment, direct accountability, low professionalization, coercive leader power, and structured tasks. If informal methods are to work well, a group will probably have a complex and dynamic environment, indirect accountability, high professionalization, persuasive leadership, and unstructured tasks.

It is important to remember that most groups are a mix of the formal and informal. Rarely does a group fall at the extremes of totally formal or informal functioning. What is important is to be able to use the information in this chapter to determine if the ways your groups function are as effective as they can be. The following chart will help you remember how the five environmental factors are related to formal and informal group procedures:

OUTSIDE INFLUENCES ON PROCEDURE

1. Stable, simple enviroment	1. Dynamic, complex environment
2. Direct, statistical accountability	2. Indirect, qualitative accountability
3. Low professionalization	3. High professionalization
4. Coercive leader power	4. Persuasive leader power
5. Structured task	5. Unstructure task

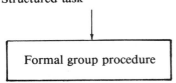

Formal group procedure	Informal group procedure

You can now bring together the results you have for each of the five checklists in this chapter. Complete the following summary form and you will have an overall assessment for your group.

Summarizing Outside Influences

1. Complete the five checklists.

2. Transfer the results from each checklist onto this summary by circling the response appropriate for each checklist.

3. Add the number of items circled in each column.

1. Environmental Checklist	Three or more no answers: stable and predictable	Three or more yes answers: dynamic, unpredictable
2. Accountability Checklist	Three or more yes answers: high accountability	Three or more no answers: low accountability
3. Professionalization Checklist	Three or more no answers: nonprofessional	Three or more yes answers: professional
4. Leader Power Checklist	Three or more yes answers: coercive power	Three or more no answers: persuasive power
5. Task Checklist	Three or more yes answers: structured	Three or more no answers: unstructured
Totals	_____	_____
	Tendency toward formal and structured group procedure	Tendency toward informal and unstructured group procedure

The column with the greater number of circled items represents the group's tendency. For example, a group might have four circled items in the left column and one in the right column. This would indicate formal, structured, and mechanical functioning. Such a group would be expected to have a fairly strong tendency toward more formal procedural and communication methods. The tendency would be stronger than that of a group with a score of three and two, but not as strong as one with a score of five and zero. If the scores went the other direction, the group could be expected to use more informal procedures and open-ended communication methods. This assessment method gives a very rough indication of the strength of a tendency as well as its direction.

Summary

There are five major factors outside the group that affect how formally or informally that group will function. These include:

1. A simple, stable or a complex, dynamic environment
2. High or low accountability to a higher authority
3. High or low professionalization of members
4. Coercive or persuasive leader power
5. Structured or unstructured tasks

In general, it is possible to predict that a group that functions in formal, structured ways will be found in a simple, stable environment. It will be highly accountable, have coercive leader power, and work on structured tasks. A group that uses informal, unstructured procedures will usually be found in a complex, dynamic environment. It will have low accountability, a high degree of professionalization, persuasive leader power, and work on unstructured tasks. These are directions of tendency rather than rigid categories. In other words, different groups function more or less formally in each of the five categories.

In Chapter 6, you will learn how to use information about your group environment so that you can match your procedure to that environment. It is important to know whether or not your group is functioning efficiently and effectively to reach its goals and accomplish its tasks. But before you can successfully match your group to its setting, you must understand how to assess the group's internal functioning. Assessing this internal functioning is the subject of Chapter 5.

REFLECTING/EXPLORING

1. Based on the checklists in the chapter, select two groups that you believe fit the extremes of group functioning: formal and informal. Now carefully apply each checklist to arrive at an overall score for each group. Use the summary form on page 57. How well does each group fit the extreme you initially placed it in? If possible, use groups in which you are a member.

2. Select a group that you believe functions in very effective ways. Again, apply each checklist and use the summary form to arrive at an overall score. Describe the procedures you believe the group uses. Then discuss whether those procedures are consistent with what you would expect the group to do based on your analysis.

3. Think about whether you work more effectively when leaders use persuasive or coercive power. Does the answer differ from group to group? From task to task? What specific information from this chapter is most useful to you in terms of your own functioning in groups?

4. List three pieces of information in this chapter you have found useful. Explain why each is useful. Then identify the next time you will be able to apply this information and describe what you will do.

5. Select a group that you believe tends to vary its procedures from formal to informal. Using the information in this chapter and information you have about the group: (1) describe how the group functions, and (2) evaluate how effective that functioning is. List at least three recommendations you would make to this group for more effective functioning. Relate these to the five factors discussed in this chapter.

CHAPTER 5

FORMAL AND INFORMAL GROUPS

In Chapter 4, we discussed the factors in the group environment which affect the group's internal functioning. The circumstances in which the work groups at the Hamburger Heaven and Le Michelin found themselves resulted in very different ways of functioning. Just as external circumstances differ, so does internal functioning. Even groups that seem similar are not exactly alike. One major difference between groups is the degree of formality in the ways groups function.

This chapter is divided into two sections. We will introduce:

1. A contingency view of group process: group functions are determined by the group's mission, environment, and members.

2. Assessment of formal and informal procedures: how best to match the internal operations of a group to its mission, environment, and members.

When you have completed this chapter, you will be aware of the external and internal factors that must be considered when deciding how a group should function. In Chapter 6, you will learn how to match a group to its situation.

Before examining the contingency view of group process, we will introduce you to the members of the city commission in Oakdale. We will contrast their formal style of functioning with the informal style used by an agency of social workers in the same community. Let's look in on the city commission meeting first:

MAYOR: Does commissioner Remmet have a comment? (Noticing that commissioner Remmet has her hand up.)

REMMET: Yes, Mr. Mayor. I am troubled by the language contained in the report of the advisory group on parks and recreation. Notice that they conclude the report with decisions. My understanding is that, according to the city charter, an advisory group can only make recommendations. Therefore, I move that we return the report to the advisory group for changes to make the language of the final section appropriate.

MARJ SMITH (Chairperson of the advisory group): Mr. Mayor, we did not intend . . .

MAYOR: Excuse me, Mrs. Smith, but we have had a motion made by a commissioner and do not yet have a second. We need a second before we can discuss this matter.

COMMISSIONER YELSMA: I will second commissioner Remmet's motion.

MAYOR: Thank you, commisssioner Yelsma. Any comments from the commission? (A long moment of silence with no comments from any commissioner.) In that case, the chairperson of the advisory group on parks and recreation has something to say. Mrs. Smith.

MARJ SMITH: Thank you, Mr. Mayor. We did not intend . . .

This excerpt illustrates the characteristics of a group that functions in very formal ways. There is a designated leader, a chairperson or a president, in most formal groups. Usually there are also an assistant chairperson or a vice-president, a secretary, and other official positions. Everyone refers to a formal agenda. Frequently the agenda has been posted or mailed to people who are interested. The group follows the agenda step by step. The chairperson is very careful to see that motions are made and seconded before discussion is permitted. If someone wants to speak, the chairperson must recognize that individual.

In this setting the proceedings seem to exhibit a sense of slowness, protocol, and exactness. Contrast the formality of this style with the informal interaction occurring in a meeting of social workers in an agency devoted to adoptions and foster care:

SALLY: The problem, as I see it, is that we are getting all tangled up in paperwork, part of it due to the court . . .

BILL: I agree, Sally, but there's no way around it.

LARRY: Why not? Why can't we streamline our procedures? It seems to me that would reduce some of the time delays.

BILL: Okay. It might cut down the total time by a few days. But I think we have got bigger issues to face. I'm still concerned about the quality of our decisions on placement.

SALLY: Oh, let's not get into that again!

LARRY: Well, I agree with Bill. It is a problem.

SALLY: Remember the last time we got into that one? We spent about five weeks worth of staff meetings dealing with it and still couldn't come up with a decent solution.

BILL: I thought we only spent one or two staff meetings on it.

LARRY: Couldn't we deal with the paperwork delays today and then move on to the placement decision problem at a later meeting?

SALLY: Don't you mean move back to the placement decision problem?

BILL: Well, I would be willing to do that.

The difference between these two groups seems clear. In the staff meeting, people call each other by their first names or simply address someone without using a name at all. Some people talk more than others. A few members may take notes but no one is making sure that everything is recorded. Ideas flow spontaneously. There are sudden changes of direction for no apparent reason. Someone tries to put together what others have said. The summary seems to satisfy most people. Members rely on their memories about past meetings. The discussion is really about the agenda of the present meeting—either no prior agenda existed or it seems to have been ignored. The participants are generalists in the sense that each is knowledgeable about the paperwork delays and the quality of placement decisions. When there are no objections, the meeting breaks up. In this setting, there seems to be a sense of abruptness, casualness, and disorganization. This excerpt illustrates the characteristics of a group that functions in very informal ways.

A Contingency View of Group Process

We subscribe to a *contingency* (situational) view of working in groups. According to this view, the way a group functions is best determined by its:

1. Mission: the goal or purpose of the group

2. Environment: the community or organization in which the group functions

3. Members: the needs and expectations of the group particpants.

Differences in mission, environment, and members account for differences in group functions.

There is no single best way for all groups to operate. Parliamentary procedure may work well in one situation and poorly in another. Random, casual conversation produces effective decisions in one group and chaos in another. Forcing parliamentary procedure on the second group could be just as destructive as encouraging the first group to use more flexible procedures.

The overall look of a contingency model is shown in the following table.

CONTINGENCY MODEL OF GROUP PROCESS

Contingency Factors	*Communication and Procedural Effects*
Group tasks	Written versus oral messages
Leader power	Fixed versus flexible procedures
Member professionalization	Scheduled versus unscheduled
Nature of the larger organization	meetings
Mission	Centralized versus dispersed
Accountability to a higher authority	leadership

The contingency factors affect *how* a group will function most effectively. The communication of procedural effects are the *ways* a group may function. Theoretically, a group's communication and procedural methods are determined by its contingency factors. Contingency theories assume that a match promotes effectiveness and efficiency and a mismatch produces problems.

Formal and Informal Procedures

The two meetings described at the beginning of this chapter are very different. The city commission meeting is formal. The social work group is informal. It is important to be able to identify formal and informal group procedures using observable characteristics.

Note that in practice, many groups use procedures that mix or combine characteristics from the extremes of formal and informal functioning. Groups are not likely to be completely formal or completely informal.

Formal procedures. Four clearly observable characteristics are associated with formal procedures:

1. Official titles and positions are assigned. Chairperson, president, assistant chairperson, vice-president, recording secretary, corresponding secretary, treasurer, personnel-committee chairperson, and vice-president for finance are examples of typical titles. Some titles give people privileges: the right to decide when particpants may speak or the order for taking up agenda items.

2. Written rules of procedure exist. Documents specify what actions the group may take and by what methods. There are rules for making motions, seconding motions, and taking a vote. There are rules for the order of speaking. New members must be introduced to the rules. They study the rules and learn about titles and positions so they can follow the group's procedures.

3. Schedules of meetings exist. Meetings are held at a stated time and in an announced place. Notices of meetings are mailed to

interested people. Meetings have stated starting and ending times. These times often are announced by the leader.

4. Written minutes exist. Minutes (written records of actions taken) are submitted for approval by the participants. The minutes serve as a record of the proceedings of the group. An agenda (a written list of business to be discussed) is used as the order of business at a meeting. The agenda is approved by the group before the meeting begins.

Formal procedures are also characterized by more subtle features. Group members are specialists. Each person has an assigned area of expertise and provides the group with information that other members are not likely to have. Part of each meeting may be devoted to having members give explanations or reports. Decision making is usually by majority or two-thirds vote. In some cases, decisions are deferred to a higher-level authority by forwarding recommendations. The higher-level authority might be a supervisor, board, or president.

Informal procedures. There are three primary characteristics associated with informal procedures. They can be contrasted to the characteristics of formal procedures. In informal group procedures:

1. Instead of titles and positions, the roles people play shift and emerge depending on who is present and what is being discussed. Identifying the leader may be impossible. The interaction between members is improvised and casual.

2. Since there are no rules to follow, turns for talking are determined at the moment by who is asked a question or who interrupts or breaks in. There is no necessity to train new members in the group's procedures. The process is shifting and improvised in nature.

3. Meetings are called as needed, rather than scheduled. Attendance may vary from one meeting to another.

Some features of informal procedures are not as obvious as these. For example, each member acts as a generalist rather than an expert. This means that each person has access to the same information as every other member. No one gives a report. Instead members share information. Decisions occur by consensus, without a vote. When it becomes clear that each person can accept the idea being discussed, someone usually makes a brief summary statement and the group goes on to other topics or the meeting ends.

The differences between formal and informal group functioning are listed in the following table.

FORMAL AND INFORMAL GROUP FUNCTIONING

Formal Group	*Informal Group*
Persons have titles and positions; there is a designated leader.	Roles emerge and shift; there is no designated leader.
There are written rules and procedures.	There is improvised and casual conversation.
New members receive specific training or indoctrination.	What informal training there is occurs in the course of group meetings.
There are written agendas and minutes.	Members sometimes take notes; people often rely on memory.
Meetings are scheduled.	Meetings occur as needed or as people are available.
Members are specialists.	Members are generalists.
Decision making occurs by voting or referral to a higher authority.	Decision making occurs by consensus.

You may be naturally drawn to either the formal or the informal procedure. Or your expectations about how groups should function might be formal or informal. In actuality, either way may be effective, depending on the contingency factors listed on page 63. Further, a combination of both types might very well be the most effective style for a particular group.

The procedures by which any group functions can be assessed in terms of formality and informality. The following checklist has been designed for assessing group functioning. Look over this checklist and think about two groups in which you have participated or that you have observed. Use two groups that present two quite different procedural styles. Observe or remember how people act and talk. Then mark each of the items in the checklist yes or no. The more yes answers, the more formal the group procedures and communication.

A Checklist for Assessing the Formality of Group Procedures and Communication

Check the following items the group members do during a meeting:

YES   NO

☐   ☐   1. Members address each other by title or last name (Mr. President, Madame Chairperson, Mr. Jones, Dr. Smith, etc.).

☐   ☐   2. Members look at or talk about written documents such as reports, letters, memos, budgets, schedules.

☐   ☐   3. Members look at or talk about procedures, policies, bylaws, a constitution or other written operating rules.

☐   ☐   4. Members make motions, make suggestions, offer seconds to motions, amend motions, and take votes.

☐   ☐   5. The group receives reports, oral or written, from individuals or groups.

☐   ☐   6. Members look at or talk about minutes from prior meetings or the agenda of the present meeting.

Check the following items group members do between meetings:

YES   **NO**

☐   ☐   7. Members write each other memos or letters (rather than telephoning or visiting each other).

☐   ☐   8. Members receive agendas of future meetings, minutes of past meetings, or other written materials about the group.

☐   ☐   9. Members know and understand the calendar of meetings for the coming months or the coming year.

If you answered five or more of these items *yes,* your group functions quite formally. Five or more *no* answers indicate informality. Once the differences between informal and formal ways of functioning are clear, the next step is to look at ways of matching the degree of formality in your groups with appropriate procedures—procedures that match the group's style. Methods for doing this are discussed in Chapter 6.

Summary

Some groups function in very formal ways. They write down records about meetings, use fixed procedures, schedule meetings, and have a single official leader. Other groups function in more informal ways: they depend on oral messages, use flexible procedures, have unscheduled meetings, and leadership is dispersed among group members. A mix of these two extremes may be the typical way your group functions. Other groups function in more strictly formal or completely informal ways. This chapter has provided you with a checklist for assessing the degree of formality present in your groups.

It is not possible to match groups intelligently to their situations unless you understand the factors that affect the ways groups function. In this chapter, we have considered the formal and informal ways a group may function. You learned how to assess the group's internal functioning. In Chapter 4, you learned about the external factors that affect the way a group functions. Now you are ready to take the information from both chapters and match a group to its situation.

REFLECTING/EXPLORING

1. Use the list of contingency factors and communication and procedural effects on page 63. Observe two groups: one that uses primarily formal procedures and another that uses primarily informal procedures. What relationships do you see between the styles of procedure and the contingency factors affecting each group?

2. Select two groups in which you participate, one that uses formal procedures and one that uses informal procedures. List the advantages and disadvantages you see in using the procedures based on the contingency factors of mission, environment, and members.

3. Select one group of which you are a member. Based on this chapter, what changes would you recommend to this group so that it might function more effectively? What characteristics of the way the group functions would you praise?

4. Attend a city commission meeting. Use the checklist for assessing the degree of formality of group procedures on pages 65 and 66. What observations can you make about the city commission meeting?

5. City commissions usually keep and publish a written record of their proceedings. Obtain a copy of the record for the meeting you attended. How accurate is the written record? How much of the actual meeting is put into the record? Do meetings of groups that you attend record more or less information than the city commission? What are the implications for the members and interested persons? What general conclusions might you draw about the difference between formal and informal procedures with regard to written records?

CHAPTER 6

ADAPTING TO ENVIRONMENTS

Above eleven thousand feet on many mountains of the Western United States, there are no large trees. There is a timber line above which large vegetation does not grow. If you climb to that elevation, you will find a variety of small plants, ranging from lichen to tiny mountain versions of the flowers in the valleys below. These plants are short and tucked into crevices to avoid the blasts of cold wind. These are plants that are adapted to their environment, to their local situation.

Groups also adapt to their environments, to their situations. There is no simple cause-and-effect relationship, however. A stable situation and relatively unskilled group members do not *cause* a group to use formal procedures. Rather, it seems to be a matter of matching procedures to its membership and situation. Such a matching enhances a group's efficiency and effectiveness. This is why we use a contingency model in this book. The contingency approach is based on the theory that there are conditions beyond the group that affect the internal functioning of the group. These contingencies, or outside factors, were the topic of Chapter 4. In this chapter, we will refer to these outside factors as a group's *situation*.

Consider the design of houses for different climates. Where it is very warm, building on stilts is practical. This is especially wise if there is periodic flooding or there are other dangers close to the ground. The areas near New Orleans might fit this description. Light breezes several feet off the ground help cool the house. A house built on stilts in warm areas, therefore, is well matched to its surrounding environment (its situation). A house built on stilts, however, is not well matched to an environment where the temperature falls below forty degrees on a regular basis. A house in the air in this situation would lose heat from the roof, walls, and floor. It is very difficult to keep such a house warm. What is an advantage in a warm, wet climate is a distinct disadvantage in a cool climate. Houses can be, and frequently are, designed to match their climatic environments (situations). Since they are built by humans, however, there is sometimes a tendency to overlook environment in favor of fashion. Some people build houses up in the air in cold climates. Others build northern style homes in very warm climates. Human decisions, both environmental matches and mismatches, are a matter of deliberate choice.

Matches and mismatches can also occur between groups' situations and the functional styles the groups choose. In this chapter, we will look at:

1. Matches and mismatches between group situations and the way a group functions
2. The stress that usually results from mismatches
3. Ways of dealing with the mismatches between the group situation and the way the group functions
4. Ways to profit from matches between the group situation and the way the group functions

Matches and Mismatches in Group Functioning

In Chapter 5, we described the formal and informal ways that groups function. When groups are in a stable environment, with high accountability, low professionalization, coercive leader power, and structured tasks, the group will probably operate in formal, structured ways. Members are likely to use formal titles, strict procedures, and a lot of paperwork. Groups in a changing environment, with low accountability, high professionalization, persuasive leader power, and unstructured tasks, tend to use more informal procedures. Members are likely to behave in more personal, spontaneous ways. There will probably be more interaction among group members.

The possible combinations of outside conditions (the situation) and the way a group functions are shown in the following table.

MATCHING OUTSIDE CONDITIONS WITH GROUP FUNCTIONS

Contingency Factors	*Group Functioning*	*Mix or Match?*	*Probable Result*
Dynamic environment, professionalized members, and complex task	Spontaneous responses, shifting roles, and meetings as needed	MATCH	EASE AND EFFICIENCY
Dynamic environment, professionalized members, and complex task	Rules of procedures, official positions, and scheduled meetings	MISMATCH	STRESS
Stable environment, nonprofessionalized members, and simple task	Spontaneous reponses, shifting roles, and meetings as needed	MISMATCH	STRESS
Stable environment, nonprofessionalized members, and simple task	Rules of procedure, official positions, and scheduled meetings	MATCH	EASE AND EFFICIENCY

Two of these situations represent matches between the group's way of functioning and the factors outside of the group that affect that functioning.

One is between the dynamic environment, professionalized members, and a complex task and meetings as needed, spontaneous member reponses, and shifting roles. The other match is between a stable environment, non-professionalized members, and a simple task, rules of procedure, regularly scheduled meetings, and official positions. In both of these cases, the match would be likely to result in relative ease and efficiency of operation. The group's methods match the demands put on the group by outside factors.

In the two other situations shown, the outside factors do not match the way the group functions. The result would probably be stress. Sometimes a group uses rules of procedure, regularly scheduled meetings, official positions with titles in a dynamic environment with professionalized members and a complex task. In this mismatched situation, stress occurs because the group cannot respond quickly and easily to the changes, shifts, and variations in its environment. In the second stressful situation, the group uses spontaneous interaction, members shift roles, and meetings are held as necessary. However, the outside conditions include a stable environment, the members are nonprofessionalized, and the group tasks are simple. Stress is likely to occur in this situation because contradictions exist between the informal group procedure and its stable environment, simple tasks, and nonprofessionalized members. As stability and sameness is required by this type of group for ease and efficiency, its procedure is mismatched.

Mismatches and Stress

When groups match the ways they function to the outside conditions of their situation, the result is relative efficiency and effectiveness. Stress is the result of a mismatch. Listen to Tonya:

> This committee is driving me crazy. We meet once a month to discuss problems. I get a problem that I want the committee to deal with. So I have to get it on the agenda. Sometimes that takes two months. Then we might discuss it for several meetings. And that may mean several months. By then, the problem is gone—or else it is a major crisis and out of our hands!

Tonya has described a mismatch between the way her committee functions and the kinds of outside conditions that seem to affect her situation. The chances are good that other committee members feel the same kind of frustration. If they do, the mismatch, and the frustration, is intensified.

What kind of a mismatch is this? Tonya's description is of an environment which changes fairly rapidly. Problems that arise either go away or get worse within a matter of three to five months. This would be considered an unstable environment. Yet the group is using formal procedures. They move at a deliberate, slow pace. As a result, at least some of the problems that come before the committee cannot be handled by them. When this occurs, the committee is bypassed. Members and other workers begin going around the committee to a higher level of authority because they can get answers faster. Committee members then begin to feel unimportant or angry. More stress is the usual result. A principle emerges here: *People in groups will feel stress if there is a mismatch between the situation and the group's way of functioning.*

Now, let's look at a mismatch that is at the opposite extreme from the one Tonya finds herself in. Paul is a salesman with an outdoor advertising company. The company designs and builds billboards. Paul wrote a memo to his boss. Paul's distress seems clear.

> Over the last six months we have experienced seven cases of dissatisfied customers who have gone to other companies. In all seven cases, the problem was that the workers who build and install the billboards did not know what the customer really wanted. As a result, the signs did not satisfy the customers.
>
> Our problem is that we do not have a good way to write up orders and get them to the shop and then to installation. Everything is done by word of mouth. I realize that we only have eight employees, but that is enough to create problems. I usually tell Fred, in the shop, what the customer wants. Then Fred draws up a design. We show that design to the customer and get approval. But Fred's ideas are only sketches. He gives them to other people to work up in finished form. There are changes. No one checks these changes with the customer. Another part of the problem is that installation does not know exactly where the sign is supposed to go. We had two cases of a sign actually being put up in the wrong place.
>
> We need to get organized around here! If we don't we will keep losing customers!

Informal procedures are often used in small groups. A group of eight is relatively small. Informal procedures do not provide controls. There often are no checks on progress or changes.

What is Paul's complaint? The group is functioning more casually than it should. The environment is stable. Once a customer decides on a sign, there is no reason to change it. The customers certainly are not changing their requirements. It seems the workers involved in building and installing the signs are not professionalized. They do not follow through and check changes with customers. No one seems to be providing strong leadership by setting up rules or by following up on orders. As a result, this work group does not seem to be functioning as formally as it could. Customers are unhappy. Paul is distressed. Other workers may feel stressed as well. Efficiency and effectiveness are low.

The contingency model can be used to identify two possible mismatches that result in stress:

1. A structured situation in which a group functions informally

2. An unstructured situation in which a group functions formally

Either situation tends to produce stress in the group members. If asked, the members probably will be able to talk about their feelings of stress. They probably will not analyze the reasons for the stress in terms of function—situation mismatch.

Mismatches between Situation and Function

The problem is clear: If demands on a group by outside conditions cannot be met effectively and efficiently by the ways it functions, stress results. The stress is usually felt by both members and leaders. What can be done about the stress? We will look at possible member responses first. Then we will look at what might be done by leaders to deal with stress.

Member responses. In the examples used in the previous section, both Tonya and Paul expressed their frustration. Stating feelings of stress may help Tonya and Paul at the moment. But it may not be enough to solve the problem. Group members can (1) try to describe and understand the problem and (2) try to change the way the group functions.

A stress-filled situation may become less intense if the reason for the stress is understood. Insight into the problem sometimes helps a group member to live with the situation. Paul's memo was an attempt to explain the problem as he saw it. More understanding might come from knowing if the other seven workers were aware of the problem. How did they view it? Tonya might have said, "Okay, this committee is not dealing with the kinds of problems I face. Maybe there is no way it can. I will live with it the best I can. I'm not paid enough to worry about this as much as I do." Recognizing, understanding, and living with conditions is one way to deal with stress.

Perhaps a more positive response would be to try to change things. This alternative is more positive because it tends to reduce stress rather than adjusting to it. Tonya could try to educate the workers around her. She could train the members of the committee. The result might be either that the committee would change its procedures or a new method for coping with the problem might be created. Perhaps a task force or subcommittee could be created.

Paul might also attempt to change things. His memo is a start. Also, he could design a procedure that would ensure that the same information reached everyone. He might develop a form for the salesperson to use in writing up the customer's order. The form could provide copies for workers at each stage of the process or it could be routed to each person involved. Paul could present his form in a *proposal.* The explanation in his memo could become part of a statement explaining the reasons for adopting the form as a new procedure. It is possible that Paul's form would not be adopted by the leaders in charge of the company. They might feel that informality is important or the company is too small for structured procedures. In this case, Paul might use a simple form on his own. He might run off copies on a duplicating machine and use the form to make sure his customers get good service. If the form works, other workers might start using it unofficially.

Leader responses. Sometimes group members are not aware of the reasons for stress, they may not know what changes to suggest, and they may not have the ability to develop, propose, and implement a change. Whether members do or do not have these abilities, it is our view that a group leader should develop ways to assess the group on a regular basis. The purpose of the assessment is to determine if there is a match or mismatch between the group's situation and the way it functions. A leader must regularly ask: Are we functioning in ways that make the best sense in terms of our situation, our workers, and the tasks we have before us? A leader can use the checklists provided in Chapters 4 and 5 to make the assessment. After using these checklists a few times, a leader may become more sensitive to signs of stress and may be able to evaluate conditions without using the lists.

A leader must be sensitive both to the conditions in which a group finds itself and the ways it functions. The outside conditions can be reviewed by looking at the demands put on the group. How heavy is the work load? What kind of competition is there from other groups? How much competition is there? How much pressure is put on the group by higher levels of authority to which the group is accountable? Thinking about the conditions in which the group is working should be a habit for an effective group leader.

The effective group leader also regularly assesses the way the team is functioning. How effectively and efficiently does the group complete tasks assigned to it? What kinds of written procedures guide the group? How many written procedures must they follow? Are there enough written guidelines? What ways exist for group members to get together with each other to discuss problems and solutions? Do members talk too formally or too informally? Should we use titles instead of first names? The leader who asks such questions regularly about both the ways the group functions and its situation will be able to make more informed, sensitive choices.

Matches between Situation and Function

It may seem unimportant to think about groups whose functions match their situations. However, both members and leaders can benefit from being alert to the possible development of a mismatch. Mismatches can develop (1) because of variations in tasks within the group and (2) as a result of large changes in the overall situation of the group.

Variations in tasks. Tasks can be simple and structured or relatively complex and unstructured. In some groups, all of the tasks seem the same, without much variation. However, some groups work on a variety of tasks. Some are complex; some are simple. A group which seems well adapted to its situation can still experience occasional or momentary stress.

Here's an example: A group of accountants in an agency were responsible for conducting rather elaborate audits of various divisions and departments. Most of the accountants were highly trained and experienced. They needed little day-to-day supervision. When the need for an audit arose, the supervisor assigned one or more accountants. They usually completed the job in several weeks or a month. These accounts drew on their knowledge of accounting and agency rules and procedures.

One day a request was made for an audit of a particular project. The project involved less than $20,000 funding. An accountant was assigned and worked for over a week on the audit. The accountant produced a rather elaborate report. The report was almost as big as the final report for the project itself. (Someone pointed this out later.) Then another request of the same type came in. The accountants were instructed to keep the audits and report simple. The supervisor issued a set of "guidelines" which were actually rules. Some of the accountants began to grumble that they might as well be bookkeepers.

What happened? A group that usually dealt with complex and unstructured tasks that required thought and knowledge suddenly found that some new tasks are very simple and straightforward. The result was minor stress within a unit that was well matched to its situation otherwise.

Several solutons are possible in such a situation: The simpler audits could be handled by less experienced accountants, even a newly hired person who could specialize in bookkeeping audits. The accountants could be educated in the idea of contingency models and the idea of matches between people and tasks. They could be asked to live with an occasional simple, structured task. A principle emerges here: *Tasks within a group can vary. This variation can create local, short-term stress in people.*

Changes in the group situation. Gradual change can occur in the overall situation of a group. Even when a match does exist, there is the possibility of a shift. In fact, most mismatches probably occur because a team continues to function in old ways when a new set of conditions arises.

The automobile industry experienced this kind of transition in the 1970s. During the fifties and sixties, the automobile industry in the United States was based on an expanding population and huge supplies of gasoline. The Big Three automobile companies competed primarily with each other. There was little external competition. Very quickly, the population increase slowed down. At the same time, gasoline supplies were cut and prices rose. Then competition came from other countries. The U.S. automobile companies had no quick way to redesign their vehicles to meet changing conditions. Their whole organizational scheme was based on long, slow evolution, not quick change.

A similar shift faced a local neighborhood association. For years, the group had functioned to provide an occasional block party, to organize a neighborhood watch for small children on their way to school, and to host candidate nights during city elections. The group was very informal. They elected officers who functioned in a very informal way. Then, within three years, two major changes occurred. First, retail stores and apartment-house developments were proposed for the land next to the neighborhood. Second, the city government decided to use a coalition of neighborhood groups to aid in planning and other functions. The changes demanded that the neighborhood association work in more formal ways. It was necessary for the group to present coherent positions and to make presentations to the planning board and city commission. The group also needed to elect representatives to the citywide coalition. These new needs implied a much more formal way of working than this group had used before. But the association officers resisted the changes. They wanted to continue the informality of the good old days. As a result, the association was ineffective—until a new group took control and started to function in ways that matched the group's changed situation. A principle emerges here: *Even when things are going well, leaders and members must remain alert to changes in the group's situation.*

Summary

All groups function within a larger situation. The way groups function may or may not match their situations. If a mismatch exists, the members of the group will experience stress. Something will not feel right. Group members and leaders can reduce this stress by introducing changes in group functioning that move the group toward a match with outside factors. If such changes are not possible, understanding the reasons for the stress can help members live with it. Even groups that have a match between the ways they function and outside conditions need to remain alert to potential mismatches. These can occur when a variety of different types of tasks exist. Mismatches are even more likely to occur when the overall situation surrounding the group changes as a result of shifts in the social, economic, or political scene.

REFLECTING/EXPLORING

1. Use the listing of contingency factors, group functioning, and probable results on page 69. Identify and describe the conditions that existed in a group of which you are or have been a member for each of the four conditions in the list.

2. For the two conditions that were or are a mismatch, describe (1) your understanding of the problem and (2) what you can do or could have done to change the situation. If you are a member of the group, describe what you might do or could have done if the leaders of your group

rejected your proposal. If you are or were a leader in this situation, describe what you could have done or could do to stay alert to the changing conditions in this group.

3. For the two conditions that were or are a match, describe any awareness you have of possible variations in tasks or changes in the group situation that may give rise to some stress. What can you do about this?

4. Describe how you might use the material in Chapters 4, 5, and 6 to help educate the members and leaders of groups that you work with in order to help prevent the stress and inefficiency that comes with mismatches. How might you present and share these materials with your co-workers?

5. Use one group of which you are a member or leader at this time. Use the checklists in Chapters 4 and 5 to assess this group. What are the results of your assessment? How might you share with your group your assessment of how well group procedures are matched (or mismatched) with your group's situation?

Section Two: Reading List

Information about the contingency model, or situational theory:

Fiedler, F. E. and M. M. Chemers. *Leadership and Effective Management.* Glenview, IL: Scott, Foresman and Company, 1974.

Johnson, B. "Contingencies and Coordination Formats," in *Communication: The Process of Organizing.* Boston: Allyn & Bacon, 1977.

Hersey, P. and K. Blanchard. *Management of Organizational Behavior,* 4th ed. Englewood Cliffs, N.J.: Prentice-Hall, 1982.

Lawrence, P. and J. W. Lorsch. *Organization and Environment.* Homewood, IL: Richard D. Irwin, Inc., 1967.

Shaw, M. E. "The Task Environment" in *The Psychology of Small Group Behavior.* New York: McGraw-Hill, 1971.

Van de Ven, A., A. L. Delbecq, and R. Koenig, Jr. "Determinants of coordinations within organizations," *American Sociological Review,* 41 (1976): 322-37.

FORMAL AND INFORMAL STRUCTURES

CHAPTER 7

FORMAL GROUP STRUCTURE

By learning about the structure of groups you observe and in which you participate, you will be able to function more effectively. You will be able to understand and work with more ease and greater success when you know the lines of authority, responsibility, and communication. In this chapter, we will examine the nature of formal group structure. Informal group structure will be described in Chapter 8. Designing, and working within, formal group structure will be the emphasis in Chapter 9.

In this chapter, we will introduce the following ideas:

1. Every group has a basic structure that includes two parts:
   a. The formal structure is represented by an organizational chart.
   b. The informal structure is represented by a communication network.

2. The formal structure includes both line and staff functions:
   a. Line denotes positions of authority and responsibility.
   b. Staff denotes positions of support and service.

3. The line functions can be understood by analyzing two factors:
   a. The echelons (levels of authority) within the formal structure.
   b. The span of control (number of people responsible to a single leader) within the formal structure.

Groups Have Formal and Informal Structures

Grand Avenue Pet Hospital in Marysville was founded in an unusual way. The veterinarians who own and operate clinics throughout the city organized the hospital about ten years ago. At that time, the doctors were accustomed to hold a monthly meeting to discuss common concerns, new methods of serving clients, and ways of supporting each other's efforts to provide better veterinary services. There were three doctors in the town who practiced veterinary medicine at the time:

1. Dr. James Bentley, a specialist in reptiles, had been in business for about five years. He owned the East Side Pet Clinic.

2. Dr. Susan Frock, specializing in birds, bought the Elm Street Pet Clinic from a retiring doctor, Ben Williams.

3. Dr. William Evans, a specialist in dogs and cats, had moved to Marysville three years before. He had been working in a large urban area animal hospital.

Ben Williams, the retired veterinarian from whom Susan Frock bought the Elm Street Pet Clinic, asked the three doctors if he could join them at one of their monthly luncheons. The doctors agreed. Ben Williams shared with the doctors his lifelong dream of opening an animal hospital that would serve all the veterinary clinics in the community. He told the doctors he wanted to provide the financial backing for a hospital and asked them if they would be willing to staff the hospital while at the same time continuing their individual private practices. Ben Williams agreed to purchase the surgical equipment for the new hospital. He proposed that the three doctors close their own clinics two afternoons a week in order to spend time at the hospital. Among them, they could staff the hospital six afternoons each week. In addition, they could rotate on-call duty at night and provide an around-the-clock emergency service that they were unwilling to offer alone at their respective clinics.

The three doctors were enthusiastic. They were especially pleased when Ben Williams agreed to serve as director of the newly created Grand Avenue Animal Hospital. The doctors decided that the hospital staff would include fifteen people: Each doctor would include his or her own paraprofessional staff on those afternoons when he or she was on duty in the hospital. In addition, Ben would have a staff of three at the hospital on a regular basis. With this background information, we are ready to examine the formal and informal structures of this new hospital.

An Organizational Chart Represents Formal Structure

The director of the new hospital, Dr. Ben Williams, oversees the entire operation of the hospital. In fact, he is the one person who is in direct authority throughout the daytime hours of the hospital. The director plus three doctors, Jim, Sue, and Bill, have the responsibility for providing service to the public. The doctors bring their paraprofessional staff from their own clinics to the hospital when they are on duty. Jim has two staff members; Sue and Bill each have three. Ben Williams, the director, has a support staff, which includes one paraprofessional in veterinary medicine, one secretary–receptionist, and one bookkeeper.

An *organizational chart* will help you visualize the formal working relationship among the group members.

ORGANIZATIONAL CHART FOR GRAND AVENUE ANIMAL HOSPITAL

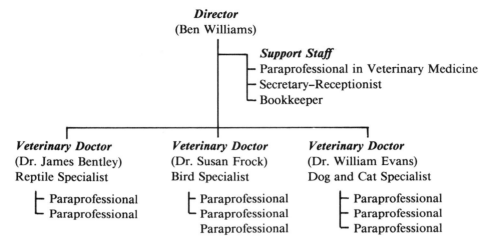

This organizational chart indicates that both the support staff and the veterinary staff report to the director. The paraprofessionals report directly to the doctors in whose clinic they work on a regular basis. This chart represents the formal structure of the group. It defines who reports to whom. The lines connecting the positions on the chart represent the lines of authority and responsibility in the hospital. These lines also indicate the formal communication links between staff members. Reports, memos, and informal notes are sent from one staff member to the person directly above or below. The organizational chart for a group includes the official positions within the group and shows how these positions are linked together. An organizational chart does not show the informal structure that exists in every group.

A Communication Network Represents Informal Structure

The organizational chart for Grand Avenue Animal Hospital outlines the pattern of formal lines of communication. However, the members of the hospital staff do not limit their communication to their immediate supervisors or to the employees over whom they have direct supervisory responsibilities. The support staff members of the hospital do not communicate exclusively with the director and the veterinarians. They provide service for the entire staff. They tend to have special relationships, or links, with the people who need more work done or whose work needs special attention. For example, Bill Evans paid his way through college by working as a court reporter. He types very well and prefers to prepare his own medical reports. Bill probably communicates less often and less regularly with Sally, the secretary–receptionist, than does any other member of the staff. Susan Frock, however, is completing postgraduate work to broaden her expertise beyond bird life. She relies heavily on Sally for secretarial work and probably communicates with her more than any other staff member, including the director. Also, Susan talks frequently with Ben Williams about the patients he previously cared for at the Elm Street Clinic. Mark, the paraprofessional assigned to the director, is still in veterinary school. Mark works closely with Bill Evans because he, too, wants to specialize in caring for dogs and cats. Mark wants to learn as much as he can about those animals. Mark and Bill talk frequently. In general, the paraprofessional staffs talk frequently across service units to each of the doctors and to each other. Their work overlaps. Together, they provide continuous care of their patients, not simply service on the days they are assigned to work in the hospital. We can plot on a chart a diagram of who *actually* talks to whom. A diagram of the informal lines of communication is called a *communication network*. The following diagram is the communication network for the Grand Avenue Animal Hospital.

A comparison of the organizational chart with this communication network shows that the formal and informal structures are very different.

1. The formal structure consists of the official lines of authority and responsibility and the official lines of communication. Sally can expect Ben to conduct an annual review of her effectiveness as a secretary–receptionist for the hospital. She can expect to hear from Ben whether she will receive a raise and if so, how much additional pay she will receive. She can expect to negotiate her vacation days with Ben.

2. The informal structure consists of the actual lines of communication among members of the group. Since Ben and the three veterinarians meet monthly to discuss hospital procedures, Susan will know about Sally's annual evaluation, her pay raises, and decisions about her vacation days before Sally knows. It is possible that Sally will hear about these issues, informally, from Susan before she hears about them formally from Ben.

Both the formal and informal structures must be taken into account if a group member wishes to understand how a group actually functions and wants to work effectively within it.

Individual work units within an organization or a community also have formal and informal structures. The formal structure seems less apparent in a small group than it does in the larger parent group. This is an organizational chart of the formal structure for the staff (work unit) that reports to Dr. James Bentley:

COMMUNICATION NETWORK FOR
THE GRAND AVENUE ANIMAL HOSPITAL

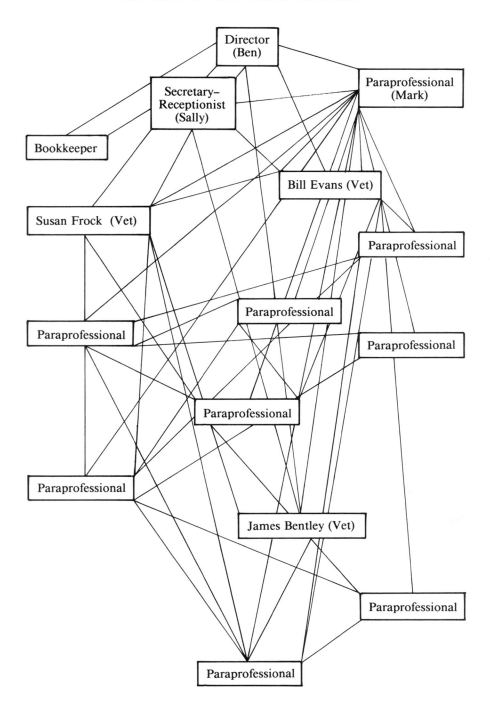

DR. BENTLEY'S WORK UNIT

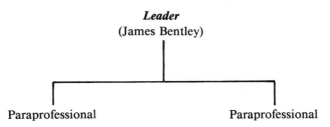

There is a leader and two members on this staff. This is the only distinction among the members of the group. Compare this to the complex formal structure of the total hospital staff. There, distinctions are drawn between director, veterinarians, support staff, and the paraprofessionals assigned to each veterinarian.

We can examine the informal structure of this same work unit in two ways. We can look at

1. Who-talks-to-whom and who-talks-after-whom

2. The pattern of contacts between people outside of group meetings

Who-Talks-to-Whom and Who-Talks-After-Whom

When examining the pattern of conversation in a meeting, it usually becomes clear that some people talk more to each other and exchange more turns between themselves than they do with others. In this way, a subgroup or clique of the larger group is created. Even in James Bentley's small staff, these characteristics are observable: José and Robin, the two paraprofessionals, work together eight hours a day in the lab of the clinic as well as at the hospital two afternoons a week. As you might expect, they interact with each other more during staff meetings than either of them do with James Bentley. Also, James usually initiates talk with José and Robin and they respond. The following diagram shows the informal structure of their small group.

INFORMAL STRUCTURE: DR. BENTLEY'S UNIT

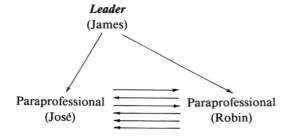

The arrows on the lines from James to José and Robin suggest that James most often initiates the talk and they respond to him. The lines between José and Robin suggest that they talk more often to each other than to James. Also, Robin initiates more talk with José than he initiates with her. Perhaps this pattern occurs because José is a new employee and Robin is training him. These patterns are typical of the staff meetings at the East Side Pet Clinic.

Patterns of Informal Contacts

The pattern of talk outside of group meetings may be similar to or different from the patterns within group meetings. Some people work closely together and have an opportunity to talk for that reason. Robin and José talk often, both because they work together in the lab and because José is learning new procedures from Robin. Sometimes group members get together outside of a meeting for the specific purpose of talking about a topic that will be discussed at the next meeting. James and José have agreed to meet so that José can evaluate the new lab trainee manual that James and Robin have prepared. José is the first employee to be trained with the new manual. The following diagram shows the informal communication that occurred among the members of this subgroup during one week:

INFORMAL STRUCTURE: DR. BENTLEY'S UNIT

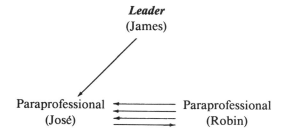

A small unit within a larger organization or community can have a very simple formal structure and an involved informal structure. This contrast can indeed be predicted in most cases. Informal group structure will be the focus of Chapter 8. In the remainder of this chapter, we will examine the features of the formal structure. First, it will be helpful to understand the differences between line and staff functions.

Line and Staff Functions

If you were to bring your pet into the Grand Avenue Animal Hospital, you might get the impression that Sally, the secretary–receptionist, is the person in authority. Sally would help you complete an initial record on your pet, assign you to a doctor, and give you prescriptions and directions for care, as well as take your payment for services and make an appointment for your next visit. You probably would not meet Ben Williams, the director of the hospital. He is the top-level authority. Actually, Sally has no formal authority at all. She performs a staff function.

Line Functions: Authority and Responsibility

Ben Williams is the highest authority as director of the hospital. This means that he has the authority to make final decisions and has the ultimate responsibility to see that the hospital functions efficiently. The term *line* refers to the line of authority and responsibility within an organization or community. The line runs from the top to the bottom of the organization. In an organization, the president is usually at the top and the line runs down through the managers to the members of their departments. In a community group, the line may run from the mayor down through the committee chairpersons to the committee members. In the Grand Avenue Animal Hospital, the line runs from the director (Ben) through the veterinarians to the paraprofessionals on their respective staffs.

When a person holds a line position, he or she can communicate officially with the person directly above or below in the line. People in line positions have both authority over and responsibility for the individuals who hold positions below their own. Similarly, people in line positions can expect that their supervisors will be in the positions immediately above their own on the organizational chart. Sue, James, and Bill report to Ben Williams, the director. The paraprofessional staff members report to Sue, James, or Bill, depending on where they are employed. Sometimes communicating up or down the line is referred to as "going through channels." For example, it probably would be appropriate for José to recommend a change in lab procedures at the East Side Pet Clinic to James, the doctor who owns the clinic. It would be inappropriate for José to make the recommendation to Ben, the director of the hospital, and suggest that Ben tell James to revise the lab procedures. Once a group member or leader knows how his or her position fits into the line of authority, then he or she knows how to function within the formal organization.

Staff Functions: Support Personnel

The lines of authority and responsibility identify the positions that directly influence the way the group functions. *Staff* functions are performed by persons in support positions. For example, a secretary who attends a meeting for the purpose of taking notes and preparing a written summary of the meeting, and who has no vote, serves in a staff capacity to that group. Sally, the secretary–receptionist at the hospital, performs this staff function when the doctors and the director hold their regular meetings. Mark, the paraprofessional assigned to the hospital on a regular basis, is a staff member. The bookkeeper is also. In the following diagram their positions are placed beside the line of authority and responsibility.

LINE AND STAFF POSITIONS

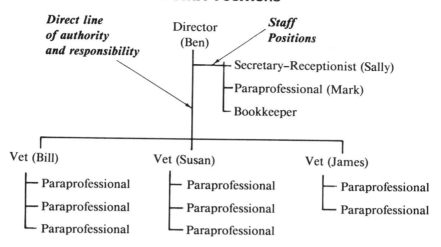

Sally, Mark, and the bookkeeper are in positions that are created to support the work of the director, Ben. Since his work involves managing the hospital, their job descriptions are related to his function. Perhaps the support role that Sally plays is the reason customers sometimes think of her as the person in charge of the hospital. She is a direct extension of the person in charge and of his work. If Sally wishes to influence the official functioning of the hospital by altering written operating procedures, she must work through a person in a line position. She has no vote at the meetings and she does not participate in the meetings in any official way. According to the organizational chart, we would expect Sally to work through the director to affect the functioning of the hospital.

Understanding Line Functions

Turn to the organizational chart of Grand Avenue Animal Hospital. You will see that the director and the veterinarians are on different levels. These levels are *echelons* in the formal structure of an organization. The higher the echelon, the greater the power (authority) and responsibility of the persons in the positions on that level. The hospital structure has two echelons: director and veterinarian.

The organizational chart of the hospital will also help you understand the concept, *span of control.* This term is used to identify the number of people a leader directs. In the hospital, Ben has a span of three veterinarians over whom he has authority. The hospital has a small, simple structure. So there are only two echelons and one span of control. The echelons and span of control for the Grand Avenue Animal Hospital are shown in the following diagram.

Echelons and Span of Control

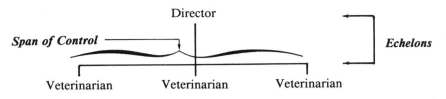

If an employee or a customer wishes to influence the policies and procedures of the hospital, this is important to know. By reporting concern or suggestion to any one of the three veterinarians, I have a good chance of getting it to the director. The director is the immediate supervisor and the final authority for each veterinarian in the hospital. There is no assistant director, no level of middle management, through which the suggestion will be filtered. If a veterinarian agrees to take a suggestion to the director, it is relatively easy to follow up with the specific veterinarian to see if the suggestion has been considered.

In a larger, more complex organization, such as General Motors, suggestions may be lost in the corporate structure. In more complex structures, a group member may need to monitor a suggestion, step by step, through the line of authority in order to ensure that the suggestion moves through the necessary formal levels of decision making. In a more complex organization, there are many echelons. Moving up the line of authority from the bottom of the organization chart for General Motors, you would see a span of control at each level. The number of positions at each level indicates the span of control for the position in line above that level. This will hold true until the very top level, where the chief executive officer, president, or board of directors is the final authority.

Formal structure is defined by the positions people hold and the relationships between those positions. The higher the position on an organization chart, the more power that position represents. Staff positions, on the other hand, are defined by their titles, such as secretary-receptionist. The lines on an organizational chart represent the flow of responsibility and authority and also the formal lines of communication. It is expected that a group member will work within the lines of authority. Going straight to the top is frowned upon. A worker who does go straight to the director instead of to the immediate supervisor will probably be asked if he or she has met with the immediate supervisor. An attempt will probably be made to send the worker back to work through the supervisor.

Many groups and work units have their formal structures defined by a set of documents. In some cases, there is a constitution and bylaws which identify various positions and titles, their responsibilities, and who reports to whom. For other groups, the organizational chart and job descriptions provided by the parent organization govern the formal structure of the group. In still others, there is a standard structure dictated by national or international headquarters. Examples of this are social or fraternal organizations such as the Elks, Rotary, or Eastern Star. By examining the written constitution or organizational chart of the orgranizations to which you belong, or which you want to influence, you can identify the lines of authority and the span of control for the various positions within the organization. Understanding the formal structure should help you work within that structure to achieve success.

Summary

There is a difference between the formal and informal structures of a group. The formal structure is defined in terms of line and staff positions. Line positions carry authority and responsibility. Staff positions are support positions that are not involved in the direct line of authority. The formal structure is built upon levels or echelons. The higher the level, the greater the power or influence of the persons holding the positions on that level. Leaders sometimes define their power by the number of persons in a level below them over which they have spans of control. Documents such as organizational charts, constitutions with bylaws, and job descriptions define the formal structure of an organization.

REFLECTING/EXPLORING

1. Obtain an organizational chart for an organization or group to which you belong. If one is not available, draw one. Identify your position. Trace the lines of authority from your position to the position at the top. How many echelons are there between your position and the top-level position? What does this information tell you about the ways in which you can successfully affect the policies and procedures in this organization or group?

2. Obtain written documents describing the formal structure of your city government. Identify the line and staff positions, echelons, and the span of control for positions at each level. How could you go about affecting policies and procedures within your community?

3. Make an appointment with the manager of a local grocery store. Ask the manager to show you the store's organizational chart and to talk about the levels of authority and how decisions are made within the store. As the manager talks, separate information about the formal structure from descriptions of the informal structure. You may want to ask questions to clarify how employees use both the formal and the informal structures.

4. Study the organizational chart for your place of employment. Obtain information about (1) the length of time persons have held their positions, (2) how and when promotions occur, (3) whether people move between line and staff positions, and (4) if they move more than one echelon at a time. What do you see as your opportunities for advancement within the organization?

5. Using the organizational chart you used in activity 4, identify the line of authority. Then identify the people in positions who actually and directly affect your work. How well do these *practices* match the information on the chart about how the organization is supposed to function?

CHAPTER 8

INFORMAL GROUP STRUCTURE

Understanding the line of formal authority and how to work with it will probably save you time, effort, and frustration. However, if you are to understand and work effectively within the total structure of a group, you must also be aware of the unofficial sources of power, influence, and information that exist among the members of your groups. These unofficial sources are not part of the formal structure. To understand and use them, you must learn about the informal structure of a group.

You were introduced to the informal structure in the beginning of Chapter 7 as a way of understanding more clearly what the formal structure does *not* include. In this chapter, we will consider informal group structure in more detail. In Chapter 9 you will learn how to work effectively with both formal and informal structures, and, as a result, you will understand how to design a structure that will promote the group task.

Four factors define the informal structure of a group. These include:

1. Degree of centralization toward one member

2. Degree of connectedness among members

3. Degree of subgrouping within the group

4. Degree of openness to outside resources or contacts

Four roles emerge out of the defining factors of the informal structure of a group:

1. Some members act as boundary-spanners when contacts outside of a group are used.

2. Some members act as linkers and liaisons when subgroups exist within the group.

3. Some members become isolates or loners and rarely communicate with anyone.

4. Some members become opinion leaders or stars because of the large number of links they have with other members.

The relationships between these factors and roles help to clarify the nature of the informal structure of a group.

We will begin by examining the four factors. First, let's introduce the group we will use to illustrate informal group structure.

We will be looking closely at the Central City chapter of Single Parents. The formal structure of the group is identified on the following organizational chart.

CENTRAL CITY CHAPTER–SINGLE PARENTS

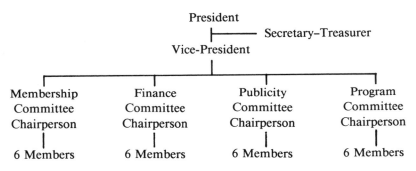

From what you know about organizational charts, you probably have noted already that the president, vice-president, and the four chairpersons of the committees are in *line* positions, while the secretary–treasurer holds a *staff* position. The staff position is paid and is filled for an indefinite period of time. However, the line positions are filled for a defined term. They are not paid positions. The line positions are filled through elections.

In contrast to the organizational chart, there is no official document that identifies the informal structure of a group. In fact, the informal anatomy of a group may change from one meeting to another, from one month to another, and from one issue to another. The informal structure *can* be observed and it can be analyzed. In fact, serious group members and leaders take into account such questions as which group members tend to work together, who seems to be most knowledgeable (and respected for the knowledge), who is the person who tends to bring information to the group from outside sources, and which members meet together for coffee or in the hallways between group meetings.

We will use dialogue between the various members of the committees who make up the governing structure of the Central City chapter of Single Parents. Then we will draw diagrams, or communication networks, to help you understand the informal structure of your own groups. In Chapter 7 you were introduced to this technique. In this chapter we will use diagrams of informal group structure. Members are shown as circles and their connections to other people are represented by lines. First, let's look at the four factors that define the informal structure of a group.

Four Characteristics of Informal Structure

As we stated in the opening of this chapter, the four characteristics of informal structure include (1) centralization, (2) connectedness, (3) sub-grouping, and (4) openness to outside resources and contacts. We will explain and illustrate each of these characteristics.

Centralization

Let's listen in on the opening of a meeting of the program and membership committee of the Central City chapter of Single Parents. First, Bill Scott, chairperson of the program committee, opens the discussion about program ideas for chapter meetings during the fall. The chapter meets every other week. This committee will present program ideas for the meetings from September through December to the chapter meeting.

BILL SCOTT (Chairperson): Well, here we are again for our quarterly programming meeting. Roger, you typically take notes. Would you do it for us today?

ROGER HARRIS: Sure. Anybody have suggestions?

MARY ROBBINS: Roger, we've never had a sailing party. What do you think about that?

ROGER: It's possible. Seems like a lot of preparation to pull it off, though.

MARY: Well, I have a friend who would be willing to provide the sailboat.

ROGER: I see. Let's make a note. (Roger writes down the idea with a notation about Mary's friend.) Any more ideas?

BILL: The Halloween Party has almost become a tradition. Shall we do it again?

ROGER: Well, if it's not too much like previous years. I'll put it on the list.

YEN LEE: I think it would be fun to have a potluck dinner near Thanksgiving. I'd be willing to have it at my home.

ROGER: O.K. It'll take a pep talk at every meeting before then to get members interested in bringing something. I'll make a note here: Who will coordinate this?

DAVE SANCHEZ: Roger, please make another note—I'd like us to bring our children to the dinner.

ROGER: (Writes *kids.*) Kids. O.K. Three meetings out of the way—what else?

DAVE: Speaking of children, I'd like to have an evening of Christmas caroling again and I'd like us to involve the children. That worked really well last year.

ROGER: (Writes down the suggestion.) I hope we're not going to make this fall a carbon copy of last fall.

DAVE: The suggestions we've made that duplicate last fall are the ones the members have asked us to repeat. After all, we're here to present to the members ideas that relate to what *they* want to do.

ROGER: How about an evening at the new roller-skating rink? That would be a new activity.

BECKY COWAN: Terrific, Roger! I haven't roller-skated since I was a child!

ROGER: O.K. I'll put it down on the list.

MARIA JUAREZ: I've been hoping we'd have a chance to go to a play together again at the civic theatre. Several members have mentioned to me how much they enjoyed the last play.

ROGER: O.K. Civic theatre. . . .

You have probably noticed a pattern in this dialogue: Bill is the chairperson of the group, but Roger is running the meeting. Roger is the central figure. He takes the notes. Every member addresses comments to him. Roger makes a comment after each member offers a suggestion. Members do not direct comments to each other. The following diagram shows the informal structure in the program committee.

PROGRAM COMMITTEE: INFORMAL STRUCTURE

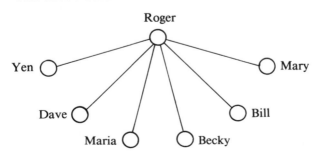

One person (Roger) is linked with every other person. Roger is the central or dominant individual. He controls the flow of communication directly. Since the members choose not to talk with each other, Roger also indirectly controls the communication. The program committee is an example of the greatest possible centralization toward one member.

Now let's listen to part of the meeting of the membership committee. The members of the chapter have expressed concern that the membership is getting smaller. At the last chapter meeting, the membership comittee was directed to look at new methods of recruiting members and report to the chapter in a month. Mary Callahan, chairperson of the membership committee, opens the discussion:

MARY: I've been thinking about what might be the best way for us to proceed today. I'd like for us to discuss this first. Jack, you seem ready to say something.

JACK BUSH: Yes, Mary. I've been thinking about how we should begin, also. You know, I'm not sure I understand the problem. Bruce, you talked quite a bit in the chapter meeting. I'm assuming you're clear about the problem. Are you?

BRUCE TAYLOR: Well, I'm not sure I see the whole picture. Maybe it's because I'm on this committee, but I am really aware that fewer people are coming to meetings. In following up on some of the members who are absent, I've discovered some have moved, a few have married and are no longer interested, others are just choosing not to attend. Yoko, we've talked. What can you add to this?

YOKO HUN: I agree with what you've said, and I want to add that the membership list shows almost no new members over the last three months. Greg, you have those records. What is the ratio between members who have left the chapter and new members?

GREG LUNDQUIST: You're quite right, Yoko. I don't have the exact figures, but we are losing members. I think that is only the surface problem. What I'm not sure about is the reason for it.

ALICE JACKSON: Greg, we've just gone through the summer months. Isn't it true that we have a history of very few new members joining in the summer?

GREG: Yes.

ALICE: Is it also true that June and July are the months when the largest number of members drop from the chapter, for various reasons?

GREG: Yes.

GRANT HOLMES: I've been listening to each of you. It seems to me we first need to survey our current membership to see how well the chapter meets their needs. I'd like some information about the level of satisfaction and some idea of how we might change any dissatisfaction before we mount a campaign for new members. Does that make sense?

You probably have noticed a pattern in this dialogue: there is no central figure. Every member talks. They pass their speaking turns on to the next person. There is a flow of communication throughout the group. As far as it is possible to observe, no one seems to be in control of the communication. Here is a diagram of the informal structure in the membership committee:

MEMBERSHIP COMMITTEE: INFORMAL STRUCTURE

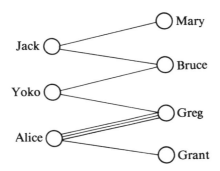

Compare this diagram with the one for the program committee. You can readily observe that the program committee has a very centralized informal structure with Roger at the helm, while the membership committee has a very decentralized informal structure. In the program committee, the effect of the centralized structure is that Roger controls the flow of communication. In the decentralized structure of the membership committee the communication flow is more spontaneous. All groups can be observed to ascertain their degrees of centralization toward one member. Most groups are not completely centralized or completely decentralized. Most can be placed at some point along a line like the following, which demonstrates the *degree* of centralization toward one member:

Centralization ——————————————————————— Decentralization

It also is possible for the degree of centralization for the same group to differ at different times. On another day with another issue the program committee may seem to function more like the membership committee. The membership committee may sometimes function more like the program committee. However, over a long period of time, a pattern in the way a group typically functions becomes apparent.

The next factor in the informal group structure is the degree of connectedness among members. It, too, is observable.

Connectedness

To understand what it means to have connectedness among members, we will observe a meeting of the finance committee of the Central City chapter of Single Parents. We will compare their meeting with that of the membership committee. The finance committee is meeting to complete the annual budget they will be submitting to the chapter at the next meeting. Hector Chavez, chairperson, has just given each committee member a copy of the most recent draft of the budget.

HECTOR: We've put a lot of work into this budget. I think this is the final draft. It may be ready to take to the membership. However, let's look at it closely one more time. Please examine those sections you've worked with the most. Also, look at the overall picture. (Silence follows as members examine the draft.)

CHRISTINE DENENFELD: Hector, I've worked mainly with the funds assigned to the president and vice-president. Brent and Julia worked with me on those. I think we've hit upon workable figures. Brent, Julia—what do you think?

BRENT HALLIDAY: Well, I still have some concern about the increase in the budget coming mainly from these positions. But cost of living *is* cost of living. It's okay with me, I guess.

JULIA CROSS: Brent, I'm concerned. Your comment sounds tentative to me. Are you sure it is okay with you?

BRENT: Yes, I just feel depressed about the rising costs of everything. It really is okay with me.

JULIA: I share your concern, Brent. And Christine, I'm satisfied we've done the best we can and that it is workable.

CHRISTINE: It's done then!

HECTOR: Jesse, Maria, Bob—any thoughts about the funds assigned to the president and vice-president? (All three express satisfaction.)

MARIA BOLT: (Changing the topic to funds for committee chairpersons.) I hate to beat an old drum but I still believe we can break away from the tradition of budgeting the same amount of money for each committee chairperson. It might offset increases for the two offices. Our committee just does not need as much money to operate as the other three committees do. I say, let's budget for what is actually needed, not on the basis of what is traditionally expected.

JESSE JENKINS: Maria, I've listened to you each meeting. I think you're finally getting through to me. Julia, you are the incoming chairperson of this committee. What do you believe your budget needs will be?

JULIA: I think I could get by with less. My company agrees that I can use my secretary and equipment and materials at work to absorb a lot of the typing and paper costs. I'd be willing to cut the allocation in half.

BOB BILLINGS: Julia, I'll go along with that—just so this decision does not set an irreversible precedent for the following year. If I were to be chairperson, for example, I don't have the resources available to me that you have.

HECTOR: Would it help if we were to provide notes with the budget that will have to be officially voted on by the members along with the budget itself?

BRENT: What do you have in mind, Hector?

HECTOR: Well, one note might read that this break in tradition is not irreversible—that we budgeted according to actual expected needs for next year only.

JULIA: We might add a statement of principle—that future budgets should be designed around actual needs.

This dialogue suggests that group members are linked together by their pattern of communication. The members in this group are tightly connected. We have shown this connectedness in the following diagram.

MEMBERSHIP COMMITTEE: PATTERN OF CONNECTEDNESS

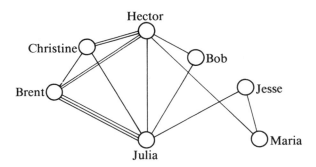

Compare this diagram with that for the membership committee meeting. In contrast to the meeting of the finance committee, the membership committee meeting is characterized by a low degree of connectedness among members. As was true with the degree of centralization toward one member, the degree of connectedness among the members of a group can be observed. It, too, can be placed as a point on a line between two extremes:

Tightly   Loosely
Connected ─── Connected

In a group of people who are tightly connected, a message introduced by any member will tend to be accurately received by other members. There will probably be less distortion because the message passes through fewer people, or links, to get to each person. There usually is cross checking among two or more members. We saw this among Brent, Julia, and Christine in the finance committee meeting. Cross checking tends to reduce distortion.

In a group whose informal structure is very loose, such as a group like the membership committee, communication occurs along a line. It must pass through each person to reach every person. Perhaps you have played a game called Gossip. In this game, a joke or story is started at one end of a line of people and repeated until it reaches the person at the other end of the line. If you have played Gossip, you can appreciate the amount of distortion, misinformation, and frustration that occurs in a communication network with a low degree of connectedness among members. One effect of low connectedness among members can be subgrouping. This is the third factor which can be observed in the informal structure of a group.

Subgrouping

In small groups, most members talk to each other. However, some talk more than others and they talk more to specific members of the group. In the finance committee meeting, Julia and Brent talked more to each other than to other members. If we were to examine more of the dialogue, this would become obvious. Julia and Brent are both in line for the leadership of the finance committee. Therefore, they have a common concern directly related to the meetings.

When a group meets, some people tend to form connections with each other. They tend to turn to each other when asking questions of the group. They usually direct comments to each other. Also, they come to expect responses from each other. These subgroups are called *coalitions*. They form out of the communication patterns among people, not because they have been appointed officially to take on a special assignment for the group. Members of coalitions often have similar self-interests in the group process. They often agree on issues.

Let's use a meeting of the publicity committee for an example of subgrouping. Jean Sharp, chairperson of the publicity committee, opens the meeting by reviewing the topic of discussion:

JEAN: I'm going to tell you right off that I am not looking forward to this meeting. As you all well know, it's the third time we've met to discuss the publicity plans for the chapter. We've asked for an extension of time in presenting our report to the chapter meeting. We're split down the middle on deciding whether or not to use TV spots this year. Hung, Frank, and Kathy—you support TV coverage. I believe it's fair to say that you all believe it's the best way to reach single parents in their homes. Charlie, George, and Jill, you don't want to ask for additional money to pay for TV spots. And, as for me, I believe we will find ways to pay for the spots and we should try it. However, I stand firm in refusing to break the deadlock with my vote. Here's how I want to begin the meeting: I want each of you to make a statement of your present position on the issue. Limit your comments to one minute. Then we will take a secret ballot and see where the six of you stand on the issue. Who will begin?

FRANK RAY: (In silence, he looks at Hung and then at Kathy.) I'm tired of this issue. We've blown it all out of proportion. As much as I want to see us try TV spots, I'm thinking this may not be a good time to do it. (Again, he looks at Hung and Kathy. No response. He sits back in his chair.) At least, for me, it's not fun to come to meetings when we hassle each other over an issue like this.

CHARLIE OSTRANDER: Well, Frank, I think you're right! Right, George? Right, Jill? (Charlie looks first to George and then to Jill. They both smile.) The timing isn't good. We've got increased costs, fewer members . . .

HUNG NGUYEN: (Interrupting.) Charlie, you know as well as I do that we've got to spend money to get new members to make more money through more dues! (Seemingly self-conscious about the emotion behind his own statement, Hung looks to Kathy and to Frank in silence. Kathy smiles. Frank seems to have a blank stare.)

JEAN: We're getting away from each person making a separate, brief personal statement. I'd like to get back to that.

KATHY KNIGHT: I've been thinking about our *timing,* too. (She pauses and glances toward Frank.) I'm not willing to wait to try TV spots another time. We'll go bankrupt if we don't do something drastic.

GEORGE LEONARD: I haven't changed my view. I have no new views. I'm totally opposed. (Charlie winks at George. Jill smiles but gives George no eye contact.)

Jean passed out slips of paper. The vote was taken and counted: two votes for TV spots, four votes against TV spots. After the meeting, Charlie, George, and Jill went out for lunch together. Hung and Kathy walked out together with Frank trailing behind them, and attempting to persuade them of the rightness of his shift of opinion. Frank refused Charlie's invitation to join George, Jill, and him for lunch.

Clearly, there are two subgroups in the publicity committee—at least, on the issue of TV spots. These subgroups are shown in the following diagram:

PUBLICITY COMMITTEE SUBGROUPS

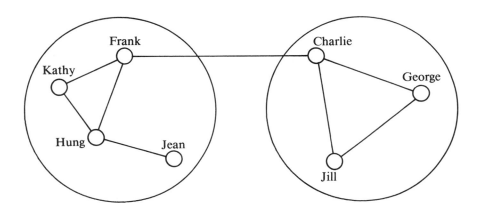

The subgroups stand out clearly. People tend to talk with others in their subgroups. They also give nonverbal clues to other members within their subgroups. There is one link, or bridge, between subgroups on this issue: Frank switches positions and Charlie relates to him. However, when asked to join Charlie's subgroup for lunch after the meeting, Frank stays with his own group.

Subgroups, or coalitions, may form over specific issues and then disband when the issue is resolved. They also may be a relatively permanent part of the communication pattern within the informal group structure. Subgrouping, too, can be plotted as a point on a line between extremes.

High Subgrouping ——————————————————— Low Subgrouping

The meetings of the membership, finance, and program committees each had low degrees of subgrouping.

Often subgrouping spills over into the time between group meetings. Members of the coalitions join each other for coffee or for lunch. Charlie, George, and Jill did this. If the groups are part of an organization, the subgroups often meet in the hallways to talk about the topics being discussed at group meetings. Sometimes members of subgroups call each other and discuss issues. Sometimes, as is the case with Kathy and Frank, they date one another. What occurs outside of meetings usually has an effect on how members view each other in meetings as well as how they relate to members of other subgroups at meetings. Like the parent group, a subgroup may be analyzed in terms of the degree of centralization toward a single subgroup member and the degree of connectedness between subgroup members. This brings us to the final factor in the informal structure of a group.

Degree of Openness

People exist outside of a group who can often provide useful information and other resources for the group. Some groups are very open to outside resources, while others may function as a closed group by having litle or no contact with outsiders. The publicity committee seemed to function as a closed group. Jean, the chairperson, asked for a time extension in presenting the committee report to the chapter meeting. Another choice might have been to report the committee deadlock to the chapter so the issue might be discussed by the members who were not on the publicity committee. References were made to the limited funds and the loss of membership. However, it seemed that no one had consulted either the finance or membership committees for first-hand information.

In contrast to the publicity committee, the program committee included some members who seemed to use information from outsiders. Dave remarked that program ideas duplicated from last year were in response to members' requests. Maria noted the interest in the civic theatre that was expressed by other members. In neither of these cases is the reference to a specific outsider. If specific people were used as outside resources, a diagram of the degree of openness to outside resources would have to include them.

PROGRAM COMMITTEE: OPENNESS TO OUTSIDE RESOURCES

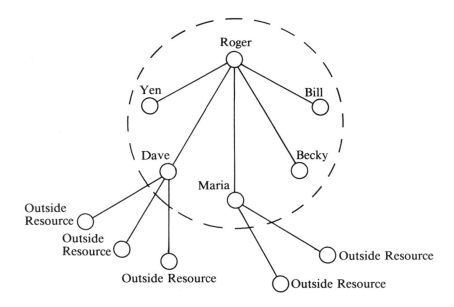

Like the other three factors, the degree of openness a group has to outside resources or contacts may be plotted as a point on a line between the two extremes.

High Openness ——————————————————————————— Low Openness

Communication beyond the boundaries of the group may provide valuable information not available within the group. For example, perhaps a member of the chapter who is not a member of the publicity committee knows someone at the local TV station and could help the publicity committee try a new, less costly approach. In some cases, communication outside the group is necessary to complete the group task successfully.

Here is a checklist you can use as a guideline in analyzing the informal structures of your group.

A Checklist of Factors Involved in the Informal Structure of a Group

YES   NO
☐   ☐   1. Is there one person (or two or three) through whom most of the information passes, and do these people make the major decisions for the group? *Yes* indicates a high degree of centralization toward one person. *No* indicates a low degree of centralization toward one person.

☐   ☐   2. Do most of the group members talk to each other frequently, regularly, and equally either in meetings or between meetings? *Yes* indicates a high degree of connectedness among members. *No* indicates a low degree of connectedness among members.

☐   ☐   3. Do members communicate mostly with a few other members in the group? *Yes* indicates indicates a high degree of subgrouping. *No* indicates a low degree of subgrouping.

☐   ☐   4. Do members of the group communicate frequently and regularly with people outside the group about group work? *Yes* indicates a high degree of openness to outside resources and contacts. *No* indicates a low degree of openness to outside resources and contacts.

Four Group Roles

The degrees of centralization, connectedness, subgrouping, and openness to outside resources are characteristics of informal group structure. Associated with each of these factors are individual roles of great importance. Without the persons in these roles, the factors would be less likely to exist.

The four roles include:

1. Boundary-spanners, members who make contacts with outside resources

2. Linkers and liaisons, members who form bridges between the subgroups that exist in the group

3. Isolates or loners, members who rarely communicate with anyone

4. Opinion leaders or stars, members who have a large number of links (connections) with other members

Boundary-Spanners

Let's first return to the program committee. Examine the diagram on page 95. Dave and Maria make contacts outside of the group. They are *boundary-spanners*. Boundary-spanners carry ideas and other resources across the group boundary. They serve two important functions:

1. Boundary-spanners act as *gatekeepers*. They open the gate to information needed by the group.

2. Boundary-spanners sometimes represent the group in meetings with other groups. Often this provides much-needed coordination between the parts of an organization or community agency.

Boundary-spanners are important to a group that depends on outside resources and coordination with other groups.

Linkers and Liaisons

The following two diagrams will help you understand the difference between a linker and a liaison. These are diagrams of the publicity committee meeting. When Jean opened the meeting by explaining the positions of each subgroup, she acted as a *liaison* between the two subgroups. She is not a permanent member of either subgroup. In our earlier diagram of the committee meeting, we showed Jean as a member of a subgroup. This was to show her agreement with one group's position. In fact, she chose not to vote and break the deadlock between the two subgroups. Diagram 1 illustrates Jean's function as a liaison. A liaison position is filled by a person who makes a bridge between two groups, without being a member of either. Committee chairpersons, supervisors, and other leaders often play this role. A group member may also serve as a liaison.

PUBLICITY COMMITTEE: LIAISONS AND LINKERS

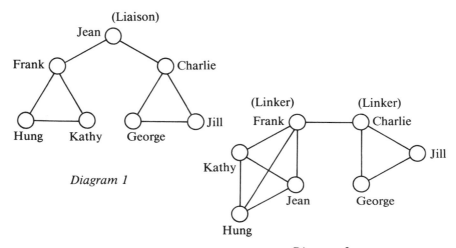

Diagram 1

Diagram 2

In diagram 2, Frank and Charlie are shown as *linkers*. Linkers are people who are members of subgroups. Yet they talk to each other, and, in doing so, they form a link between their subgroups. In this case, the communication seemed one way. Charlie talked with Frank and received little or no response. To be effective, linkers must have freer exchanges than Frank's with Charlie. Their linking seems to have occurred only on the issue of TV spots. The two subgroups probably reverted to a liaison structure after the vote. By this time, Jean would no longer be a part of the subgroup of Frank, Hung, and Kathy.

Liaisons and linkers are key individuals because they tend to coordinate and unify the separate subgroups. If all the members of the committee are to have access to needed information, they will probably receive it through the committee's linkers and liaisons. If these roles are not filled in a group that has a high degree of subgrouping, communication among all group members does not often occur. Ineffective communication may well result in both ineffective group process and a useless group product.

Isolates and Loners

Someone who does not regularly communicate with other group members is isolated from the group process. Turn to the diagram of the publicity committee on page 101. Notice that the link to Jean is one way. This is a result of the fact that, by her choice not to vote, she isolated herself from the decision-making process. Isolates or loners usually have at least some links with the group. However, in comparison with other members, their degree of connectedness is at a very low level. A person who missed a meeting has no contact with any group member before the next meeting might be thought of as totally isolated for the period of time between meetings. The effect usually is that the absent member requires some briefing at the next meeting before he or she functions at the level of the rest of the group members.

Opinion Leaders or Stars

A group chairperson or member who has a high degree of influence with the rest of the group plays the role of opinion leader. In the meeting of the program committee, Roger was put in an influential position when the chairperson asked him to take notes and when the members directed their comments to him. Sometimes a person who is put into a position of influence as Roger was does not remain influential except for the period of the meeting.

Opinion leaders are referred to as stars because they have a large number of links with other people. On a diagram, their communication pattern looks like a star.

OPINION LEADER COMMUNICATION PATTERN

Opinion leaders who remain in that role for a long period of time usually have the respect of the other group members. If a group has an opinion leader, others must yield influence to the person in that role.

Opinion leaders can be identified by their characteristics. Here are seven characteristics usually associated with opinion leaders:

1. They are highly competent in group functions related to completing tasks.

2. They are competent in relating to group members in open and direct ways, task specialists who have learned human-relations skills.

3. They tend to support the social norms or rules of the organization of which their group is a part. They are not viewed as deviants.

4. They usually have access to information and resources such as mass media, technical journals, conventions and conferences, and books.

5. They are open, sociable, and accessible to other people.

6. They may be in positions of any rank or level within an organization or community, but they tend to seek advice or information only from someone at a higher rank or level.

7. They are more innovative than other people in the group and they tend to focus on creativity and change.

Not only are these characteristics typical of opinion leaders, but other members must recognize a person as having these characteristics before that person can become a long-term opinion leader.

The roles of boundary-spanner, liaison or linker, isolate or loner, and opinion leader may be filled by different individuals. However, one person may fill more than one role at a time. For example, Jean, the chairperson of the publicity committee, was a liaison, perhaps an opinion leader, and perhaps also a boundary-spanner in her role as a chairperson who probably met with chairpersons of other committees or with officers. She also was an isolate for a brief time when she chose not to vote on the issue of TV spots.

Here are questions that you may use in identifying the persons who fill key roles in your groups.

Questions for Summarizing Key Positions and the People Who Fill Them

1. If there are subgroups, who belongs to them? (List the subgroups and their members below.)

2. If there are subgroups, who serves as a linker with people in other subgroups? (List linkers below.)

3. If there are subgroups, who is not a subgroup member but serves as a liaison by helping subgroups communicate with each other? (List liaisons below.)

4. Which members serve as the boundary-spanners in the group by regularly communicating with people outside of the group and bringing information in, or taking information out of the group? (List the boundary-spanners below.)

5. Who rarely communicates with other members and acts as an isolate or loner? (List isolates or loners below.)

Combine the information from questions 1–5 by listing the key people in the group—linkers, liaisons, boundary-spanners, and opinion leaders. (Remember that the same person can be a linker, boundary-spanner, and opinion leader.) List a person only one time no matter how many roles he or she plays.
(List key people below.)

(List the isolates or loners below.)

By using this checklist, you will become more aware of who the people are who tend to help your group function with a certain amount of centrality, connectedness, subgrouping, and openness to outside resources. You also will discover whether your group tends to have any members who seem isolated from the informal group structure and the overall group process. Your understanding of the informal structure in your groups will become more sophisticated as you learn to observe the dynamics of the process that occurs among the four factors and the four roles.

Factors Affecting Groups

The factors of the informal structure combine in ways that are specific to a particular group. The roles that exist, the people in those roles, and the ways members respond to the key people affect the informal structure. Even though each group is different, it is possible to make four general observations about the relationships among the four factors and the roles associated with them.

1. In a highly centralized group, the objective for members is to obtain the understanding, agreement, and approval of the person or persons at the center—usually the opinion leader. They probably represent the power source. When there is a high degree

of decentralization, the appropriate strategy is to obtain understanding, agreement, and approval from a larger number of people. The linkers, liaisons, boundary-spanners, and opinion leaders are especially important people.

2. If there is a high degree of connectedness among members, a leader or member can assume that by communicating information to one person, the message will reach almost every other person. Low connectedness among members may result in a much less rapid or complete information exchange throughout the group. As a result, structures with low connectedness are probably easier structures to manipulate or control but more difficult structures in which to share information with everyone.

3. If a high degree of subgrouping exists, the member or leader must be able to work with the subgroups or coalitions in order to complete a task. At least, members or leaders must be able to work with those who have power in the subgroups. In addition, liaisons and linkers become much more important. They serve to bridge the spaces between subgroups. If there is less subgrouping, action can be directed more toward the whole group.

4. An informal structure that includes a high degree of openness to outside resources obviously provides an opportunity for an exchange of information between a group and persons in the organization of community. The usual result is that the group's work is related to the parent organization in realistic and useful ways. However, there sometimes can be an information overload from the outside. If an issue, such as instituting the use of TV spots, is announced outside of the meeting before the plan is finished, the committee might be bombarded with data from outside regarding ways and means of implementing the plan. In addition, too much information flowing out from the committee may prematurely destroy the idea before the committee has the opportunity to work up a presentation that is feasible. A closed structure reduces information overload. Another result of a closed structure may be that information needed for a solution may not get to a group, even though that information exists outside the group.

Now that you have an understanding of the nature of formal as well as informal group structures, we will turn to some of the ways you can work with these structures. In addition, we will present methods of designing groups to meet your needs. This information will be especially helpful if you have the opportunity to influence the make-up of newly formed groups. Using and designing the formal and informal structures of groups will be the focus of Chapter 9.

Summary

Informal group structure can be observed and diagrammed. A diagram gives a graphic picture of the patterns of interaction that exist between group members. The informal structure has four major features: (1) the degree of centralization toward one or a few members, (2) the degree of connectedness, (3) the degree of subgrouping, and (4) the degree of openness to outside resources and contacts. A group can be analyzed in these terms to obtain a picture of its overall informal structure.

A group can also be analyzed on the basis of the roles individuals play: liaison, linker, boundary-spanner, opinion leader, or isolate.

The four factors and the four roles together constitute the informal structure of groups. Understanding how they function in your groups will help you work effectively within their informal structures. This awareness also will assist you in designing group structures that are functional.

REFLECTING/EXPLORING

1. Observe a community group. You may want to attend a city commission meeting or, if it is available to you, watch a commission meeting on cable television. Before the meeting begins, draw circles on a piece of paper to represent the seating arrangement of the people in the group. Place each person's name beside the circle that represents him or her. When the meeting begins, draw lines between the circles to stand for the flow of communication between people. Do this for fifteen to twenty minutes of the meeting. What observations can you make about centralization, connectedness, subgrouping, and openness? What roles seem to exist and who functions in these roles? Refer to the checklist on page 104 for a review.
2. Observe a group of which you are a member or leader. Complete the checklist on page 104. How typical is the information you have summarized? What long-term communication patterns seem to exist in your group? What effect do you believe they have on the way the group functions? How might you share this information with the group?
3. Identify the key positions in the group you used in activity 2. Use the checklist on pages 108 and 109. What relationships do you see between the people in these roles and the information you collected in activity 2? What do you believe is the effect on the way your group functions? How might you share your observations with others in your group?

4. Think about the ways you function in the group you used in activities 2 and 3. What roles do you fill? What roles would you like to fill? How do you affect the way your group functions?

5. Review the relationships between factors and roles on pages 109 and 110. How many of these are true of the community group meeting (activity 1)? How many are true of your own group meeting (activities 2, 3, and 4)? What observations would you make for either of these groups that differ from the relationships presented on pages 109 and 110?

CHAPTER 9

WORKING IN AND DESIGNING GROUPS

A surgeon must understand anatomy. Without a clear working knowledge of it, the surgeon's efforts might be fatal for the patient. Similarly, a group member cannot function well without a clear understanding of the structure of the group. While the lack of such knowledge usually will not totally destroy a group's effectiveness, group functions will probably be complicated by chronic miscommunication.

Maryanne was associated with Elkton Community Theater Association. The association had a long local history. The organization included a board of directors, twelve people plus a full time executive director, and a staff of three, which included two secretaries. Maryanne wanted the theater to produce the musical, *Man of LaMancha,* during the new season. Maryanne received statements of support from a number of people in the community, including several season patrons of the Community Theater Association. She approached the board about producing the musical. Her project was not even considered by the board. Why? Because Maryanne failed to understand the formal structure of this group. Technically, Marsha Owens, the executive director, supervised the staff and reported to the board. However, the bylaws show that the executive director also served as the chairperson of the board of directors. Almost every member of the board itself was selected by the executive director. Any play chosen for production was chosen by the executive director. Formally and in fact, Marsha Owens *was* the real and total power in the organization. Signatures and support from season patrons did not matter to Marsha Owens. Maryanne failed in her attempt.

The information in Chapters 7 and 8 on the formal and informal anatomy of groups should help you avoid the kind of failure Maryanne experienced. Knowledge alone is not enough, however. It is important that you also understand how to put your knowledge to use, so you can function effectively within your groups. Also, if you have an opportunity to influence the composition of new groups in your organization or community, it will be helpful for you to know how to design a group. Working in and designing group structures are the topics of this chapter. The chapter is divided into three major sections:

1. Using knowledge of group structure to work within existing groups.

2. Designing formal group structures.

3. Influencing informal group structures.

We will begin by focusing on how you can use your knowledge of both formal and informal group structures to work within existing groups effectively and efficiently.

Working within Existing Groups

Knowing which positions and persons within an organizational or community structure carry the most influence and power is important information for successful group work. If you compare Chapter 7 with Chapter 8, you will notice that our discussion of the formal structure of groups did not require dialogue. You can understand the formal structure of a group by examining organizational charts. In Chapter 8 we provided you with extensive dialogue so that you might better understand the characteristics that indicate a group's informal structure. While the formal structure provides you with information about which *positions* are designed to have power and influence, the informal structure helps you understand which *people* really exercise power and influence in a group. Sometimes a comparison of the organizational charts and the communication networks for the same group shows that people in positions of power and influence within the formal structure are also the persons with power and influence in the informal structure. But this may not always be the case. In Chapter 8, the person who chaired the program committee was in the position of formal power and influence. But Roger, who took the notes and became the central focus of the meeting, was the person who actually exercised the most influence during the meeting of the program committee. It is important for you to understand how you can work within both formal and informal structures, since the official and actual power and influence may not coincide. Let's begin with the formal structure.

Working within Formal Structures

Maryanne probably would have been more successful if she had known about the formal relationships between the executive director and the board of the Elkton Community Theatre Association. There are two sources of information she might have used:

1. She could have asked. People in a group usually are willing to give this information. (If you completed the activities at the end of Chapter 7, you have this information about one or more of the groups of which you are a member.) Group members and leaders

can be relied upon the describe the people who have formal titles and who hold official positions of influence. Sometimes they also volunteer stories of situations in the past to illustrate "how the system works." Maryanne's case could easily become such a story in the future. People interested in influencing the season's playbill at the Elkton Community Theater could profit from Maryanne's story. They could then spend more time influencing Marsha Owens, the executive director, than in collecting signatures from season patrons.

2. The second source of information about a group's formal structure consists of the various written documents that establish the committee, board, or group as part of a larger organization. These documents may include constitutions with bylaws and organizational charts. The positions within the organization are customarily identified and defined in terms of duties and responsibilities. The written documents often include information on who reports to whom. Terms of office and other useful information may be provided. If an organizational chart exists, it includes diagrams of positions and titles held by people within the structure. It shows which positions are superior and which subordinate to other positions within the organization. In addition to the organizational chart, there are often formal documents that describe the functions of each position. These are called *job descriptions.*

Such written documents explaining the formal structure are available for most groups. However, it is useful to talk with people in an organization to discover the extent to which their documents represent their actual practice. Since it is difficult to include all the details of operating procedures in a written document, talking with group members and leaders helps to provide a more complete understanding.

After you study the written documents and conclude your informal conversations with individuals in a group, you probably will have the following types of information:

1. A list of the officers, leaders, or managers

2. A list of the persons who work closely with and support the officers, leaders, and managers (administrative assistants, secretaries, and aides)

3. A description of the authority, responsibility, and duties associated with the major positions

4. A description of the relationship between the formal positions and those who actually hold these positions.

This information is indispensable when you want to know who to approach in order to accomplish your goals. However, this information alone is not enough for effective work with groups. It is also necessary to use informal group structure effectively.

Working within Informal Structures

Jim was a young, conscientious social worker in a family and marriage counseling agency. Jim was an avid reader. He attended conventions and conferences, and kept up with his field. As a result, Jim felt strongly that some newer methods of marriage counseling could be used effectively in his agency. He wrote an agency proposal designed to implement the new ideas. Jim contacted several people on the agency staff. They seemed to think his ideas were good. Jim got permission to present the proposal at a staff meeting.

After his presentation, Rachel spoke up first. She politely but firmly indicated that she would not support the proposed changes in counseling methods. Within five minutes the staff members had begun discussing other topics. Jim felt confused and hurt. Only later did he discover that while Rachel had no formal title or position, she was very influential with the other social workers. Her influence resulted from her role as liaison between the two subgroups. For five years, she had successfully coordinated the work of these two divergent groups in the agency. She saw Jim's ideas as a threat to the working relationship she helped to maintain.

Jim did not understand the informal structure of his work group. Rachel was a key influence. Had Jim talked with her first, he might have been more successful in understanding how to present his proposal in a way that would be acceptable. He could have attempted to enlist Rachel's support. Jim could have used the information in Chapter 8. If you use these ideas, you will be able to identify:

1. The subgroups that exist in a larger group

2. The opinion leaders in both large groups and subgroups

3. The liaisons and linkers who create bridges between subgroups

4. The boundary-spanners who communicate between the group and outside resources

Subgroups and individual members represent a background against which you must see decisions before you take action. In preparing proposals and in deciding on your persuasive strategies, it is important to know who the members of subgroups are. Note the opinion leaders, liaisons, linkers, and boundary-spanners as well. These influential members often wield as much power as the formal leaders in a group.

It also is important for you to think about the four factors of the informal group structure. It is important for you to know the extent to which:

1. The members of the group are connected with each other. In a tightly connected group, information flows quickly. Rapid transmission of information to all members is possible. However, it is difficult to maintain secrecy when information is confidential or when premature disclosure might defeat a proposal. In a loosely connected group, a much slower process of dissemination occurs. It is possible for one or two people to try a new idea or plan without everyone else knowing.

2. The group is open or closed to outside resources. Open groups are characterized by a free flow of information to and from the outside. Often open groups are fairly adaptive and innovative. Such groups are easier to work with when you want to make suggestions or propose new ideas. Closed groups typically change less rapidly and may require a very formal approach in presenting new ideas or suggestions.

3. The group is centralized or decentralized. A centralized group implies that one or two people are at the center and have the focus of attention. In a decentralized group, it is important to direct communication to a large number of people.

The understanding you have of a group's formal and informal structures will enable you to function more intelligently. This knowledge will help you when you initiate proposals as well as when you decide whether to support the proposals of others.

Designing the Formal Structure of Groups

As a member, you can use your knowledge of group structure to help your groups function more effectively. Group leaders and other persons in positions of power in the formal structure of organizations and communities can literally design their group structures to promote effective functioning. Designing the formal structure is far easier than shaping the informal structure. While the factors and roles of the informal structure cannot be controlled, they can be influenced. In this section, we will focus on designing the formal structure. In the next section, we will provide information on influencing the informal structure.

The formal structure of many groups is designed according to tradition. People who form groups use a model they have seen or used in the past. Sometimes, too, a larger parent organization imposes a specific structure. For example, local churches must often use the formal structure dictated by national or international church discipline or leaders. Whatever the source of the formal structures, four practical principles can be used as guidelines in designing or revising formal structures:

Principle 1: The formal structure of a group should include all the offices and positions needed to make the group legal and consistent either with other similar groups or with the requirements of a larger organization.

In a missile manufacturing plant, a work group usually includes a supervisor and at least one secretary, with perhaps a file clerk. A dentist's office includes a receptionist (who often serves as the bookkeeper, also), a chairside assistant, a dental hygienist, and a dentist. A planning or zoning board would include a chairperson and an assistant chairperson. The typical volunteer organization might include a president, vice-president, recording secretary, corresponding secretary, and a treasurer. Where there are legal requirements, clearly they must be followed. An affirmative action officer is an example of a position necessary in most large organizations. The person in this position implements national and state requirements for affirmative action. Where there are no legal requirements but social norms or expectations exist, the group is often designed to fit these expectations. If the formal structure includes offices, then the next principle follows logically:

Principle 2: All offices and positions and their relationships and responsibilities should be described, so that the task or mission of the group can be met.

Simply naming the positions is not enough. There must be a minimal description of what duties are involved in the positions. In Chapter 4, we discussed the written documents used by formal groups to describe the positions. These documents eliminate duplication of effort. They help people understand who reports to whom. The documents include the responsibilities identified with each position. Here is an example:

Recording secretary: The recording secretary shall take the minutes of all meetings of the board and see to it that the minutes are typed, reproduced, and distributed to the president, vice-president, treasurer, corresponding secretary, and the chairpersons of the committees on finance, publicity, membership, and programming. The reproduced minutes shall be available to the persons listed above no later than one week before the next meeting of the board or five days after the meeting for which they have been taken, whichever comes sooner. In the event the recording secretary cannot attend a meeting, the recording secretary will contact the corresponding secretary who will act as the recording secretary for that meeting. If there is any question as to an action taken in a meeting before the minutes are distributed, the recording secretary shall contact the president of the board for clarification. At the beginning of each meeting, as dictated by the official agenda, the recording secretary shall introduce the minutes of the preceding meeting and request clarification and comment and then approval. Once the minutes are approved, they cannot be changed. The approved minutes will then be typed, reproduced, and distributed in final form with notice of approval (Approved Minutes) displayed prominently at the top of the first page.

Notice the extreme detail and the attempt to cover a variety of possible situations. Very little is left to the imagination of the recording secretary. Models of such descriptions exist in the form of constitutions and bylaws of existing organizations.

In a small, informal group, a written job description might be nonexistent or it might be very brief:

> The recording secretary is responsible for taking the minutes at every meeting and seeing that everyone gets a copy after the meeting.

This description gives the secretary wide latitude. Flexibility is appropriate in a group where there is a need for rapid response to issues or problems and where people are highly trained and professionalized.

Principles 1 and 2 are related to a basic problem in designing formal group structures: How many people should be included? A group can consist of as few as two people working together on a task. A human-service agency relies heavily on volunteers. It has a paid staff of four but a board of directors consisting of twenty-four people! Our answer to how many people should be involved brings us to principle 3:

> *Principle 3:* A group should have the smallest number of members possible who have all the resources and points of view needed to meet the goal or mission of the group.

Groups should be as small as possible. This is the first part of the principle. However, the group needs to be large enough to include the resources necessary for completing its tasks according to the goals of the group. If the expertise of four people is needed to solve a problem (an accountant, a lawyer, a public relations person, and a salesperson, for example), four is the smallest possible size for the group. Absence of any one of the specialties will result in an ineffective decision. Similarly, if coordination is required among six different neighborhood associations, the best group size is six.

As group size increases, there is more complexity as well as more time spent in sharing information accurately and completely. Sometimes groups are large beccause of tradition. Sometimes there are other reasons: A group must have enough technical skills and resources available to make decisions and solve problems. There must be enough people to provide the necessary resources. In some cases, members must provide representation of a number of constituencies and interest groups. If there are seven distinct camps in a larger organization, or fourteen well-defined interest groups in a community, their representative groups have to have at least seven and fourteen members.

Sometimes the smallest number necessary is more than ten or twelve. This is quite large. Large groups can be unwieldy. Meetings are more difficult to manage. Not everyone has the opportunity to speak in meetings. If this is the case, the designer of the group should establish formal subgroups (committees, subcommittees, or task forces). This leads us to the final principle for designing formal structures:

> *Principle 4:* A large group should be divided into subgroups based upon logical task subdivisions. The subgroups should be described in terms of their objectives or goals and relationships to the larger group and to each other.

When subgroups are created, it is necessary to prepare written documents describing them. Here is one example:

> *Finance Committee:* The finance committee shall consist of the treasurer, who shall act as the chairperson, and four members elected by the membership. Members shall be elected for two-year terms of office. Two members shall be elected each year to provide for continuity. The finance committee shall report to the executive committee on a regular basis. The finance committee will prepare and present an annual budget, prepare and present quarterly reviews of the current budget, and oversee unbudgeted expenditures. In addition, the finance committee shall arrange for an annual external audit of the financial records of the association.

This description lists the duties of the committee and specifies its relationship to the executive committee.

These four principles for designing the formal structure of a group are simple and practical. They are based upon past experience and research. The principles are derived from the experience of groups that function effectively and efficiently. They will provide you with guidelines when you design or revise the formal structure of your groups. It is important for you to add to these guidelines information about how you can successfully influence the informal structure of your groups.

Influencing the Informal Structure of Groups

The informal structure of a group emerges as a result of the various ways the factors and roles described in Chapter 8 are combined in a specific group situation. The informal structure cannot be designed in the same way as the formal structure can be formed. However, the informal structure can be influenced. We have ten recommendations for you.

Five factors seem to be very influential in altering informal group structures. These factors include:

1. Group size

2. Similarities of group members

3. Norms or rules about formality and informality

4. Seating positions or work-station locations

5. Design of the task

We will give you two sets of recommendations that take into account these five factors.

The first set of recommendations is useful if you want to influence a group in the direction of (1) minimum subgrouping, (2) a high degree of connectedness among members, and (3) high decentralization. The recommendations include:

Recommendation 1: Include as few group members as possible.

Recommendation 2: Select group members for their similarity with each other in terms of education, background, experience, ethnic origin, race, and expertise.

Recommendation 3: Establish norms of informality so that people use first names and not titles in addressing each other.

Recommendation 4: Design group tasks so that everyone must be involved in the completion of the tasks.

If it follows these four recommendations, a group will tend to become more cohesive and efficient.

Groups that are cohesive and efficient may still have some problems. The problems that occur, oddly enough, stem from the high degree of similarity among group members. For example, similarity may violate affirmative action and equal employment opportunity laws as well as other ethical considerations. And, if people are similar to one another, they may not have enough variety of expertise and knowledge to work effectively on a wide range of problems or tasks. A lack of creativity and innovation often results when group members are very similar.

The second set of recommendations are useful if you want to move a group toward (1) greater centralization, (2) less connectedness, and (3) more subgrouping. The recommendations include:

Recommendation 1: Create as large a group as is manageable.

Recommendation 2: Select group members who are dissimilar in terms of such factors as education, background, experience, ethnic origin, race, and expertise.

Recommendation 3: Establish norms of formality so that people are addressed by title or by title and last name.

Recommendation 4: Arrange seating positions or work stations so that people are isolated from one another and cannot communicate quickly and easily.

Recommendation 5: Design group tasks so they can be completed either by one person or by a few people working in sequence.

If followed, these recommendations will result in much less communication among group members. Members will draw closer to others who have similar backgrounds. Thus, subgroups will form. Physical locations and shared tasks also may be a basis for subgrouping.

It is important to note that these recommendations are based on prior research which suggests that these five factors taken together do influence informal structure. However, there is no guarantee that, if one recommendation alone is implemented, it will make a major difference. The communication and work patterns in a group become habitual. Attempts to influence or change the informal group structure may require that months or years pass before the new patterns replace habitual ways of relating and working.

Summary

Knowledge of the formal and informal group structures can be used effectively by a group member. The member should study the documents defining the formal structure and should obtain information from other members about officers, leaders, and their duties. Understanding informal group structure includes the ability to identify subgroups (interest groups or coalitions), and the ability to identify key individuals (opinion leaders, liaisons, linkers, and boundary-spanners). The overall characteristics of a group (the degrees of openness, connectedness, and centralization) can also help in knowing how and when to communicate.

Leaders often have the opportunity to design the formal structure of groups, making them more effective. Four principles to use as guides in designing formal structure are (1) include all the offices and positions needed to make the group legal and consistent with social and cultural norms, (2) prepare written documents that include descriptions of positions, duties, and relationships among positions, (3) control group size to include the smallest number of people necessary for completing a job, and (4) create subgroups such as committees or task forces, if a large group is unavoidable. These four principles are the major points to remember when designing new groups or redesigning the formal structure of existing groups.

Informal group structure cannot be designed, but can be influenced by leadership decisions. The key influences are group size, similarity of group members, norms of formality or informality, physical arrangements for seating or work areas, and the way tasks are to be completed. By deliberate manipulation of these factors, a group can be informally structured to be more or less centralized, cohesive, and connected.

REFLECTING/EXPLORING

1. Obtain all of the written documents available to you that pertain to a group of which you are a member. These documents may be written directly about your group. You also may want to ask for written documents that describe groups to which your group reports or written docu-

ments that pertain to groups that report to your group. Make sure you have the materials listed on page 115. Then talk with group members and key people in your organization or community who are related to your group's work. Determine to what degree the information in the written documents matches the actual practice in your group and organization.

2. Obtain a constitution, bylaws, and descriptions of offices or positions for a volunteer agency in your community or for a professional association of your choice. Most nonprofit groups will be willing to honor your request. Examine the procedures and job descriptions. Might they be used as models for creating written documents for your group or for suggesting revisions in the existing documents used by your group?

3. Review the characteristics of informal group structure (page 116). Choose a group and write a specific description of its degrees of connectedness, openness, and centralization. Base your specific descriptions on the characteristics identified on page 116. What conclusions can you draw about the most effective ways to initiate new ideas in the group you've described?

4. Choose a group. Compare its formal structure with the four principles listed and discussed in this chapter. How well does the formal structure of your group match the principles? How well does the formal structure of your group match its interpersonal and work needs? What suggestions might you make for redesigning the formal structure of your group?

5. Examine the informal structure of the group you used in activity 4. Describe (1) group size, (2) similarities among group members, (3) "rules" of formality and informality, (4) seating positions, and (5) the design of tasks. How would you describe the effect of these five factors on the degree to which your group seems to be centralized, connected, and subgrouped? Would you recommend any changes for more effective group work? List these recommended changes. How might you share these and any suggestions you have from activity 4 with your group?

Section Three: Reading List

Bacharach, Samuel B., and Edward J. Lawler. *Power and Politics in Organizations.* San Francisco: Jossey-Bass, 1982.

Cummings, H. W., L. W. Long, and M. L. Lewis. *Managing Communication in Organizations: An Introduction.* Dubuque, IA: Gorsuch Scarisbrick Publishers, 1983.

Farace, R. V., P. R. Monge, and H. M. Russell. "Communication in Organizational Groups," and "Communication Patterns in Organizations—Macro-Networks," in *Communicating and Organizing*. Reading, MA: Addison-Wesley, 1977.

Gordon, W. I., and J. R. Miller. *Managing Your Communication: In and For the Organization*. Prospect Heights, IL: Waveland Press, Inc., 1983.

Hunt, G. T. *Communication Skills in the Organization*. Englewood Cliffs, NJ: Prentice-Hall, Inc., 1980.

Myers, M. T., and G. E. Myers. *Managing by Communication: An Organizational Approach*. New York: McGraw-Hill Book Company, 1982.

Shaw, M. E. "The Social Environment: Group Structure," in *Group Dynamics: The Psychology of Small Group Behavior*. New York: McGraw-Hill, 1971.

PEOPLE AND THEIR RELATIONSHIPS

CHAPTER 10
MEMBERS OF THE GROUP

Each person in a group has needs and motives. Each person also has behavior patterns and habits. Taken together, they are the person's *personality*. Personalities of group members affect how a group functions. Let's look at two examples, Joanne and Ralph.

Joanne discovered that her sense of humor worked well for her in meetings through junior and senior high school. If there was tension in a group, she could tell a joke and everyone would laugh. Her humor was timely and appropriate. This was evident to her because she was reinforced for her humor. Joanne learned to use her humor in every group. It served a purpose in most situations.

Joanne's skill with humor serves another purpose for her. She feels as though other group members like her. When she tells jokes, people laugh. When they laugh, Joanne feels good. Joanne wants to be liked, and the response of other group members to her helps her meet her need to be wanted.

Ralph is a very shrewd and analytical person. He learns quickly. He remembers key facts. He can analyze a problem and get to the core of it. Ralph's father taught and encouraged this way of thinking. "Everything has a cause; everything has a solution." When there is a problem to be solved in a group, Ralph's logical thinking places him in high demand. He is a valuable group member.

The skill Ralph uses also helps him personally. Ralph likes to do things efficiently and effectively. He takes great pride in seeing a project completed. This is especially true when the result works well. The ability to analyze problems effectively usually leads to good results. Thus, Ralph's behavior helps him satisfy his needs: he is successful and he is held in high regard.

Both Joanne and Ralph use their skills in groups to satisfy their personal needs. Groups provide settings that help individuals meet their needs. Effective individuals are also likely to see beyond their personal needs to the needs of the group. An effective group member thinks the needs of the group are very important. In all of these instances, human needs are a powerful factor affecting group process and outcomes.

127

We'll examine three points of view toward human needs in this chapter. These include:

1. A model of human needs
2. A model of how needs are translated into behavior
3. A model of human behavior styles

A Model of Human Needs

Psychologist Abraham Maslow identified five levels of human needs. Maslow's list of needs is shown in the following table.

MASLOW'S HIERARCHY OF NEEDS

1. Physiological	Hunger, thirst, need for air, etc.
2. Safety and defense	Security against want, protection from attack, etc.
3. Social acceptance	Belonging, being liked and loved, etc.
4. Self-esteem and achievement	Strength, competence, confidence, freedom, accomplishment, self-respect, earned respect from others, etc.
5. Self-actualization	Creativity, innovation, development of new skills, insight, acceptance of self and others, etc.

Maslow believed that needs occur in definite levels. The lower-level needs must be satisfied before higher-level needs come into play. For example, a group member who has not eaten for a long time and has a terrific headache will be more concerned about meeting physiological needs than about social acceptance. Four of Maslow's need levels are especially important in learning about groups. These include (1) safety and defense, (2) social acceptance, (3) self-esteem and achievement, and (4) self-actualization. We'll examine each one of these in turn.

Safety and Defense Needs

Some people have had bad experiences in groups. Their ideas were not accepted. They were ridiculed or ignored. From such experiences, some people have learned to distrust and even avoid group situations. Sometimes they are forced to meet with a committee or task force. When this occurs, these people tend to defend themselves psychologically from the risks of defeat or ridicule. They use several methods. One typical way is to *minimize involvement*. Talk as little as possible. Speak only when spoken to. Another way is to *defer to others*. Do not take a position on an issue. Find out which way the vote seems to be going and vote that way. If you state an idea, attribute it to someone else: "Jack has a way to handle this situation, if we want to try it." These are some of the ways to protect oneself from the dangers of working in a group.

Social Acceptance Needs

Some group members have a high need for affection, acceptance, and approval. They want to be liked by everyone in the group. Such people act so that others will like them. They smile and nod a lot. They agree with everything and everyone. If forced to take a position, they nearly always go with the majority. A strong need to be accepted leads to conformity.

Self-Esteem Needs

There are group members who want to get work done, like Ralph, in the example cited earlier. They want to meet objectives and see results. They are motivated by a need to achieve mastery, and a need for esteem. They do not want to be liked as much as they want self-respect and admiration for their accomplishments. Instead of smiling and nodding, these members are more likely to present ideas, to look for the best possible answers, and to argue about the best way to manage a situation. Other group members may become angry with these people. However, they see the goal as getting the work done, not pampering group members.

Self-Actualization Needs

Maslow's theories became popular during the sixties and seventies, when there was much emphasis on the individual. He believed that when an individual's first four levels of needs were met, that person could then go on to achieve, create, and enjoy a lively and unique life. For Maslow, self-actualization is using all of one's inner creative and innovative potentials, exploiting them to the fullest. The self-actualized individual continually creates new, higher goals.

Maslow's theory of motivation influences groups in two ways: (1) individual group members have personal needs, and (2) the group as a whole has needs—it is moving toward *group-actualization.* A group member may benefit a group by seeing that the needs of the group are met. The member who acts from an individual need for belongingness and love may help group members get along with each other. The member who is pursuing a need for personal achievement may at the same time help the group meet its goals and finish its tasks. The group member who feels accepted and highly respected is more likely to be able to concentrate on the group. This person will be able to contribute to the people *and* the goals, the relationships *and* the work. One will not receive more emphasis than another. The group process will be more balanced.

When there is a balance between the need satisfaction of the members and the need satisfaction of the group, an individual member need no longer worry about whether "my idea" gets accepted. The goal is to accept the *best* ideas. No longer is it important to worry about whether I am liked by group members. The goal is to have people work together and feel *mutually* satisfied. The self-actualized person is able to move beyond individual needs to see the group as a total, functioning unit.

Needs Translated into Behavior

Our needs are a basic part of our lives. They motivate us. We can suppress some of them for a time, but they cannot be denied for long. Sometimes in moments of crisis, our needs become apparent to others, even though we wish they would not. Needs are observable in behavior.

Paul Hersey and Ken Blanchard provide a simple model of how needs (motives) are translated into specific actions. This process is shown in the following diagram.

TRANSLATING NEEDS IN BEHAVIOR

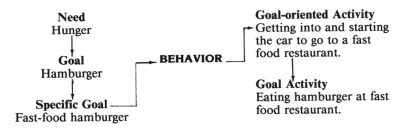

Needs (motives) are general: hunger, for example. There are many ways to satisfy hunger. Many different foods exist, and there are many different ways of preparing those foods. Hunger is translated into a *specific goal:* a hamburger at a fast food restaurant. The *specific goal results in behavior* because the goal is one definite idea among all the possibilities that exist. The first behavior is called *goal-directed behavior:* it starts the process of satisfying the need. In our example, goal-directed behavior would mean getting into the car to drive to a restaurant. The second kind of behavior is the *goal activity:* in this case, eating the food. By chewing and swallowing, the need or motive is reduced. The person is no longer hungry and goes on to other thoughts or behaviors.

Let's look at these same ideas in the context of group work. Joanne feels pleased when her group's final products are neat, clean, and complete. This is a motive (need) for Joanne. When her group must produce a report, Joanne's need comes into play. She engages in goal-directed behavior: she volunteers to oversee the typing and production of the report. She will make plans for getting the work done. As a rough draft is approved by the group, Joanne moves into her goal activity: she supervises the typing. She sees that mistakes are corrected. She asks professionals to draw figures and charts. As the work nears completion, Joanne finds satisfaction in it. But she will be pleased when she sees the final product only if it meets her standards.

Joanne, like other people, learns how to satisfy her needs. There are many ways to satisfy hunger and a number of ways to produce a neat, clean, and complete final report. There are also many methods to motivate people to work together, to like each other, and to get work done quickly and efficiently. People learn these different ways to meet their needs.

This learning process results in habits (patterned ways of doing things). People create patterns. All an individual's habits or patterns represent that person's *personal style.* People have styles in working in groups, too. There are hundreds of different personal styles and many ways to classify them. We believe the classification system developed by Thomas and Kilman is helpful in understanding human behavior in group situations.

A Model of Human Behavioral Styles

According to Thomas and Kilman, human behavior falls on a line from *assertive* to *nonassertive* and along a line from *competitive* to *cooperative.* If these two lines are placed across each other, four possible styles result:

1. Assertive and competitive

2. Assertive and cooperative

3. Nonassertive and cooperative

4. Nonassertive and competitive

In group work these four styles are called:

1. The Fighter

2. The Team Player

3. The Nice Gal/Nice Guy

4. The Individualist

The following diagram shows the possible combinations of styles.

COMBINATIONS OF PERSONAL STYLES

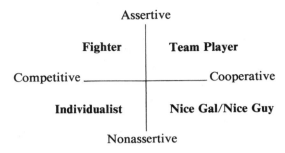

The Fighter. Fighters enjoy arguments and debates. They test ideas in a competitive way. They favor throwing all ideas into the "discussion," believing that the best one will survive. People who use this style usually have been successful at introducing (or forcing) their ideas on previous groups. They can speak forcefully and clearly.

The Nice Gal/Nice Guy. Nice gals and guys are at the opposite pole from the Fighters. They want people to get along together. They seek harmony in a group. This style involves giving in to keep the peace. Rather than competing, the Nice Gal/Nice Guy prefers to find an answer that is acceptable to everyone. It is important to them that all group members have a chance to present their ideas.

The Team Player. The Team Player combines elements of the Fighter and the Nice Gal/Nice Guy styles. The Team Player wants to get the best ideas stated and put together in an effective solution. However, the Team Player *also* wants members of the group to accept the result and get along with each other. A good idea accepted by only a few people will not satisfy the Team Player. A combination of unrelated ideas acceptable to everyone is not acceptable, either. The Team Player tries to find the best ideas acceptable to the largest number of group members.

The Individualist. The Individualist is nonassertive and competitive at the same time. Individualists want the group to do what they want. If the group will not accept their answers, Individualists are likely to become silent and uninvolved. Individualists may be very effective in their jobs. They may not be particularly effective group members. People who start their own businesses are often Individualists.

Some of the behavioral characteristics of the four personal styles are summarized in the following table.

CHARACTERISTICS OF PERSONAL STYLES IN GROUP BEHAVIORS

Style	Talking Versus Listening Behavior	Typical Group Behavior
Team Player	Balances talking and listening.	Much interaction; much statement making, information seeking, agreeing and disagreeing.
Fighter	Prefers talking and asserting.	Much statement making and disagreeing; much interrupting.
Nice Gal/ Nice Guy	Prefers listening and accepting.	Much information seeking and agreeing; not much interrupting.
Individualist	Prefers minimal communication.	Few interactions.

Personal styles are not static personality traits. Styles are learned methods of personal operations. Most people can change from one style to another to some extent. They can also add elements of another style to their own. A good analogy is clothing styles. Many people are able to dress appropriately for different situations. They change their clothing styles to fit the occasion. They also keep up with changes in business and social dress. Similarly, many people also are capable of being Fighters in situations that demand or encourage that style. They may revert to their original styles for other situations.

There are three factors which seem to influence the style a person uses:

1. *Learned behavior from the past.* Most people tend to develop patterned or habitual ways of acting. As stated earlier, group members bring these patterns with them to group meetings. They affect the group.

2. *Role or vocation.* Patterns of behavior are related to different roles and vocations. The group leader (a role) is expected to be informed about the issues that come before the group. A police officer (a vocation) is expected to be emotionally controlled and businesslike. An airline attendant (a vocation) is expected to be cheerful, friendly, and outgoing.

3. *The group social norms.* Groups become used to functioning in specific ways. Those ways that are comfortable and effective tend to be repeated. These first become the group's habitual pattern of behavior and ultimately its norms. Some groups encourage a lot of joking. Others use a stated or unstated rule: Strictly Business All Day Long.

All of these factors—the individual, the role or vocation, and the group norms—influence the style a particular person uses in a committee meeting, a staff meeting, or even in dealing with a co-worker.

It would be a mistake to think that styles are stereotypes. Styles can be put on and taken off. Jim is not always and only a Team Player. Jill is not always and only a Nice Gal. Probably, Jim uses the Team Player style most of the time. Yet when he deals with issues that are very important to him, Jim shifts to the Fighter style. Some people are able to shift among all four styles as the situation demands.

Personal styles do have an impact on group functioning. Every group has two basic requirements:

1. Members ought to add resources to the total effort.

2. Members ought to coordinate their actions.

Each individual ought to bring something to the group: individual technical skills, a special viewpoint, an ability to work with people. However, these individual resources are of little use to the team effort if they are not coordinated. When technical ideas are needed, they must be brought forth. When a personality clash develops, interpersonal skills are needed. The group must see that appropriate resources are used at appropriate times.

When members are assertive and cooperative, they add resources and coordinate people. Nonassertive people do not always speak up or give the group their ideas and skills. Competitive people try to win as individuals rather than promote a team effort. Ideally, every member of a working group should be a Team Player, adding resources and cooperating with other team members. However, some members are not Team Players.

Groups profit from a blend of styles. A work unit which consists only of Fighters is likely to generate many good projects or programs, but may get mired down in a war between people trying to get their pet projects funded or given priority. A group in which there are only Nice Gals and Nice Guys might be a pleasant place to be, but not a good place to work. Everyone would be so concerned with not offending anyone else that few ideas would be proposed and few programs would be suggested.

EFFECT OF PERSONAL STYLES ON GROUP FUNCTIONING

Style	Adds Resources	Coordinates	Effectiveness as Team Member
Fighter	yes	no	medium
Team Player	yes	yes	high
Nice Gal/Guy	no	yes	medium
Individualist	no	no	low

As time passes, group members are likely to become specialized. Some deal with task functions. Others deal mostly with interpersonal functions. To get work done, members must perform certain specialized functions: making plans, setting standards, obtaining compromises. The following list shows some of the typical functions associated with the four personal styles.

1. Team Player	Synthesizing ideas
	Assessing risks
	Summarizing status
	Negotiating solutions
2. Fighter	Setting standards
	Generating ideas
	Testing ideas
	Providing expertise
3. Nice Gal/Nice Guy	Encouraging participation
	Providing compromises
	Reflecting feelings
	Supporting others
4. Individualist	Providing ideas
	Criticizing answers
	Defending ideas

When a group is composed of people with different styles, these specialized functions are more likely to be performed effectively. This is less true when a group has members whose styles are virtually the same or when a group has only one or two styles among its members.

When a group of people have different styles, there is likely to be conflict. There are wide differences between Fighters and Nice Gals/Nice Guys. There are times when they will get on each others' nerves. This is an inevitable result of diversity.

A group with a uniform style has much less conflict. This group, however, pays the penalty of missing some important functions that are performed by members who have styles other than the one represented. Ideally there should be an optimum blend of diversity and similarity.

Let's look at the styles and functions present in one group. Note that most of the members have both a primary (usual) style and a secondary style.

STYLES AND FUNCTIONS IN ONE GROUP

Group Members	Primary Style	Secondary Style	Functions Usually Performed
Alice	Nice Gal	Team Player	Smoothing over differences, getting cooperation
Jan	Fighter	Individualist	Planning, scheduling, and budgeting
Frank	Fighter	Team Player	Generating and defending ideas
Maria	Team Player	Nice Gal	Integrating different ideas into one good answer
Susan	Team Player	None	Mediating and arbitrating to get consensus
Ed	Nice Guy	Individualist	Providing support for ideas when they are accepted by others
Preston	Team Player	Nice Guy	Seeing possibilities for reaching consensus

By being aware of the differences in personal styles, group members can be more understanding and tolerant of one another. Therefore, it is important for members and leaders to assess the personal styles of group members, as well as the functions performed by each member. This was done for the group shown above and can be done by you for your group.

Diversity of styles ensures creativity and effectiveness. Adequate similarity promotes effective levels of cooperation. An effective group ought to have a diversity of styles. The group must also have members who can fulfill the most critical functions needed to get the group's work done effectively. These include both task and interpersonal functions.

Summary

In this chapter we considered the members of the group. We used Abraham Maslow's model to study human needs. Four of the need levels he identified strongly affect group behavior: (1) safety and defense needs, (2) social acceptance needs, (3) self-esteem and achievement needs, and (4) self-actualization needs. We extended self-actualization needs to apply to groups as well as to individual members.

Hersey and Blanchard's model helped us to identify how human needs (motivations) are translated into behavior. Finally, Thomas and Gilman's theory of human behavior styles provided four styles of behavior usually present in groups: (1) the assertive–competitive style (Fighter), (2) the assertive–cooperative style (Team Player), (3) the nonassertive–cooperative style (Nice Gal/Nice Guy), and (4) the nonassertive–competitive style (Individualist). Groups that have all of these styles represented are likely to perform all important group functions. They *will* experience conflict. However, conflict is a necessary part of creative, effective decision making. If all four styles are present in a group, both task and interpersonal needs will be managed.

REFLECTING/EXPLORING

1. Consider a group of which you are a member. Describe the needs you have which this group membership seems to satisfy. Use Maslow's five levels of needs. See if you can describe the needs every other member brings to the group. How does membership in the group seem to satisfy these needs? What have you learned about your group by identifying members' needs?

2. Using the needs you have described for yourself in activity 1, trace each into specific behavior by using Hersey and Blanchard's model. Do you see a personal style (pattern of needs) that you bring to your group? What is the personal style (or styles) you use in this group? How do you think your style affects the group?

3. Repeat activity 2. Use one or more other members of your group. How does their behavior affect the group? How does it affect you as a member? What is your usual response to each member's behavior?

4. Use Thomas and Kilman's model of human behavior styles. Identify a specific group situation in which you have used one of the four personal styles. Do this for each of the four styles. Describe the situations and your behaviors. What function do you think your behavior served for each situation?

5. Use Thomas and Kilman's model of human behavior styles. Identify the primary style you believe you use in a group. Identify the primary styles you believe other group members use. What functions do you believe these styles serve for your group? Do you believe there is a balance between task and interpersonal functions? How might you report this information to your group?

CHAPTER 11

MEMBERS AND THEIR RELATIONSHIPS

Part of the complexity in working on a team comes from having to deal not only with individuals but with their relationships. Sally is a member of a committee with Jim. But Jim cannot deal with Sally as a single person. Instead, Jim must take into account the obvious facts that Sally has a strong friendship with Helen and that Sally often pairs with Jeremy in voting on certain issues before the committee. Sally's relationships with Helen and Jeremy are as important as any personal qualities Sally might have.

Relationships are one reason that large groups become more difficult to work within and to control. Notice how the number of possible relationships increases as the number of group members grows.

POSSIBLE RELATIONSHIPS AMONG GROUP MEMBERS

Number of Group Members	Possible Relationships
2	1
3	6
4	25
5	90
6	301
7	966

Once a growing group gets beyond five or six members, the number of possible relationships among them expands rapidly. In this chapter we will examine two methods of analyzing relationships between people. One involves studying three major factors in a relationship: Who controls whom? Are these two people attracted to or repelled by each other? Do they share personal feelings with each other? These three factors are commonly referred to as control, bonding, and intimacy. The other method involves classifying relationships as either formal or informal.

Control, Bonding, and Intimacy

Because the factors of control and bonding are so closely interrelated, we will consider them together.

Control and Bonding.

Control is a measure of dominance in a relationship. Is one partner dominant and one submissive, or do they tend to have relatively equal voices in joint decisions? *Bonding* is a measure of the degree to which the two persons are attracted to each other. They may be friendly toward each other or repelled by one another.

Control and bonding are illustrated in the following diagram.

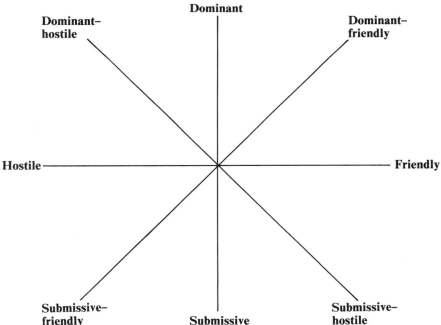

CONTROL AND BONDING

The diagram is based on a two-dimensional model of interpersonal communication developed by Leary. The vertical (control) dimension is labelled *dominant* and *submissive* while the horizontal (bonding) axis is labelled *friendly* and *hostile*. Combining these four positions results in the four combined categories shown in the diagram. We will use Joe and Mary and this diagram to help you understand the concepts of control and bonding in groups.

Relationship condition 1. The relationship between two group members may be relatively equal.

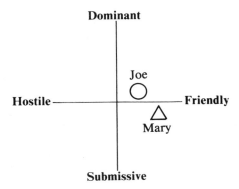

Relationship condition 2: On the other hand, one person (Mary) may be dominant over the other (Joe). Joe is submissive.

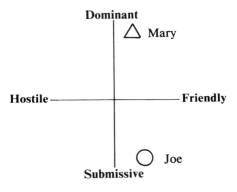

Relationship condition 3: Many combinations are possible within relationships. Some are considered unstable. For example, two people may be attempting to control each other.

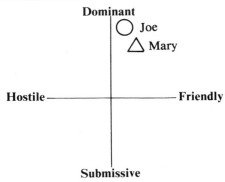

This is likely to be a highly unstable situation. One of two results is likely: (1) one person will win out and dictate, or (2) one person will leave the situation. Relationship conditions 1 and 2 are more likely to be stable. This means they will continue for a longer period of time. If one person is willing to submit to another, the dominant–submissive relationship is stable. Similarly, if both people are willing to compromise and negotiate, then neither has very great control. They are relatively equal and can maintain their relationship for quite a while.

Let's look at stability in terms of friendliness and hostility.

Relationship condition 4: Two people can be friendly. In this situation, Mary and Joe are friendly.

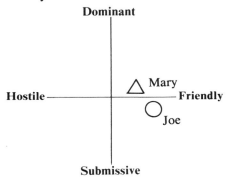

Relationship condition 5: In contrast, two people may be hostile toward each other.

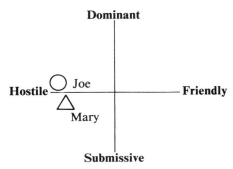

Both relationship conditions 4 and 5 are stable relationships. Instability only occurs if one person acts in friendly ways and the other responds consistently with hostility. It is then likely that the friendly person will begin to become hostile. The other possibility, of course, is that the hostile person will shift toward a more friendly posture.

Intimacy

The third important dimension in a relationship is *intimacy*. Some people get to know quite a bit about each other. They freely discuss their hopes, frustrations, and feelings. They come to understand each other. Each can predict how the other person will respond in certain situations. Other pairs, however, maintain a much more distant relationship. They learn relatively little about each other.

Getting to know another human being is a little like peeling an onion. People, too, have layers of personality which can be "peeled" away. The outermost layers are social. They are the "face" a person learns to put on in order to be acceptable to others. This face may include common courtesy and protocol, as well as a personal style. The smiles that a person uses in daily conversation manifest this face.

In a close relationship, two people get beyond the outer layers expressed in surface conversations. Beneath outer social layers lie goals and dreams, failures and disappointments, and inner feelings. Most people keep these layers hidden. Occasionally people are willing to talk about them. Even deeper within are the "secrets," those deep, private thoughts people have about their past or about their fantasies. This information is not often shared, even with very close friends.

Another way of looking at this inner and outer knowledge is with the well-known Johari Window. The following diagram shows the Johari Window.

THE JOHARI WINDOW

	Known to self	unknown to self
Known to others	Public (Open)	Blind
Unknown to others	Private (Hidden)	Unknown

Notice that the Johari Window is divided into four sections:

1. Public. There is some personal information which is known to the individual and some which is not. Some information is known to others and some is not. If information is known to the self and known to others, it is *public*. Commonly, such information includes a person's name, hobbies, interests, marital status, attitudes, opinions, and so on. Public information is usually readily available to anyone who asks and obviously known by the person involved.

2. Private. *Private* information, on the other hand, is known to the self but not to others. For whatever reason, a person chooses to

keep this information from others. It may include dreams and fantasies, negative experiences from the past, and items which the individual sees as faults or failures.

3. Blind. Although it may seem strange to some people, there is information to which the self may be *blind*. This is information that is available to others but not to self. What kind of information? Nervous habits and behavioral peculiarities often fall into this category. One person is unaware that she says "you know" a lot in conversation. Another may be unconscious of the fact that he blinks his eyes rapidly and repeatedly when the tension increases in a group. Most people are also blind, to some extent, to other people's perceptions of them. Another group member may think I don't take other people's feelings into account. Many people are blind to the fact that they are liked and appreciated by others. This occurs because we rarely talk about these things in social and public life.

4. Unknown. Finally, there is an area in the Johari Window which is *unknown* to both the self and others. Some information in the subconscious is never consciously considered by a person. Because it is private and remote, it is not known by others.

By talking to each other about matters that are important to them, two people learn more and more about each other. As the layers of the "onion" are peeled, more of the self is visible to others. The public area gets bigger and the private area gets smaller. In many situations, people also get feedback from their co-workers and peers which allows them to see themselves more accurately. Thus, the blind area gets smaller. Revealing important information about the self and getting feedback from others combine to make the public area larger and the private and blind areas smaller.

A larger public area usually indicates more openness and intimacy between people. *Intimacy*, then, means that people know important things about each other, things shared with them directly by that person. Intimacy can help in a work group because people are better able to gauge what to say and how to say it when they know each other well. If the sharing is mutual between two or more members of a group, there is a larger area of intimacy.

Formality and Informality in Relationships

Most of us work in groups. We have positions and roles in these groups. This fact suggests another way of looking at the relationships among group members. Relationships are of two general types in a group situation, particularly in a work group. They are either formal or informal. *Formal* relationships are a result of organizational or group positions, job titles, and job descriptions. For example, Cindy is the chairperson of a task force in the PreHub Corporation. Andrew is a member of that task force. Cindy and Andrew have a formal relationship as chairperson and member. This relationship can be seen in action when the task force meets. Andrew will defer to Cindy in her role as chairperson. Informal relationships occur outside structural or official positions and roles. Cindy and Andrew may be friends. They discuss many issues outside the task force. They know a great deal about each other. They and their spouses have gone out socially to dinners and concerts. Thus, they also have a relationship as friends.

Formal Relationships

Formal relationships are often defined by the organizational chart referred to in Chapter 2. Some of the possible formal relationships are shown in the following list.

1. Superior–subordinate

2. Crisscross
    superior–someone else's subordinate

3 Co-workers, peers, colleagues
    two managers
    two employees

4. Technical or Task Relationships
    professional–paraprofessional
    journeyman–apprentice
    expert–beginner

Two people may have a dominant–subordinate relationship (supervisor–employee). Two people may also be co-workers. Co-workers are two people of the same rank who work in the same group (the supervisor or manager of one unit and the manager of another unit).

Formal relationships may be based on technical expertise. There are experts and beginners, journeymen and apprentices, professionals and paraprofessionals in most organizations. Although all are employees, some have more power or prestige as a result of seniority, education, or special skill. The professional teacher working with a classroom aide is an example. The staff physician working with doctors in training is another example.

Informal Relationships

Informal relationships are social. They do not depend upon positions or titles. Informal relationships exist with:

1. Friends	5. Relatives
2. Enemies	6. Partners
3. Acquaintances	7. Competitors
4. Strangers	8. Members of a coalition

Friendship is a very common informal relationship. It may occur either between peers or between superiors and subordinates. (In the orthodox view of leadership and management, a supervisor was not supposed to have friends among the workers. In practice, it happens fairly often.) Co-workers develop friendships among themselves. They might bowl together, or share an interest in a hobby. Often they have similar backgrounds and education.

There are other informal relationships which develop around tasks and work. People form *coalitions.* There are informal groups of people who have the same kind of job, or similar problems in getting a task accomplished. People whose jobs involve preparing paperwork for a manager may get together and "gang up" on the boss for their mutual self-interest. Coalition formation is fairly common in work units and committees. Members have certain self-interests and band together with others who share them. Obviously, no one draws up a formal chart of who belongs to what coalitions and then has it signed and distributed to everyone in the organization!

Although no one is likely to draw up a formal chart showing the coalitions or other informal relationships in a group, it sometimes pays for a member to do so privately. It helps in understanding what is going on in the group. It may help in getting things done. The following is one possible way of drawing up such a chart.

CHARTING INFORMAL RELATIONSHIPS IN A GROUP

	Mary	Frank	Naomi	Al	Jo
Mary	X	Friendly Equal Close	?	Neutral Equal	Friendly; M. over J.
Frank	—	X	Hostile N. over F.	Neutral Equal	Equal Neutral
Naomi	—	—	X	Friendly Close Equal	Hostile N. over J.
Al	—	—	—	X	
Jo	╱	—	—	—	X

The members of the group are listed both horizontally and vertically. This forms a *matrix*. Each block (cell) in the matrix represents a potential relationship between two group members. The observable relationship which exists between the two persons can then be described briefly in the blocks. In this example, coalitions exist between Mary and Jo, and between Naomi and Al. Key people seem to include Mary dominant over Jo, Naomi dominant over Jo, and Al as the "swing vote" between coalitions.

In some informal relationships, one person makes the decisions and exerts control. The other is dependent and does not object to being controlled. Carl always decides, for example, where he and Jack will go to lunch. Jack does not mind. Knowledge about such dominance patterns in a subgroup is helpful in understanding that group.

Summary

In this chapter, we have examined two methods of looking at the relationships between group members. The first uses the criteria of control, bonding, and intimacy. The second contrasts formal and informal relationships. Only formal relationships are found on an organizational chart. However, it may be useful for you to define the informal relationships that exist in your groups. They affect the way your groups function as well as the group outcomes. The two-dimensional model of interpersonal communication, the Johari Window, and a matrix of interpersonal relationships are provided as ways to assess these informal relationships.

REFLECTING/EXPLORING

1. Using the two-dimensional model of interpersonal communication, plot your informal relationships with other members of a group to which you belong. What conclusions can you draw from this diagram about the effect of these relationships on your group's efforts?

2. Using the same or a different group, draw a matrix and describe the informal relationships among all the group members. Compare this to the formal relationships that exist in the same group. What are your conclusions?

3. Draw a Johari Window for yourself as you relate to two members of a group to which you belong. How accurately do your diagrams reflect the amount of public information that exists between you and the two other persons? What do you see as the effect on the way the group functions?

4. Describe a formal role you have within a group (member, leader, secretary, treasurer, subcommittee chairperson). Describe the ways you believe a person in this role should function with other members. Use the two-dimensional model of interpersonal communication. Are the ways you expect yourself to behave in your formal roles consistent with your informal relationships with people in your group?

5. Use the Johari Window. Draw a window for the person in one of your groups you relate to the most and another for the person you relate to the least. How do they differ? How do your relationships with these two people affect the way the group functions?

CHAPTER **12**

INTERPERSONAL SKILLS

The executive board of the Hampton Mental Health Association met on Friday afternoon with disastrous results. Briefly, here is what happened. According to observers and participants:

The chairperson, Bob Jones, started the meeting at 2:00 P.M. He immediately introduced a motion to reduce the budget for the coming year by twenty percent, with most of the cuts coming from the program on alcoholism and drug abuse. Bob started his proposal persuasively. He used a wide variety of facts and figures to back up his argument. The staff and other board members were stunned. They had not expected Bob to make such a proposal. Yet everyone knew the budget had to be cut.

After a few minutes of brief, quiet responses from the other board members, the executive director indicated that she wanted to speak. Martha Evans responded to Bob's proposal in a very controlled but obviously angry way. Her hands were shaking. She spent a few minutes supporting the alcohol and drug abuse program. Then she proceeded to attack Bob. Martha's main argument was that Bob had not consulted anyone on the staff or the board before making his proposal. She accused him of pulling a "dirty trick," of hitting below the belt. No one had an opportunity to prepare counterarguments.

Bob responded angrily to Martha's counterattack. The two of them argued back and forth for almost twenty minutes. A power struggle was in full swing between the top administrator and the chairperson of the executive board.

Jerry, the vice-chairperson, interrupted them: "I think we need a spirit of compromise here. There are good points on both sides of this issue. I would like to see all of us discuss those points and then make a rational decision. We don't have to take all or most of the cuts out of alcohol and substance abuse. We can spread them out. We do not need to make some of the cuts. Can't we compromise?"

Bob answered quickly, "No. I stick by my proposal."

Martha said, "I am willing to compromise, but we have to support the alcohol and drug abuse program."

That triggered Bob. He launched into another round of justifications for his proposal. Jerry tried again: "I get the idea that the two of you are talking past each other. Martha, what do you think Bob is suggesting?"

Martha replied, "I heard him say that he wanted to eliminate the drug and alcohol abuse program—for all practical purposes. He is suggesting almost a seventy-five percent cut in that program to reduce the overall budget by twenty percent."

Jerry kept trying, "Bob, what do you think Martha said?"

Bob replied, "She has taken the position that our cuts should be across the board and not from the drug and alcohol abuse program. I cannot go along with that. We need to target the cuts in the least effective program or the one we can most afford to cut back. Other agencies are dealing with substance abuse. We don't have to . . ." And so Bob went on with his argument.

During the time this was going on, Carrie was fidgeting in her seat. She was clearly upset by the proceedings and seemed to want to say something. But she didn't. Later, Carrie admitted that she was bothered and angered by the conflict. She also noted that she had been approached by Bob earlier about his proposal. She did not support his idea, but the proposal itself set her thinking about ideas for handling the budget cuts. And then she had a brainstorm: one way to totally avoid a drastic cut would be to seek more funds or to join with another agency or program to share program responsibilities. The idea was particularly appealing to Carrie. She knew that there were two other agencies in the county dealing with substance abuse. In one case, at least, the agency was swamped with work and understaffed. Wouldn't a staff-sharing arrangement be possible? It was worth investigating.

Unfortunately, Carrie never offered her ideas. She sat and fidgeted instead. When asked later why she did not jump into the discussion, she said there was no opportunity.

The meeting lasted over two hours and was finally adjourned without resolving the issue. Lots of bad feelings resulted. What went wrong? Who was to blame? Bob made an error in introducing a proposal without checking with other people. After that, everyone was at fault. The problems stem from a lack of interpersonal skills.

In this chapter, we will discuss the interpersonal skills that will help group members meet their individual needs as well as the needs of the group. These skills also will help the group effectively use relationships between members. This chapter includes three sections:

1. *Two requirements for teamwork.* These requirements include (1) combining individual resources, and (2) coordination and cooperation.

2. *Five required interpersonal skills.* These skills include (1) assertiveness, (2) listening, (3) negotiation, (4) conflict management, and (5) timing.

3. *Interpersonal skills and group relationships.*

Two Requirements for Teamwork

Teamwork involves a group of people coordinating their efforts to meet a shared goal. There are two key ideas here, effort and coordination. Given a goal, a group has to do something to move toward the goal, to get the work done, to complete activities, to finish materials. Meeting group goals requires (1) combining individual resources, and (2) coordination and cooperation.

Combining Individual Resources

The usual reason for having work done in a group is that the efforts and expertise of more than one person are needed. If one person could do the task, one person would have been assigned to it. Some groups, however, are made up of people with different viewpoints or who represent various units or departments within the organization or community. In such a case, the group is formed because the work to be done requires taking into account all of these different viewpoints. When a variety of abilities is needed or when various viewpoints must be represented, forming a group is the logical response.

Individual group members may be selected because they have specific technical skills or expertise. The accountant is needed to manage income and expenses. The lawyer is needed to make recommendations on legal matters. In a human-service agency, the social worker knows ways in which clients can be treated and supported. In an industrial setting, the engineer can understand and work with problems of design. Working together, these specialists can combine their resources for successful group outcomes.

As noted above, sometimes groups are formed to provide representation for various views or units. Members of these groups are not selected because of their technical specialties. In a hospital, a committee may be formed to review the problems of laundering linens. Who ought to be on the committee? Obviously, someone from the laundry. Someone from nursing should be on the committee because the nurses supervise the making of beds. The transport area must be represented. These are the people who carry the clean linens to the units and remove the used bundles to the laundry. Someone from the central administration should be involved to make sure costs are considered in making a decision. This group consists of representatives of the various work groups affected by the laundering of linens. In this kind of group, the individual is not so much a technical expert as a representative of other people, all of whom have a stake in the decision. Group members must communicate the needs of the groups they represent.

Whether a group is formed on the basis of technical expertise, representation, or a combination of both, the group must have the appropriate mix of resources (skills and views) to get the job done effectively and efficiently.

Coordination and Cooperation

Each group member must communicate in order to add to the overall resources of the group. Individual contributions must be coordinated in order to perform the task. By *coordination,* we mean taking into account what other people are doing to get the job done. If Mary is making up name tags for a conference and Ernie is getting programs printed, the two need coordination to make sure they are using the same title for the conference and the same logo.

When two or more people coordinate their actions, they are combining their skills and expertise rather than using them individually. Coordination is a key issue in group work. Not only must the marketing person, accountant, lawyer, and engineer set forth their opinions and ideas, but they must take into consideration what each other person is saying. In some situations, coordination is possible because all four talk to a chief executive who then makes a decision based on their input. But that is not group work. It is four individuals talking in sequence to an executive. To function as a group, the accountant, the lawyer, the engineer, and the marketing representative must hear and use what is being said by the others.

For the coordination of efforts to occur at the task level, the group members must *cooperate* at the interpersonal level. The accountant is not a robot or module, replaceable by any other accountant. Instead, the accountant is Dick, a fun-loving individual who likes practical jokes and puns. He is quite easy to get along with. He is patient and able to explain complex issues in accounting to laypersons. In other words, Dick is a cooperative person. However, Geraldine, the lawyer, is cool and humorless. She also is very busy. She is overworked and this, therefore, makes her feel impatient. When Geraldine thinks that she can no longer influence the group decision, she simply leaves the meeting. Clearly, Geraldine is less cooperative than Dick.

Thus, group members must not only have expertise and be willing to communicate. They must also be willing to coordinate their efforts with others. They have to cooperate with every other person in the group. The group's need for expertise, communication, coordination, and cooperation helps to define the major interpersonal skills required for group work.

Five Required Interpersonal Skills

Five interpersonal skills are required of effective and efficient group members:

1. Assertiveness
2. Listening
3. Negotiation

4. Conflict management

5. Timing

Timing is a super skill affecting the other four skills. Timing makes it possible to use each of the other skills in the most appropriate ways. Possession of these five skills will enable a group member to work more successfully in meetings, teams, and committees.

Assertiveness

Perhaps the easiest way to define assertiveness is to say that it falls between passivity and aggressiveness.

Passive Behavior. Some people are shy. They do not like to speak before a group or in a group. Perhaps they feel inadequate. Sometimes this results from past experiences when they felt silly or embarrassed. Unpleasant past experiences tend to encourage an individual member to be more passive. Carrie's behavior is an example of passivity.

There also are people who speak up in group meetings but do it in ways that make their contributions sound indefinite. For example, a direct statement might be: "We need to consider the costs of that proposal." The indirect or passive version: "Maybe we could look at the possibility that it might be expensive to do that." This second statement includes many *qualifiers*. Maybe we could . . . the possibility that . . . . it might be expensive . . . : All of these expressions qualify (soften) the statement involved. The qualifiers seem to turn what could have been a statement into an apology.

Another passive way of speaking is to end a statement with a question or request: "We might want to consider the costs of this, don't you think?" or "Shouldn't we consider the budget here?" If someone in the group does not answer the question, or if someone says "No," the idea is lost. The group decision may be less workable because the budget was not considered.

Aggressive Behavior. Aggressiveness is the opposite of passive behavior. Few people are too aggressive. Absolute, dogmatic statements are aggressive: "Without question, this is the *only* way we can solve this problem." Aggressiveness is often shown by interrupting others or refusing to be interrupted. An aggressive individual may also change the topic in a meeting without consulting others.

Aggressiveness in one person usually produces frustration, defensiveness, and hostility in others. A passive individual may be liked but not respected. Many people have confused passivity with being courteous or "nice." When they try some assertiveness, they think it is aggressive behavior. However, assertiveness is not aggressive.

Assertive Behavior. Assertiveness is the middle ground between aggressiveness and passivity. In group meetings, a member behaves assertively by speaking up when it is appropriate. Assertiveness involves speaking forcefully enough to make a point and be heard. Assertive behavior does not include (1) putting unnecessary qualifiers on statements, (2) apologizing for ideas, and (3) asking questions instead of stating ideas. Passive behavior leads the people who use it to think that their ideas are not worthwhile or are not needed by the group. It is important for group members to realize that they have been selected to be members of the group for the purpose of sharing their ideas and experience. Stating those ideas and opinions is the only way to make them available to the group.

Listening

Most people think of listening as passive. People sit and listen. People sit back and listen. Listening, however, is an *active* process. It involves focusing one's attention. It may include paraphrasing what has been heard either silently to oneself or in a statement to the speaker. Listening well means hearing what is being said between the words, and noting what has been left out. It includes taking nonverbal cues into account. For the effective group member, there are three levels of listening:

1. Paying attention (attending behaviors)
2. Listening for understanding
3. Empathic listening

Using Attending Behaviors. *Attending behaviors* include nodding the head, smiling, using direct eye contact, sitting forward, and saying "uh-huh." Most of us learned these behaviors early. We use them without conscious thought. Unfortunately, these behaviors can also be used without listening. They can be used without paying attention and without really being interested in what another person is saying. This is sometimes called pseudo listening, or false listening. Some people may look very attentive while their minds have wandered to other things. They probably will neither understand nor remember what the speaker is saying.

Using attending behaviors can help you listen more effectively. By sitting forward, using direct eye contact, nodding the head at those moments when an idea seems clear to you, saying "uh-huh" to indicate you truly understand, smiling when a smile fits the speaker's meaning, or raising your eyebrow when you experience confusion, you will focus your attention on the speaker. Attending behaviors can help a listener stay in the present with the person who is talking.

Listening for Understanding. *Listening for understanding* takes even more effort than attending behaviors do. There is no way this kind of listening can be faked. The listener must want to understand. In addition to using attending behaviors, three learnable listening skills are involved:

1. *Asking open-ended questions.* Open-ended questions are questions that cannot be answered simply with a yes or no. They are the *who, when, where, why, what,* and *how* questions. Here are some examples:

   1. Who was involved in that project?
   2. When did that happen?
   3. Where were the staff managers when the crisis occurred?
   4. Why do you think they reacted that way?
   5. What happened?
   6. What can be done now?
   7. How was that decision made?

2. *Paraphrasing, summarizing, or repeating what the other person has said.* Here are some examples:

   1. You seem to be saying that . . .
   2. Let me see if I can put that into my own words . . .
   3. I want to see if I can give a brief version of your proposal . . .
   4. If I understand you, you're saying that . . .

3. *Seeking clarification.* Seeking clarification may involve asking for more explanation, description, or instances. Here are some examples:

   1. I'm not sure I understand what you are saying. Could you put it in different words?
   2. I don't think I'm clear on this. What do you mean by "deflating the dollar"?

You can use these questions in a meeting. They will provide you with active ways to listen for understanding.

Empathic Listening. *Empathic listening* involves listening "between the lines." Empathy means putting oneself into the position of another. It involves trying to see from someone else's point of view. Obviously, when people talk, they use words. Empathic listeners are sensitive to what is *not* being said in words. They use the nonverbal cues that accompany the message. Facial expression, pauses, body position, and distance are nonverbal cues. So are voice tone, rate, and pitch. Does the speaker seem calm or tense? Relaxed or emotionally involved? Positive and happy, or depressed and negative? Highly involved in the message or simply saying what someone else has said? All of these hidden messages need to be heard, interpreted, and checked out if the listener is going to *really* understand what is going on in a group meeting. This is particularly important when there is conflict and disagreement.

One of the problems in the executive board meeting used at the beginning of this chapter had to do with listening. Bob Jones, the chairperson, and Martha Evans, the director, stopped listening to each other. This happens when people feel strongly about an issue and become angry. Both Bob and Martha took positions. Neither wanted to hear what the other was saying. Instead of asking questions, repeating, or seeking clarification, the two locked horns. Each probably spent the time while the other was speaking putting together arguments. Neither listened at all. Listening is a key skill for just this reason: If two people do not listen to each other, they are bypassing each other. They respond not to what is said, but to what they want to hear or what they think was said.

Listening can be a very powerful skill. An effective listener often becomes influential in a group. Information is power. The person who acquires and understands facts, arguments, and suggestions is one who will be able to come up with reasonable compromises and rational decisions. Information is acquired through listening, not talking. The amount of information members hear determines how much information will be considered in completing the group task. The ability to listen empathically to the feelings and ideas of others helps people feel understood. Listening has a powerful effect on interpersonal relationships.

Negotiation

Even with active listening and almost complete understanding of each other, people may still have different opinions on what will and will not work. This is the time for *negotiation.* Let's go back to the opening board meeting. Part of the problem between Bob and Martha resulted from their inability or unwillingness to negotiate. Bob started by making a statement that sounded final and absolute. There seemed to be no room to negotiate. Martha responded in kind. Both took positions, opposing positions.

In their book, *Getting to Yes,* Roger Fisher and William Ury have provided a useful way of looking at the negotiation process. Their method aids in reaching an answer with a minimum of bad side effects. It has been used in a variety of situations involving disagreement. It is very similar to some problem-solving methods.

The key to the Fisher and Ury system is to understand the difference between *taking a position* and *seeking a self-interest.* Bob took the position that the substance abuse program would have to be cut in order to reduce the budget. Martha took the position that Bob acted improperly in making the proposal without consulting staff or board members before the meeting. What self-interests does each person have at stake? Bob wants to see the budget reduced. This is a legitimate interest. It is one that is shared by all the board members and Martha. However, Martha's interests probably include wanting to preserve staff morale and perhaps wanting to continue some political plays among agencies in the county. If both Martha and Bob had stated and agreed upon their interests, a satisfying solution might have been worked out. It might have included some reduction in substance abuse, but have spread the rest of the reductions across the other programs. It might have included ways to get more support for the agency. The problem was that Bob already had an answer (position) and Martha did not like it.

The Fisher and Ury negotiation strategy is radically different from the familiar adversary methods that involve the parties in taking fortress positions and going through a series of compromises to reach a middle ground. In those negotiations, people first take an "up-front" position. Privately, they decide on a "fall-back" position, making note of the items they are willing to trade for something else. The Fisher and Ury method encourages the negotiating parties to seek a solution that satisfies the interests of everyone. There are no winners or losers.

The Fisher and Ury negotiation style can be particularly effective in cases where people have been assertive in stating their views and have listened to each other. At that point, the possibility for creative negotiation exists.

Conflict Management

Conflict cannot always be resolved. Research indicates that some conflicts are ongoing, sometimes lasting for decades. Long-term conflicts emerge out of real differences between people. These might be differences in habit or temperament. Jack likes to have an orderly but leisurely meeting. Susan wants to have a quick meeting to fix whatever currently is a problem. Jack and Susan could go on fighting over this difference for years. Susan tends to think long meetings waste her time. Jack might feel irritated over Susan's tendency to leave the meeting after half an hour.

With Bob and Martha there is a power struggle. These two people "run the show." As chairperson of the executive board, Bob is elected by the other board members. He is probably used to having his way in his own business. Martha is the executive director of the agency. She runs the agency on a day-to-day basis. Both have considerable power. When Bob makes his suggestions, Martha very possibly interprets these as an attempt to take over her power. She responds as expected: with anger. The underlying issue here is not the budget reduction. It is the power of these two people. This is often the case in conflict situations.

We are wise to view the situation between Bob and Martha as a problem of *managing* conflict, not resolving it. Neither Martha nor Bob is likely to back off and give up power. Both want it. Bob is not going to resign. Martha probably will not resign either. So they need to find a way to work together. The well-being of the agency demands that they create ways to work with each other in spite of their differences over power.

Three steps are helpful in managing conflict:

1. Recognizing and confronting

2. Bringing the issues out in the open and dealing with them directly

3. Working out a way to allow everyone to feel respected and needed in the work situation

These steps represent an assertive way to manage conflict. But many people run from conflict. This can be dangerous. Differences do not simply disappear with time; sometimes they get worse. It is important to confront conflict. This means directly and openly stating those differences. Bob and Martha would be well advised to meet with each other and frankly talk about the issue of power. There is no way their differences can be managed if they talk about budgets or how to conduct meetings or some other surface issue. If the real issue is power, that is what needs to be discussed.

It is important to realize that when the real issue is discussed directly, the conflict becomes threatening to the people involved and to their egos. If one person loses as a result of discussing the real issue, there is a real danger of even worse conflict in the future. The people involved must be able to work out their differences so that they feel that their opinions are heard and respected. This may take a series of meetings.

Conflict management is a skill. In many ways, it is the highest level of skill. It may also be the most difficult skill to acquire. Confronting someone with whom you have differences is not easy. Talking directly with that person implies a willingness to change as well as a desire to have the other person change. True mutual understanding is needed. Conflict management requires assertive behavior, listening skills, the ability to negotiate, and appropriate timing.

Timing: The Super Skill

Group members may be able to use the four interpersonal skills just discussed and still not be successful. They might be using the skills in the wrong place or at the wrong time. Imagine the problems that might occur if someone decides that the time to be assertive is in the middle of a conflict that desperately needs some empathic listening from everyone involved! Suppose that a person with an idea that might solve the problem decides that it is more important to really listen and understand others rather than to be assertive! There are guidelines for when to use the interpersonal skills. These are not hard-and-fast rules. They do not cover all situations. However, they will serve as a useful guide. We have arranged the guidelines according to the particular set of interpersonal skills involved.

Guidelines for Timing Assertive Skills

Assertive behavior is needed:

1. When you have resources (information or an opinion) needed by the group and which no one else can provide

2. When time is at a premium

3. When you have strong feelings based on your values and ethics about a decision or solution to a problem

4. When conflict exists between other persons and you can provide a way to solve a problem or get to a decision that bypasses the conflict

5. When efficiency and effectiveness outweigh group goals of teamwork and developing personal relationships

These situations may occur within a single meeting. Sometimes a group begins working smoothly and then gets bogged down. Assertiveness can be useful then.

Guidelines for Timing Listening Skills

Skills of effective listening come into play:

1. When other members of the group have expertise, knowledge, or opinions and you need the information they have

2. When there seems to be confusion or uncertainty among group members and people are searching for an answer or solution

3. When teamwork and improving relationships are important

4. When minority views have not been shared in the discussion and the input and votes of these members are needed

The effect of listening is to encourage other people to take part in group efforts. Often the result is that people feel important, involved, and understood.

Guidelines for Timing Negotiation Skills

Negotiation skills are needed:

1. When there are two or more conflicting proposals on the table and a single decision is needed soon

2. When there is conflict over ideas, as opposed to personality clashes

3. When technical problem solving will work and there is time enough to seek a creative solution that will satisfy all parties

Negotiation takes time. It usually cannot be accomplished in ten or fifteen minutes. The payoff is the resulting consensus and harmony within the group.

Guidelines for Timing Conflict-management Skills

Conflict management is used most appropriately:

1. When there is clear evidence of anger and hostility and work is stopped because of these emotions

2. When the frustrated or angry people withdraw by not participating in discussions, by leaving, or by not attending meetings

3. When disagreement exists because of differences in the basic values or in the lifestyles of the people involved

4. When the disagreement within a group has existed for a long time and seems to affect nearly every problem or decision that comes before the group

Someone must bring the conflict into the open so that group members can discuss it directly. Indirect conflict management often results in backbiting, sarcasm, and silence. These behaviors may divide a group. Sometimes it is not possible to repair the divisions that result from indirect conflict management.

Effective group members must be sensitive to, and must understand, the current situation. Effective group members should have interpersonal skills. They must use the skills appropriate to a specific situation. This requires the super skill of timing.

Interpersonal Skills and Group Relationships

Both formal and informal relationships within a group depend on interpersonal skills. The efficient and effective use of interpersonal skills permits relationships to be developed and maintained. Improper use of the skills or failure to use them results in the breaking down and even ending of relationships.

To work as a team, group leaders and members must develop and maintain relationships. Any relationship depends on mutuality. Each person must talk and be heard. Each person must listen and try to understand. This implies a combination of assertiveness and listening skills.

In some unrealistic versions of interpersonal relationships, people simply speak their minds and they are automatically understood. In the real world of work, life rarely is that simple. No two people are exactly alike. Jack has a personal style that differs from that of Sarah. Jack grew up in a home where conflict was avoided. Sarah was raised in a family where the talk at every family dinner was a debate over politics, religion, foreign affairs, and personal topics that any member of the family wanted to discuss. These differences in early training will be seen in the ways Jack and Sarah take part in teamwork. The result often is conflict.

Negotiation and conflict management are absolutely vital skills for maintaining relationships over the months and years that people may work together. Individuals must learn how to live with their differences. They should take time to celebrate their similarities. Effective group members will be able to manage conflicts among them in a manner that allows their relationships to be civil and respectful. It is not necessary that everyone like each other. It is necessary that each person feel accepted and respected as a member of the group. Practicing interpersonal skills will help you develop the personal style you need for effective group work.

SUMMARY

A group, committee, board, task force, or team needs the expertise of its members to solve problems and make decisions. It needs the views of its members, especially if they represent departments or units within the organization or community that must provide input for the group's decisions. At the same time, the group needs coordination and cooperation among its members. The members cannot go off in different directions.

These needs in group work can be met with four basic interpersonal skills: assertiveness, listening, negotiation, and conflict management. A fifth, the super skill, is timing in the use of the other four skills. Assertiveness is needed to get opinions and ideas into the discussion. Listening is needed to make sure that ideas and opinions are heard and understood. The skill of negotiation helps group members seek answers that satisfy the greatest number. Conflict management allows a group to ride through the rough seas of deep disagreement. A sensitive, alert group member is aware that these skills are needed at different times and in various situations. An effective group member knows how to use the super skill of timing.

By using the interpersonal skills appropriate to each situation, group members will have a better chance of getting along with each other. They will be able to build and maintain their relationships. All members of the group will be involved in the work of the group. The result will be a group that holds together through difficult times as well as in moments of success.

REFLECTING/EXPLORING

1. Examine the reasons for your membership in various groups. Is your membership based on expertise, representation, or a combination of both? Do you behave differently when your membership is differently based? Explain.

2. Describe a group meeting that, in your opinion, was not effective. Dis-

cuss what could have been done to make the meeting more effective in terms of coordination and cooperation. What could you have done?

3. Use a scale from 1 to 5, with 1 standing for seldom and 5 standing for usually. Rate yourself on each of the four skills (assertion, listening, negotiation, and conflict management). Ask yourself, do I use each of these skills at the most effective time and in the best place? Identify specific times when you did and specific times when you did not. What might you do to improve your timing with each skill?

4. Use one of your groups that meets regularly. Use the scale in activity 3. Rate each member on all four skills. What observations might you make based on the result of your evaluation? When and where might you share your observations with the other group members?

5. Use the same group you used in activity 4. Describe the situations in which you expect conflict to occur in this group. Describe what you believe is the cause of the conflict. How might you use the four interpersonal skills and timing to help manage the conflict?

SECTION FOUR: READING LIST

Information on motivation and group member styles:

Blake, R. R. and J. S. Mouton. *The New Managerial Grid.* Houston, TX: Gulf Publishing, 1978.

Hersey, P. and K. Blanchard. *Management of Organizational Behavior,* 4th ed. Englewood Cliffs, NJ: Prentice-Hall, 1982.

Macoby, M. *The Gamesman.* New York: Bantam Books, 1977.

Maslow, A. *Motivation and Personality.* New York: Harper & Row, 1954.

Thomas, K. and Kilman. *Conflict Mode Instrument.* San Diego, CA: Learning Resources Corp., n.d.

Information on relationship and ways of relating with people:

Leary, T. *Interpersonal Diagnosis of Personality.* New York: The Ronald Press, 1957.

Luft, J. *Group Process: An Introduction to Group Dynamics.* Palo Alto, CA: National Press Book, 1970.

Shostrum, E. L. *Man, the Manipulator.* New York: Bantam Books, 1967.

Information on interpersonal skills:

Egan, G. *Interpersonal Living.* Monterey, CA: Brooks/Cole Publishing, 1976.

Fisher, R. and W. Ury. *Getting to Yes: Negotiating Agreement without Giving In.* New York: Houghton, Mifflin, 1981.

Information on assertive behavior:

Alberti, R. E. and M. L. Emmons. *Your Perfect Right.* San Luis Obispo, CA: IMPACT, 1970.

Bower, S. and G. Bower. *Asserting Yourself: A Practical Guide for Positive Action.* Reading, MA: Addison-Wesley, 1976.

Lange, A. J. and P. Jakubowski. *The Assertive Option: Your Rights and Responsibilities.* Champaign, IL: Research Press Co., 1978.

GROUP PROCESS

13
GROUP PROCESS WITHIN MEETINGS

Valerie spoke to Fran about the meeting they had just left:

> I noticed something tonight. When the meeting started, we all seemed a little uptight. There was some tension, I thought. Everyone seemed to be trying to guess about what we were supposed to be doing. But as the discussion continued, we seemed more sure of ourselves. I saw people actually relax. At the same time, they seemed to get more involved. And then I could actually see the sense of relief when Sarah made the suggestion about putting the two different programs together into one. People seemed to leave feeling good.

Valerie has given a description of the process that occurred for one group in one meeting.

If we observe a meeting or participate in one, a basic fact becomes clear: there are changes over time. There are differences in how people react to each other. There are differences in how they face the job at hand. These shifts constitute *group process*.

Every group has a basic structure. Group structure is made up of the stable, consistent features of a group. Structure includes the communication network among group members: who usually talks to whom. Group structure stays relatively stable for months, even years. A group continues to have a leader, linkers and liaisons, and opinion leaders. However, within this basic structure, there are shifts in the ways people communicate with and relate to one another. These changes represent process within the structure.

In the next two chapters, we will examine how group process changes during meetings and how group process changes as a result of what occurs between group meetings. Finally, in Chapter 15, we will help you learn methods to influence group process.

In this chapter, then, you will concentrate on observing and describing changes that occur in group process during a meeting. You will learn that:

1. New ideas create disturbance

2. Changes in group process are related to the task

3. Changes in group process occur at the relationship level

We will discuss each of these topics.

New Ideas Create Disturbance

When ideas or suggestions are presented that are new to a group, people feel tension and disturbance. Even if the idea may have a positive effect, the newness of the information usually results in feelings of stress. Members may not understand the new idea. A suggestion may conflict with standard, traditional, or habitual ways of working together. The tension that results must be reduced or eliminated. Group process is living and changing.

To reach a clearer understanding of new information, members will talk about the idea. They will compare it to the other ideas currently in use. They will examine the pros and cons. In this process, they will find out where they stand in relation to the idea and to each other.

R. F. Bales suggested that new ideas introduce tension into the group process. Bales thought of changes as a series of movements in the group that became more and more faint. These movements are composed of responses, and corrections to those responses, by group members. The reactions move back and forth from negative to positive until a satisfactory solution emerges. Let's examine this process of change in an example from an actual group meeting.

PROCESS OF CHANGE DURING A GROUP MEETING

New proposal.

1. The following idea was introduced in a staff meeting: Task assignments should be based on seniority. The most senior people should be assigned the most difficult tasks.

Immediate negative reaction.

2. Two staff members rejected the idea. They observed that different people have different task expertise. A junior staff member might be better suited to some difficult tasks. (Other staff members recognized that these two people happened to have some of that special expertise and they were junior members.)

Positive correction to negative reaction.

3. Another staff member supported the idea of seniority. (Group members noticed that this person was in the upper third of the group, based on seniority.)

Mild negative correction to positive response. Door opened to satisfactory solution.	4. One staff member suggested that seniority alone was not a good criterion. He wanted to use several criteria.
Positive response. Satisfactory resolution developed.	5. Three other members supported this idea. As a result, seniority, special expertise, and current workload were presented as three important criteria.
Previous negative response reversed.	6. Both of the staff members who opposed the original idea supported the new proposal.
Mild negative response.	7. A person who had not yet spoken suggested that they just continue assigning tasks the way it had always been done, by simple rotation.
Lack of response dampens negative reaction.	8. No one supported this idea. No one spoke against it, either.
Satisfactory solution.	9. Someone suggested taking a vote on the idea of using three criteria. It passed unanimously.

Notice that the idea of seniority created problems or disturbances in this group. Not everyone liked the idea. There was a split. Some people rejected the idea while others supported it. Then a change in the proposal was suggested. It emerged from the discussion. The modified idea was more acceptable to the group members. It was particularly acceptable when compared to the existing method.

We used a key word in group process in this description: *emergence.* People talk, discuss, argue, compare, and suggest. Ideas emerge from this process. Proposals are not simply accepted or rejected. They are changed. Sometimes entirely new suggestions are made, explored, modified, and negotiated even after a previously discussed suggestion seems to be the final solution. Group members who are comfortable with and able to use the tension energy that comes with new ideas will be better able to weigh available information. They will also be better able to arrive at the most effective decisions.

Task-related Changes

When a group is working on a task, changes in group process occur in four phases:

1. The orientation phase
2. The evaluation phase

3. The emergence phase

4. The solution phase

The Orientation Phase

In the early stage of discussing a new problem, group members attempt to define the task. They share information about the problem. Sometimes they tell lengthy, detailed stories of how their jobs or units are affected. They attempt to clarify what they mean by the problem. In this phase, they tend to pool information for the purpose of defining the problem, task, or issue facing them.

The Evaluation Phase

The amount of information exchanged tends to diminish as the meeting continues. The number of opinions exchanged tends to increase. This change in the type of sharing reflects a shift from defining the problem to working on possible solutions. Opinions are introduced when members talk about what should be done and how. The talk seems more focused and less ambiguous in this phase than in the orientation phase.

The Emergence Phase

Usually each member is aware of the point at which a workable solution begins to emerge out of the discussion. More statements of support are made for one proposal than for others. The supporting statements tend to be repeated. Fewer and fewer objections are raised to the proposal that begins to stand out as a possible answer. At this time, the talk may become more general. Statements seem more indirect and wordy. Members find ways to "disagree agreeably."

The Solution Phase

In this final stage, a solution to the problem is accepted. There is less introduction of new ideas and less sharing of opinions. The talk is mainly for the purpose of interpreting how the solution will work. Disagreements seem to be at a minimum and talk of coordination and cooperation is common.

In terms of task-related changes in group process, members start with defining the problem, then progress through conflict over possible solutions to end with one solution.

While change is occurring at the task level, it is also happening in interpersonal relationships.

Changes in Emotional Tone in Groups

As the group moves through the phases of solving a problem, members respond emotionally. Most members feel involved in one solution or another. They have personal interests in one aspect of the problem or another. Emotional changes occur in individuals. These result in social changes among group members. Let's examine some of the changes that may occur as a group works through the phases of solving a problem.

The Orientation Phase

In this phase, people feel each other out. They may engage in sparring, much as boxers do. Some may feel relief that the issue is finally being discussed. Some may see the topic for discussion as permission to talk about the stress they may have felt because the current system is not working for them. Others may feel frightened because changes may occur. They feel more comfortable with the current system because they know it. A new computer may streamline accounting procedures, yet the senior accountants who know little about computers may feel frightened and anxious about the possibility that their department will be computerized. The orientation phase can be full of unknowns. Some see it as a challenge. Others see it as frightening.

The Evaluation Phase

Once the possible solutions have been stated, members feel a sense of relief. The sparring is over. There is a focus to this phase: members may choose to share their opinions of how one or more possible solutions will work for them and for their departments. As opinions are shared, group members may begin to support others who seem to agree with their views. Thus, coalitions are formed.

The Emergence Phase

One solution emerges as the most acceptable because the members who spoke for it seemed persuasive. It also emerges because others who did not support it are willing to compromise. The solution often emerges out of disagreement. Members who supported the losing solution may have strong feelings if the issue is important to them or their department. As a solution emerges, coalitions formed in the evaluation phase may dissolve.

The Solution Phase

At this point, one solution has been selected. While open disagreement may be at a minimum, strong feelings of disapproval and disappointment may exist among those members who preferred a different solution. Yet, the talk is focused on how to make the solution work. In most cases, this kind of talk tends to unify the group. There is a sense of relatedness among group members. This is a result of having been a part of a group going through the process of expressing differences in order to negotiate a common solution.

Overall, group meetings move from fairly closed, indirect, and distant behaviors and feelings in the early stages to more open, direct, and close behaviors and feelings toward the end. It is common to experience wide-ranging shifts in the emotional tone of a meeting. Communication may flow smoothly at first. It may slow down in the evaluation phase. The orientation phase may be characterized as slow and awkward. Then talk flows smoothly once more when a solution begins to emerge.

Taken together, the combined emotional changes of each member affect the mood (climate) of the group. Changes and shifts in work and feelings are a natural part of group process.

A person who likes to see work completed may feel frustrated when the group is enjoying itself at the expense of finishing a task quickly. Another who prefers to socialize may find a group dull when it is being very serious and productive. Both people must learn to adapt to the sequence of moods that occur within group process.

The key question to ask is this: Is the group's inability to complete a task caused by lack of needed information, skills, or creativity? Is it because members do not want to talk, are fearful of the unknown, or don't trust each other? If this is the case, it is a relationship issue. Work must be stopped and interpersonal factors discussed. If there is a lack of information or skill, the group probably should adjourn until the needed information is obtained or until new members with the necessary skills can be added to the group.

SUMMARY

Group process is not static. Changes in the behavior of individual members and in the total mood of the group occur over time. The changes may be so small they are not noticeable. Changes may be quite obvious and extensive. Changes in routine usually result in feelings of stress among members. The introduction of any new idea creates disturbance. As a new idea is discussed, negative and positive comments are exchanged about the idea until a mutually satisfactory solution emerges.

The changes that occur in group process (1) are related to the task of the group and (2) also occur at the relationship level. When working on a task, a group usually moves through four phases: (1) the orientation phase, (2) the evaluation phase, (3) the emergence phase, and (4) the solution phase. Task-related changes in group process start with defining the problem, move through some conflict over possible solutions, and end up with a solution. Moving through these phases at the task level causes changes in interpersonal relationships. During the course of a meeting, groups move from fairly closed, indirect, and distant behaviors and feelings to more open, direct, and close behaviors and feelings.

If a group finds itself unable to complete a task, two questions about group process may prove helpful: (1) Is more information or are different skills needed? (2) Are we willing to talk with each other and trust each other? In either case, work on the task should be stopped. If information or skills are needed, they should be obtained. If the trust level is low, interpersonal factors should be discussed before proceeding.

REFLECTING/EXPLORING

1. Observe a group attempting to solve a problem. This may be a meeting of your city commission or council or it may be a meeting of a small task force in your church, community, or at work. As you observe, describe the flow of conversation back and forth from negative to positive. Plot each comment as positive or negative on a line. What did you learn about changes that occur with the introduction of a new idea in this specific situation? If you have the opportunity, repeat this activity with a different group and compare the results of the two groups.

2. Compare two group meetings that you participated in recently. Select one meeting in which the flow of discussion seemed to move quite smoothly. Select a second meeting in which discussion seemed to bog down. How do you account for the differences in the way the two groups were able to arrive at their solutions? Take into account both the task level and the relationship level of group process.

3. Observe a group. This may be one in which you are a member. As the group attempts to solve a problem, watch for each of the orientation, evaluation, emergence, and solution phases. Describe the specific behaviors that are related to each of the four phases. What occurs in the group process that permits you to identify the point where the group leaves one phase and moves into the next phase? Describe the behaviors you believe are related to the task level and those behaviors that are part of the relationship level in the group's process.

4. Patterns sometimes occur in group process. Each time a group discusses a new problem or issue, it tends to behave in the same way. What patterns do you see in the process of a group you observe regularly or a group of which you are a member? Which of the patterns are helpful to group decision making? Which stand in the way of making effective decisions? How might you present this information to the group?

5. Take part in a group meeting at which new information is being presented. As you participate, keep a record of your feelings. List your feelings in the four categories that match the four phases. When the meeting is finished, examine your list of feelings. To what extent do you view your feelings as being related to the task level in the group process? To the relationship level? What statement might you make about changes in group process based on your record of your own feelings?

14

CHANGE AND DEVELOPMENT IN GROUPS

A Greek philosopher once described life as a process. It is constantly changing like the water flowing in a river. Change certainly is a fact of life in groups. Groups have a life span, just as people do.

Some groups have a very brief life span. They may be formed to work on a specific task that can be accomplished in a one-hour or a day-long meeting, over a weekend, or during a three-day session. When the task is finished, so is the group. An example of a group with a very brief lifespan is an accreditation team. This kind of group usually includes about six people. The members are teachers, school administrators, and citizens named by a state department of education. Its purpose is to review the overall program of a local school system. The team's work is done and the team no longer exists as soon as its report is submitted to the appropriate state agency. The members of the team may not work together again as a group.

Many groups have longer life spans. The personnel department of Oakridge Community Hospital will probably exist as long as the hospital does. However, the group process does not remain static. Members of the group may change as employees retire and others are hired. Members may be absent from meetings occasionally, affecting the process. As the group moves from task to task, changes occur in its process not only because the tasks differ but because members of the group are interested in one task more than another.

When the personnel director at Oakridge is out of town, meetings may be shorter than usual or even cancelled. When the group is conducting an internal review of the way the personnel department functions, group members may have strong vested interests in the results. Feelings may not be as strong when they are reviewing the procedures for using a new government regulation on affirmative action in hiring policies. Levels of interest may vary widely among members. Variations in people, procedures, tasks, and the situation itself result in changes in the group process.

In the last chapter, we discussed the changes in group process that occur in a single meeting of a group. In this chapter, we will analyze the changes that occur from meeting to meeting over the lifetime of a group. One of the characteristics of group process is difficulty in predicting what these changes will be. Who knows when Carlotta will decide to experiment with her level of involvement in the group? Who can predict when Kelly will feel ill and stay home for several meetings, creating a whole new pattern of relationships and procedures? However, it is possible to understand and predict some changes.

In this chapter, we will help you identify the changes that can be predicted. In Chapter 15, you will learn how to influence changes in group process both during a single meeting and over the life span of the group. This chapter has two parts. The first covers the changes that occur as a group develops a stable and workable structure. We will introduce you to three predictable changes. These include:

1. The degree to which a group depends on leadership.

2. The degree to which members feel accepted by each other.

3. The ability of the group to complete specific tasks.

The second part of the chapter deals with the changes that occur in group process after a basic structure has been achieved. These changes may be either internal or external:

1. Predictable internal changes may result when (1) shifts occur in the personal lives of members, and (2) repetition results in boredom.

2. External factors predictably change group process when (1) new members are introduced, (2) variety exists among tasks, and (3) shifts occur in the levels of authority to which the group is responsible.

Let's begin by examining the three areas of predictable change that may occur while a group is struggling to find a workable structure.

The Search for Structure and Stability

When a group is newly formed, the first meeting is the beginning of the life of that group. Individuals come together to work on a specific task in a specific time and place. Look at two groups:

Group One: This group was created by the mayor of Centerville to plan and oversee the year-long bicentennial celebration for the town. The group members are citizens who do not know each other. They will meet for the first time in January. They know their group will be eliminated two years after the first meeting.

Group Two: This group was created by the principal of Centerville High School to plan the school's participation in the same celebration. Students, teachers, and parents will serve on the committee. One parent and one teacher have served on another committee together. Two of the students were in a class taught by one of the teachers. Yet, as these people come to the first meeting of *this* group, it is a new beginning with a new task at a new time. They will begin work by discovering a stable and comfortable way of working together.

The members of both of these committees spend time and effort discovering their basic structure. In searching for stability and a structure for their group work, predictable changes will occur in the areas of dependency on leadership, member acceptance, and ability to complete specific tasks.

Groups may begin with a number of individuals in undefined roles and relationships. The group develops a structure with defined member relationships. The group may be given some initial structure. The chairperson or secretary may be appointed. There still remains the process of defining and regulating. This process continues until a stable, workable routine emerges. Let's examine each of the areas of predictable change in turn.

Degree of Dependence on Leadership

Ambiguity, or a lack of clear structure, results in feelings of frustration in the members. Different individuals and groups seek structure in different ways. Some people and some groups expect the leader to provide the structure. If the person who created the group or an appointed leader outlines how the group will function, these people are very satisfied.

Let's look at the first meeting of the Centerville Bicentennial Committee:

The mayor of Centerville started the meeting. She gave each member a booklet. The booklet included a list of the five major activities the mayor wished to suggest for the celebration. A description of five subcommittees was also included. Each subcommittee was to work on one of the suggested activities. The mayor included dates for monthly committee meetings for the next two calendar years. After the mayor explained the five subcommittees, she called the attention of the group members to the lists indicating on which subcommittee each committee member would be asked to serve. As Tom Merrill and Carrie Rush left the meeting, they introduced themselves to each other. Then Tom said, "You've got to hand it to her. The mayor sure knows how to organize a group and get things done quickly." Carrie replied, "If there's anything that I feel frustrated about, it's going to a meeting and wasting time. I know exactly what I am to do and when I'm to be here to do it. I like that."

When the leader provides a structure, most members will be more than willing to live with it. However, the procedures and plans suggested by a leader can also reduce the involvement and participation of group members. Perhaps when Tom and Carrie agreed to be members of the committee, they started to think about the group task. When they went to the first meeting, they may have had some ideas for the celebration. But, when the mayor listed the five major activities for the bicentennial year, Tom and Carrie did not make additional suggestions.

Sometimes members counter or rebel against the suggestions made by a leader. Listen in on the conversation of Bill Riley and Sam Green as they left the same meeting:

"Well, she's done it again!" Sam continues, "You know, Bill, I almost declined to be on this committee, but I thought it would be good publicity for my business. The mayor is a dictator! Why does she even form a committee to 'plan' the bicentennial celebration when she knows darn well she's already made up her mind and only wants people to carry out her orders!" Bill shook his head and replied, "Well, I'm willing to meet once a month. You're right. It's good for business. But I'll tell you one thing. If she expects me to put in any time other than the meetings she's scheduled today, she's got another think coming! If there are any problems in pulling off this celebration, they're the mayor's problems, not mine."

Bill and Sam will reduce their involvement in the committee's work because they do not like to be told what to do and when to do it. Instead of depending on the leader for structure as Tom and Carrie are happy to do, Bill and Sam are *counterdependent*. They want to take on the task and work through it in their own way. They rebel against the tight structure provided by the mayor. Their counterdependence may be observed in a lack of regular attendance, leaving meetings early, or even dropping out (if they become completely frustrated).

During the third meeting of the group, this conversation took place:

MAYOR: Bill, we need to have some material laundered for the July 4th pageant. You've done that for us in the past. We'll need drapes and some costumes cleaned.

BILL: Listen, Mildred. I'm willing to be on this committee. I'm willing to sit here and make it look like we've come up with this celebration. But I'll be darned if I'll do your laundry! Do it yourself. I'd sure hate to be your husband. (With this, Bill walks out of the meeting.)

Bill's reaction to the mayor was strong. He started out disliking the committee and the mayor, but restrained his feelings for the good of his business. Then, as a result of not expressing himself earlier in more appropriate ways, he blew up. The mayor, we might add, responded in kind. She pointed out that Bill had known all along about the structure of the celebration and the committee and should have expected to be asked to launder the materials.

Counterdependence may be seen in attacks on either the leader or the structure the leader has strongly recommended for the group. In some cases, there might be sabotage, as the counterdependent person works outside the group to create trouble for the group or to avoid supporting it. The degree to which the leader provides structure and the degree to which members are willing to depend on the leader for structure creates change in group process as the balance is worked out between leader and members.

Attitudes among Group Members

As groups progress from one meeting to another, the feelings of group members change toward one another. Some people feel left out. (After Bill walked out of the meeting of the bicentennial committee, the mayor adjourned the meeting and Sam caught up with Bill in the parking lot. Bill said to Sam, "You know, just because I own a laundry does not mean I should be used. I've got some good ideas for this celebration. She only thinks I'm good enough to wash clothes.") Bill did not feel involved at the level he wished to be. He felt left out.

Sometimes the group task does not interest a member. Some people who become disinterested continue attending meetings while others do not. Others even drop out. (Bill finally did resign from the committee even though he thought it would be good for his business to be involved.) Sam shared Bill's feelings but continued to attend meetings. He knew it would help his business to be seen as a member of the committee. After all, he was a new businessman in the community. However, since he was associated with Bill by other committee members, especially by the mayor, he was very cautious about what he said in meetings.

At the opposite extreme, some members feel fully accepted by the group and become heavily involved. After the sixth meeting of the bicentennial committee, Carrie talked with Tom: "Imagine," said Carrie, "the mayor asked me to take Bill's place on the subcommittee in charge of the 4th of July celebration! Now I'm on two subcommittees! I feel really important. And Sam invited me to have lunch so he could fill me in on what the subcommittee is doing. I am so pleased to be a part of all this!"

Feelings can vary greatly from one meeting to another. This is true for a single individual. When Sam told Carrie she would be in charge of laundering drapes and costumes her feelings soared. Her initial feelings of high enthusiasm later changed to feelings of concern about whether she would have time to take on the extra work in the evenings. The group mood may shift also. Before the mayor told Bill he would be in charge of laundry details, the group seemed full of energy, excited about the events for the 4th of July celebration. Then when Bill left, the silence that remained masked feelings of embarrassment, confusion, and concern. When changes in feeling are related directly to members' feelings of acceptance, these changes affect the work level, the interest level, and the relationships among members and between them and the leader.

Group Effectiveness

Some people believe groups ought to be able to do everything; committees can solve any problem. The opposite view is that committees are a waste of time and should be distrusted. From one meeting to another, group members' ideas about this very issue vary. If we look once again at the bicentennial committee, we will discover that as excited as Carrie was about being on two subcommittees, she was the person who began the seventh meeting of the committee with this comment:

> "I have given our work a lot of thought since last month's meeting. It seems as though we come here once a month and do little more than report to each other what is happening in our subcommittee. I am on two subcommittees now. That takes more time than I am willing to devote to this work. I think we should have a meeting of this committee less often—every other month. Then we could devote more time to the subcommittee where the *real* work gets done. If the mayor wants to know what's going on, she can attend subcommittee meetings."
>
> Tom responded favorably. He went further. "You know, I have about decided that the subcommittee I'm on, the one to determine who to honor at the Veteran's Day celebration, does not really need to exist. The mayor has given us the instructions for the celebration. It's just a matter of following through. Certainly, someone in your office, Mildred, could follow through on your instructions. In fact, four of the six members on our subcommittee have quit. I think it's because a committee was not necessary to do the work as it's outlined. I'd like to take Bill's place on the other subcommittee. That will take some of the extra work and pressure off of Carrie." And so it was: The Veteran's Day celebration subcommittee was eliminated and a secretary in the mayor's office completed its work. The main committee met only every other month. Occasionally, the mayor would drop in on subcommittee meetings on alternate months to stay abreast of their work.

There is a very strong possibility that, over a period of several months, the issues of dependence on leadership, feelings of acceptance among members, and the ability of the group to complete a task will affect the way the group functions. Perceptive members and leaders will be able to observe these issues and comment on them in order to help the group discuss them and move through them in productive ways.

Any member who effectively helps a group move through these issues may be seen as exerting leadership. Both Carrie and Tom showed leadership in their suggestions to change the procedures for group meetings and committee work. Most groups have appointed leaders. The mayor chaired the bicentennial committee. However, sometimes appointed leaders may emerge from the group membership. Tom replaced Bill as subcommittee chairperson. He was appointed by the mayor as a result of his request to assume the work Bill had been doing before he resigned.

The mayor eventually called a meeting of the committee and asked, "What are your feelings about this committee and its work?" The members who felt she had dictated the form and details of the celebration spoke up. They were surprised to find, however, that others on the committee liked that approach. Meanwhile, the people who wanted structure and direction were equally surprised to find that some people were upset. Individual differences were aired and everyone was able to get along better afterward.

Someone will emerge, just as Tom did, as the spokesperson for a group or as the most influential member. Even if the formal leader has been named, there will still be informal leadership emergence. It will affect group process. Ernest Bormann studied leadership emergence in newly formed groups. His analysis indicated that leaders tend to emerge by a method of *residues:* People are slowly eliminated from consideration as potential leaders until there is only one person left.

According to Bormann, several people are eliminated in the first stage because they lack the necessary knowledge or skill. They may also be eliminated because they do not talk very much. In a group of five people, two may be eliminated in the first half of the meeting because one simply does not seem to know what he is talking about and the other is very quiet. That leaves three people in contention for the leadership role.

Bormann describes two ways in which leaders may emerge after the first round of eliminations:

1. In the first method, there are two people who are seen as the logical leaders. The third individual left in contention then becomes a "swing person." This person is able to support one or the other of the main contenders. If this third person consistently supports one of the two contenders, the result is a leader plus a "lieutenant." (The leader is the contender being supported and the lieutenant is the person giving the support.) The other main contender then has secondary status. The leadership emergence process is over.

2. The second method is more complex and time-consuming. Essentially, each of the two main contenders acquires a lieutenant. Then there is a two-against-two split. In a five-person group, the one remaining person becomes the "swing person." This tied struggle could go on for a long time.

The dynamics of leadership emergence is occurring at the same time that the degree of dependence on leadership, the degree of membership acceptance, and the question of whether or not the group can complete its task are all being resolved. When these essential issues are decided, a workable structure for the group has been determined.

Continuing Changes in Groups

Once a stable structure evolves, the group process does not become static. There are various factors that tend to disrupt and destabilize the functioning of a group. Some of these are internal factors. Other destabilizing factors are external to the group.

Internal Factors

Internal destabilizing factors include changes that occur even if there are no shifts in membership and no changes in external situational factors that might affect the group. Internal factors primarily include (1) changes in the personal lives of members, and (2) the boredom that results when group work becomes repetitious.

Changes in the Personal Lives of Group Members. Personal life changes vary: moving to a new home, having a child, having a child leave to attend school or get married, getting married or divorced, earning a degree in a related field, and so on. People do not leave their personal lives at home. Even when personal changes occur that are not work related, they affect work.

Sometimes personal issues are work related. For example, Bobby enrolled in a business administration program and completed a master's degree. As a result, he became a more informed and analytical contributor to the discussions when the sales staff of Allen Electric met each week.

The changes resulting from Bobby's increased competence and involvement did not stop with him. For example, as Bobby increased his involvement, Marilu was used less frequently as a resource person. Marilu felt resentful. She began to withdraw from the group. Prior to the change in Bobby's behavior as a group member, Marilu and Bobby had formed a coalition. They seemed to think alike. They supported each other on all issues that came before the sales staff. Now Marilu decided to undercut Bobby and formed a coalition with two salespersons who tended to take positions opposed to Bobby on nearly all issues. Change in personal lives results in continuing change in the group process throughout the life of the group.

Changes Caused by the Boredom of Repetition. Human beings are capable of creating change for the sole purpose of avoiding sameness. Carlotta, who talked a great deal in the first ten minutes of a group, decided to experiment with remaining silent. As a result of Carlotta's change in behavior, Maria and Kamali talked more frequently. This shifted the entire pattern of interaction in the group. Carlotta was bored with her role and wanted to try something different. Boredom occurs with the task as well as with the roles a member has. A group that works seriously and consistently for five weeks may experience a change in mood and work level in the sixth meeting because one or more group members are bored with the task. Alternatively, they may be bored with the serious style the group seems to use. If the group lightens up for a meeting, it may not finish the expected amount of work for that day. However, at the next meeting, the members return with renewed interest and energy and accomplish more work than expected. When one member becomes bored and changes his or her behavior, that change has an affect on the other members and the entire group process.

External Factors

Destabilizing external factors may include (1) the introduction of new members into the group, (2) variation in the type of tasks assigned to a group, and (3) shifts that occur in the levels of authority to which the group is responsible.

Introduction of New Members into the Group. Nearly all groups experience turnover. Members resign or their terms of office expire. Other members are hired or elected. The new members must be integrated into the group structure. They need to discover where they fit in terms of power and influence as well as in terms of friendships and coalitions. When new members are added, old coalitions disappear. The entire power structure of the group may have to be realigned when one very influential member is transferred to another department. Groups are constantly in the process of seeking structure for this reason. Group process is not a single track to a state of stability, but an ongoing attempt to deal with changes in membership.

Variation in the Tasks Assigned to a Group. Group tasks change over time. After they developed a very useful way of dealing with work assignments in the plumbing department at Jason Hardware, some of the employees joined the union. Management and employees both had to adjust to differences between union and nonunion personnel. The group process in the plumbing department changed.

At Designs Unlimited, the drafting department was given the task of implementing a quality-improvement program. This project did not require much creativity but did require patience and an understanding of employee motivation. The drafting department had prided itself on the creative solutions it produced, even when given very difficult technical problems to solve. The change in the type of task was overwhelming to the members of the department.

Notice what happens when a creative group has to shift gears. Karl, Cassandra, and Toby had been the most effective group members. They provided literally hundreds of good ideas for products and services. Then they were faced with the problem of quality improvement. At first they presented some useful ideas. However, creativity is not the most important resource for obtaining higher quality. Suddenly, Jack emerged from the background. He understood the problem of motivating line employees to see the need for reducing errors. He understood the problems and attitudes of the workers. Almost singlehandedly he replaced Karl, Cassandra, and Toby as the richest resource in the group. Changes in tasks affect the group process by changing the ways people work together.

Shifts Occur in Higher Levels of Authority. Often when changes occur in the levels of management to which a group is accountable, compensatory changes occur in the structure of the group. When new management takes over, there are stricter guidelines or guidelines are relaxed. Procedures rarely remain the same. Sometimes management personnel remain, but their directives change. If an organization is faced with very little competition, then suddenly finds itself confronted with a shift in its market, it is natural that guidelines will change throughout the organization. Certainly, United States automobile companies have experienced the effects of this type of change. The appearance of any change in laws, regulations, competition, or production levels will have an impact on the committees, work groups, task forces, and teams within an organization.

Groups are changing constantly. Change occurs as basic structure is achieved, continues as that structure is affected by shifts among members, variations in the task, and alterations in the situation within which the group works. Group process *is* change.

SUMMARY

Some groups exist for a matter of hours while others exist for years. In both cases, changes occur in group process both during a single meeting and over the life span of the group. This chapter examined changes that occur over the long-term existence of a group.

Long-term changes fall into two categories: (1) those changes that occur during the time that a new group is working out a stable and functional basic structure, and (2) changes that occur once the basic structure is achieved. One characteristic of group process is that change can occur quickly and unexpectedly. In spite of this feature, some changes are more predictable than others.

Three areas of predictable change exist in the initial stages of group process when members are determining the basic structure for their group. These include (1) the degree to which a group depends on leadership, (2) the degree to which members feel accepted by each other, and (3) the ability of the group to complete specific tasks. Changes in these three areas are observable in the talk and behavior of members.

Changes that occur in group process after a basic structure has been achieved are either internal or external. These changes occur because various factors disrupt (or destabilize) the structure of the group. The most common and predictable internal factors include (1) shifts that occur in the personal lives of members, and (2) changes in the way members work together as a result of boredom with the work itself. External factors that predictably change group process include (1) the introduction of new members into the group, (2) the introduction of variety among the tasks, and (3) the shifts that occur in the levels of authority to which the group is responsible.

Any member who helps the group move through the changes in group process may be seen as providing leadership. Ernest Bormann described leadership emergence in newly formed groups by a method of residues.

Members are eliminated from consideration as potential formal or informal leaders until there is only one person remaining to do the job.

The ability of a group member or leader to predict and to observe changes in group process is a skill that is basic to knowing how and when to influence the group process.

REFLECTING/EXPLORING

1. Observe the first meeting of a newly formed small group in your organization or community. The group should have five to seven members. Does the appointed leader outline the task or leave it up to group members to structure? Notice how members react to the way the task is presented. What observations can you make about the degree of dependence on the leader for structure?

2. In the group you used for activity 1, observe the informal leadership emergence process. How would you describe the emergence process as it occurs in this group? Was it a process of emergence by residues?

3. Review your involvement as a member of a small group over at least three separate meetings. Describe the degree to which you felt accepted by other members. How did this level change in each separate meeting? How did it vary over the three meetings? What do you see as the effect on group process?

4. Review the last three tasks that one of your groups completed. You might use the group you reviewed in activity 3. Was your group the best place for these tasks? Might another person or group within your organization or community have been able to do this work more efficiently or effectively? Explain.

5. Select a group of which you are a member. Analyze the internal and external factors that affected the group process after the basic structure evolved. Do this by selecting two internal and two external factors that you believe significantly changed the way the members of your group work together. Describe these changes in terms of their effect on (1) group process, (2) task completion, and (3) your degree of involvement with the task and other group members.

15

INFLUENCING GROUP PROCESS

The Pinedale Church was governed by a board of seven persons in addition to the minister. The board consisted of the elected leader of the congregation, a treasurer, a secretary, and the chairpersons of the committees on finance, membership, mission, and buildings. To understand process in this group, some information about the members is needed.

The Elected Leader. A woman in her forties, fairly quiet, very well respected, and a life-long member of the church.

The Treasurer. A young man whose occupation is accounting, precise and careful, fairly conservative in financial and social matters.

The Secretary. An outgoing woman in her mid-thirties, a housewife who enjoys the church as a change from her daily chores, somewhat erratic in her performance as secretary (sometimes minutes are produced, sometimes not).

The Chairperson, Finance Committee. An older man who has been a member of the congregation for forty years, a middle-of-the-road person who always wants to do what is best for everyone, quite logical and practical.

The Chairperson, Membership Committee. A young career woman in her early thirties, married to the treasurer, no children, very much concerned about the church's responsibility to young adults, single adults, young marrieds, and dual-career families, and quite outspoken.

The Chairperson, Mission Committee. An engineer in his early forties with a strong social conscience, wants to see the church do more for the poor and powerless in the community, lacking conversational skills, sometimes antagonizes people with his views.

The Chairperson, Buildings and Grounds Committee. A very conservative woman in her early sixties, married to a former leader of the congregation, very concerned that the church maintain its image in the neighborhood and local community, a direct, blunt person who defines her role as an advocate for the members of the buildings and grounds committee.

The Minister. In his early forties, this is his third church; has become very sensitive to the feelings of the congregation and its various interest groups as a result of being ousted from his last church; has been with this church for only eight months.

Now that you have met the members of the board, we will describe what happened over the course of two of their monthly meetings.

The first meeting occurred in October and every board member attended. The minister opened with a brief prayer and a few words on comments and concerns from the members of the congregation. The leader of the church then asked for reports from each of the board members. This took up the next twenty minutes or so. There was little comment. The reports varied with the people. The secretary and membership chairpersons gave fairly lengthy statements. The chairperson of the finance committee gave his report in less than two minutes.

The next agenda item was to be a discussion of an upcoming membership drive. The chairperson of the membership committee presented the plan developed by her committee. The plan's primary emphasis was on approaching people in apartment buildings as well as those in traditional one-family homes in the neighborhood. After hearing the membership proposal, the chairperson of the buildings and grounds committee objected to the emphasis on apartment dwellers. Her point was that they moved often and showed little or no interest in community and religious activities. A polite but obviously hostile encounter took place.

There was a series of irrelevant statements by the secretary. The chairperson of the finance committee made some attempts to compromise and appease the warring members.

Then a complication occurred. The chairperson of the mission committee started to defend the membership drive goals. But in the process he inserted his favorite project—serving the poor and powerless. This caused the chairperson of the building and grounds committee to respond with anger. The treasurer also entered the fray. Now the argument was over mission as well as membership and the two issues were tangled together. The minister remained quiet during this part of the meeting.

The elected leader of the church sought to stop the argument by announcing that the decision on the membership drive would be postponed by one month. This meant that the drive itself would be postponed from February to March.

This confrontation took almost an hour. The minister then introduced a request from a neighboring church for an interdenominational worship service on a Sunday in March or April. The idea received general support although the chairpersons of the mission committee and the membership committee were noticeably quiet. The interdenominational service was approved by a unanimous vote with every board member voting.

The leader suggested that the meeting end. A motion to adjourn was made and approved. The treasurer and the chairperson of the membership committee (husband and wife) left together with the chairperson of the finance committee and the secretary. The chairperson of the mission committee left alone. The chairperson of the buildings and grounds committee also left alone, although she looked for someone to walk with out to the parking lot.

The elected leader and the minister stayed after the meeting. They went to the minister's office and discussed the conflict in the board meeting for about thirty minutes. They came to no conclusion about how to manage the situation. They left together. Later in the week, they met again over lunch and tried to develop a way of dealing with the membership-drive issue at the next meeting.

Meanwhile, the chairperson of the membership committee and her husband, the treasurer, discussed the issue at home. He was not totally supportive but understood her concerns. He agreed that the membership committee had developed the plan as a group. During that same week, the chairperson of the buildings and grounds committee called the elected leader, the minister, and the chairperson of the finance committee on the telephone. She lobbied against the plan presented by the membership committee. She suggested that the plan be sent back to the committee for revision, with instructions that a plan similar to those of past years be presented at the next meeting.

The stage was set for the November meeting.

The meeting began in a similar way—brief prayer and comments from the minister and reports from the board members. However, the chairperson of the mission committee was not present. His place was taken by a member of his committee. The treasurer had to leave early in order to get back to his place of work to finish a report. The chairperson of the membership committee introduced the same plan that was presented in the previous meeting. There was little comment. The chairperson of the buildings and grounds committee voiced her disagreement but indicated that she would not stand in the way of the plan. During the meeting, the secretary talked on, sometimes bringing totally irrelevant topics and stories into the discussion. Obviously there was some irritation on the part of the other people in the meeting as a result of her intrusive and wandering conversation. Finally, the elected leader called for a vote. The secretary and the chairpersons of the finance and membership committees, as well as the elected leader and the minister, voted for the plan. The chairperson of the buildings and grounds committee voted against it. The plan was approved by a vote of five to one, with two members absent.

The description of these two meetings of the board at the Pinedale Church illustrates change in group process. The five factors involved in these meetings include:

1. A standing disagreement between the chairpersons of the buildings and grounds committee and the mission committee. This became evident in the first meeting.

2. The complication of the membership-drive plan. This happened when the chairperson of the mission committee introduced the mission issue into the discussion.

3. The secretary's random and inconsequential talk in both meetings.

4. The lack of involvement of the minister and the elected leader in the arguments.

5. The conversations between the two meetings. Apparently, the chairperson of the buildings and grounds committee found little support for her objections to the plan.

The net result of the group process was that the plan was accepted with ease at the second meeting.

The focus of this chapter is the question of how group processes such as these can be influenced. There is no question that group process can be influenced. Sometimes it is harder to do than at other times. We will examine methods of influencing group process at different times. These include:

1. *Influencing group process during a meeting.* This involves (a) diagnosing the process, (b) attempting to influence it indirectly, and (c) attempting to influence it directly.

2. *Influencing the process between meetings.* This type of influence occurs through (a) talking about the last meeting with members, (b) meeting as subgroups between meetings, and (c) developing proposals or suggestions between meetings.

3. *Influencing the process over a long time.* Two effective ways of having long-term influence on the process include (a) using postmeeting reaction sheets and (b) training group members.

The remainder of this chapter will be devoted to these topics.

Influencing Group Process during a Meeting

Perhaps the most difficult time to attempt to influence the group process is during a meeting. When a group has deadlines to meet, but members seem to be in a very relaxed mood and little work is being accomplished, it may seem impossible to shift to high task accomplishment. Yet the effective group member or leader must try to help the group make such a shift. This means that the group process must first be "diagnosed."

Diagnosing the Process

If you ask for an appointment with a doctor, he or she will ask a series of questions. The purpose of these questions is to help diagnose what is happening inside of you. The group member or leader who wishes to influence group process at the time it is occurring must also begin with a diagnosis. Is conflict occurring? If so, is the conflict over differences of opinion about how the group should work together, about the task itself, or is it basically a clash among personalities?

There are two views from which group process can be diagnosed while it is occurring. The first one is the *personal perspective:* Mary wants the group to work faster and more intently on the task. The group is not working in these ways. Mary concludes that the group is avoiding the task because it is Friday afternoon.

The second view provides a wider perspective because it takes into consideration the *viewpoints of other people* and of the group as a whole: Mary observes that group members are talking about their plans for the weekend. They are not getting down to business. Mary recalls that the group has just finished a very difficult and time-consuming task. She wonders if the group may need time to adjust or change its focus from the completed task to this new work. As she observes the group, it seems to Mary that members who were opposed to each other's views in the previous meeting are eagerly talking to each other about weekend plans. Mary concludes that the informal talk, even though it seems irrelevant to the task at hand, may help the group concentrate on the task at hand and finish it efficiently once the group shifts to the present work.

There are several possible interpretations of the meeting of the board at the Pinedale Church. The conflict could have resulted from the ongoing differences between the chairpersons of the buildings and grounds committee and the mission committee. It also might have been an indirect result of the passive leadership shown by the elected leader and the minister. Each of these people probably would have a different interpretation of the process as it was occurring and even long after the meetings finished.

It is not useful to set an ironclad rule about whether to act on a personal view or on a broader perspective. If a group member strongly believes in a position or has strong convictions that a specific suggestion will work effectively, he or she probably should argue for that position or suggestion. On the other hand, if the way the group members work together seems highly important, then diagnosing the process from the perspective of other people and the group as a whole may be necessary. Group members and leaders should bear these two possible ways of viewing a situation in mind and use them as general guidelines. They can then make decisions about how and when to influence group process that will show sensitivity to individuals as well as to the group as a whole.

Once a diagnosis is reached, the next step is to make an attempt to change what is occurring in the group meeting. This can be done indirectly or directly.

Indirect Attempts to Influence Group Process

Indirect attempts to influence group process usually involve talking and acting in ways that suggest a change should occur. But the suggestion is never directly put into words. Common indirect methods include (1) hinting, (2) sarcasm, and (3) withdrawal. We will describe each of these methods and observe members of the board of the Pinedale Church as they use them.

Hinting. The church leadership meeting is in progress. Some clear differences of opinion have been stated politely. However, tense facial expressions, low voices, and periods of silence followed by people talking over each other suggest that the members of the board have deep feelings. The secretary says, "wouldn't it be a nice place to live if everyone could just get along in this world?" This clearly is a *hint* that the people in the meeting should try to get along with each other. However, the message is not directly stated to the particular people involved. Instead, the secretary makes a general statement to the whole group. The issue does not appear to be the process of *this* meeting and the differences that exist among *these* people. The issue seems to be people getting along in this world. Sometimes a hint may be responded to in direct ways. The minister could have responded, "Are you saying that you want the members of this board to express their differences in ways that show personal respect for each other?" The minister did not respond this way. He responded with silence. It is very easy to ignore a hint.

Sarcasm. Sarcasm is another indirect method. It is a substitute for honestly expressing anger or frustration. In the middle of the conflict in the first meeting of the board, the treasurer said, "If this argument gets any more heated, the plastic is going to melt on our notebooks!" A more direct way of stating his observation might be: "I am feeling frustrated with the continual bickering and fighting." The sarcastic comment is a substitute for such directness. The use of sarcasm helps a person voice an opinion in an indirect way. Just as with hinting, a sarcastic statement can be ignored easily even when the indirect message is understood quite clearly.

Withdrawal. Some group members use withdrawal to voice their opinions indirectly. Teenagers frequently use this technique by going to their rooms, shutting their doors, and "letting silence speak" for them. The group member who withdraws may begin to read, doodle on a note pad, or look out a window. The person who withdraws does not react to the events as they occur in the group. This lack of response (withdrawal) is intended as a message. Some group members may pick up on the message and say, "We've not heard from Mary on this issue. Mary, I'd like to know your opinion." The withdrawal message is not picked up directly, it is interpreted privately by those who notice it. Often it is not interpreted in the way the sender intended it to be. How can anyone know what someone else's silence means? Boredom? Sickness? Anger? No opinion? Unless another member chooses to confront indirect methods used, the message will not be understood. It probably will not affect the group process in a helpful way.

This is true of all the indirect methods. When a member responds indirectly, another member must observe that response and confront the hint, sarcasm, or withdrawal in order to bring the message into the discussion. People who present their statements in indirect ways risk losing their influence. If other members do not choose to pick up on the message, the effect is as though the indirect statement had never been introduced.

The alternative is to initiate ideas and opinions directly. These methods are riskier because they may be rejected. However, direct methods are more effective because they will be heard. They become part of the discussion.

Direct Attempts to Influence Group Process

Direct attempts require members to work openly within the group process. Instead of using hints, sarcasm, or withdrawal, group members and leaders try to describe what is happening from their own points of view. The secretary asked, "Wouldn't it be a nice place to live if everyone could just get along in this world?" Instead, she could have said, "I don't like conflict. Right now I really feel uncomfortable with the way we are talking. Let's discuss what we can do about it. I have a suggestion." A direct attempt to influence the group process usually results in confrontation of the issues by the group. Of course, members may ignore the direct attempt or engage in conflict. However, other people will at least respond to such a direct approach. They will often consider the issue. Most of the time, directness results in more directness.

It is important for group members to confront both negative and positive issues directly. The board meeting at Pinedale Church included negative examples. Conflict and anger caused the difficulties. Groups need to discuss positive situations as well. Too seldom do group members share with each other statements like, "I really like working in this group. We get work done. We really seem to like each other. I feel useful and excited when I am working with all of you!" The overall result of sharing positive comments is mutual appreciation among members.

Whether negative or positive, attempts to influence the group process in direct ways mean talking about what is happening at the present moment. Statements are made about the here and now: *this* place and *this* time. It is important for group members to talk about events as they occur. When weeks or months pass, thoughts and feelings about a situation have also passed and been forgotten or distorted. It can be very dangerous to delay talk about problems. Emotions fester. Complications develop. Talk about the issue immediately. If it cannot be resolved, at least people are able to discuss it and express their feelings openly at the time those feelings are being experienced. They will have the benefit of hearing similar opinions and feelings from others. The result usually is less frustration and inner turmoil.

Here is a useful rule of thumb: If I have strong feelings about this process, probably other people have them, too. In other words, if I feel upset and frustrated at lack of progress in a group meeting, the odds are that other group members feel the same. If I state my feelings, others will be relieved to know they are not alone. Then the problem, why we are not working as efficiently as we would like to be, can be discussed directly.

If direct attempts to influence group process are not used, people often discuss their feelings and opinions after the meeting. Sometimes they do this with other group members. Sometimes they talk to outsiders.

Influencing Group Process between Meetings

When groups interact directly and effectively during meetings, there is little need to think about the group process that may occur between meetings. Few tasks or emotional issues are left unresolved after an effective meeting. However, there are many times when meetings are not effective and a large amount of group process occurs between meetings. This happens primarily in situations that are very "political," in both the positive and negative sense. Wherever factions and interest groups are at work, conversations occur between meetings. These are discussions on how to manage the next meeting. Plans for maneuvering and negotiating are designed between meetings. Discussion is centered on (1) interpreting the previous meeting, (2) meeting as subgroups, and (3) developing plans to be presented at the next meeting.

Talk about the Last Meeting

Often, when people leave a meeting, they do not clearly understand what occurred. Talk between meetings helps to clarify understandings about the group meeting. Members do this as a matter of course. Recall the conversations that took place between the board members of Pinedale Church: The chairperson of the membership committee and the treasurer (wife and husband) talked at home. The chairperson of the buildings and grounds committee phoned three board members in an attempt to lobby against the membership-drive plan. The elected leader and the minister met twice. The talk that occurs between meetings usually has an impact on the next meeting. In fact, most people talk between meetings because they *expect* that talk to have an influence in the next meeting. The following discussion between the chairperson of the membership committee and the treasurer occurred at their dinner table:

MEMBERSHIP CHAIRPERSON: Why do you suppose Mildred (chairperson of the buildings and grounds committee) always opposes these plans?

TREASURER: Well, she sees it as a threat. I mean we do have a big mortgage on the sanctuary. We need to have people join the church who will pledge and pay the pledges.

MEMBERSHIP CHAIRPERSON: Oh, I know. We don't want to drive those people away. We want to get more people committed. We want to involve some of the younger people, too.

TREASURER: Mildred thinks she represents a really strong group in the church.

MEMBERSHIP CHAIRPERSON: I know. I know. But she always seems to treat me the way my mother did when I wanted to try something new. "You'll get in trouble." I don't like that. I am competent. And so is my committee.

Notice that the chairperson of the membership committee sees the meeting in terms of a mother–daughter struggle. This view probably would be a total surprise to Mildred, the chairperson of the buildings and grounds committee. Some of the discussion between husband and wife simply restates the obvious: Mildred is conservative. Mildred represents a conservative group in the church.

This conversation will probably have two effects on the chairperson of the membership committee: First, it will reinforce some existing attitudes about Mildred. Second, it will result in her deciding to take a position and go ahead with the membership drive plan, no matter what. In this way, processes that occur between meetings can affect the group process at the next meeting.

Simply talking about a meeting with one or two other persons can help create understanding about what happened in the last meeting. It can also provide action plans for future meetings. Some people go a step further. They call together a significant subgroup to talk about past events and to plan for the future.

Subgrouping between Meetings

When members meet in subgroups between meetings, the effects may be negative or positive. Consider possible negative outcomes first. If a group of seven like the board of Pinedale Church meet once a month, but word gets out that four of them meet for lunch two or three times between meetings, distrust may develop among the three people left out. This distrust may lead to strain at the group's meetings. In this group, subgrouping will appear as an obvious attempt to affect votes. It may be looked upon as devious.

One positive advantage of meeting in subgroups between meetings is the possibility of working out a plan that can be submitted to the whole group. This usually happens in one of two ways, openly or secretly. In the open method, the subgroup may have been requested to meet and draft a plan to present at the next meeting. Or the group announces that it will be meeting. When the whole group meets, they can begin with the recommendations of the subgroup. This is a useful and practical way to affect group process between meetings.

In the secret method, the subgroup meets without informing other group members about the meeting. Highly political situations sometimes result in secret subgrouping between meetings. The purpose of the meeting may be to get enough votes to pass a motion. It may be held to gather notes to defeat a suggestion with which subgroup members do not agree. In this situation, the subgroup may devise strategies for voting or for using the rules to prevent a vote.

The choice between open and secret meetings depends on the openness and directness of the group process in regularly scheduled meetings.

Whether subgroup meetings are held openly or in secret, they result in the development of a plan or proposal.

Developing a Proposal between Meetings

In addition to conversations about the past meeting and meeting as a subgroup, there is a third way to affect group process between meetings. Sometimes there is a heated discussion in a group meeting. It is very difficult to respond creatively or to move beyond immediate, definite positions and issues. Away from the meeting, members may think more clearly and flexibly.

If group members are tangled in a complex problem or a conflict, the period between meetings is a very practical time to develop options. In the case of the board of the Pinedale Church, the minister and elected leader could have talked about the membership plans, and gone to the chairperson of the membership committee. It might have been possible to make a few minor changes in the emphasis of the membership drive. Apartment dwellers could have been approached at the same time as current members who pledge and follow through. Perhaps current members could have been visited early. In fact, some of the current members might have been potential members of visitation teams. Such a proposal would have reduced the opposition of the chairperson of the buildings and grounds committee.

Effective problem solving and decision making include the development of several options that can be explored as part of the process of choosing a solution. Presumably the membership committee had already done this. After the meeting was the time to go back and modify the plan enough to make it acceptable, or at least less objectionable, to a key member. In fact, taking the time to modify the plan might have resulted in bringing the two chairpersons into an effective working relationship. That would have improved their personal relationships as well as helping to make the membership drive a huge success. This kind of effort often requires making effective use of the time between meetings.

Group process is not only influenced during and between meetings. Changes occur and can be influenced over long periods of time in those groups that meet for months or years.

Influencing Group Process over a Long Period

As time passes, a group's processes are influenced by the ways people act and react, by their personalities, by the tasks, habitual patterns, and historical events that occur within the life span of the group. Group processes can be influenced over the long term in at least two ways: (1) by using postmeeting reaction sheets, and (2) by training members. We will examine each of these.

Postmeeting Reaction Sheets

One of the simplest, easiest, and least-used methods for influencing group process is to ask members to assess that process at the end of each meeting. The recommended procedure for using reaction sheets has four steps:

1. Hand out the reaction sheets at the end of a meeting. Collect them before members leave. Usually sheets are not signed.

2. Someone compiles the results and prepares a summary. This usually is the leader.

3. Before the next meeting, or at its beginning, the results are circulated.

4. A brief discussion of member reactions to the summary occurs at the beginning of the meeting. This indicates whether procedures should be revised or altered.

There are several reasons for following this four-step procedure. Forms are completed anonymously to encourage each member to fill out the reaction sheet honestly. It is important that each person get a copy of the results. The group process belongs to the members as well as to the leader. Members have both the right and the responsibility to understand and to solve group problems. Discussion of the reaction-sheet summary at the beginning of the following meeting encourages the members to voice their opinions. The discussion openly and directly invites each member to take part in influencing the group process *during* the meeting.

Usually a postmeeting reaction sheet consists of five to ten statements that can be rated quickly on a scale. A space for open-ended comments follows the specific statements. The following reaction sheet is typical of those used to assess interpersonal relationships and group functioning. These questions concentrate on the basic issues in interpersonal relationships discussed in Chapter 11: dominance, friendliness, and openness. In some of the questions, members describe their own reactions ("I talked"), while in others, members describe other members ("Other people listened") or the group as a whole.

POSTMEETING REACTION SHEET

Directions Read each item carefully. Respond honestly. The space at the end of the form is provided for your comments, concerns, and suggestions. Do not sign your name to the sheet.

You will receive a summary of results either before or at the next meeting. The summary will be discussed at the beginning of the next meeting. Your observations will be welcomed.

1. I talked . . .

    ___ far too much   ___ a little too little

    ___ quite a bit too much   ___ quite a bit too little

    ___ a little too much   ___ far too little

2. The group discussions were . . .

    ___ dominated by one person   ___ fairly equal

    ___ dominated by two or   ___ totally equal
         three people

    ___ dominated by a group
         of people

3. I listened and understood what others were saying . . .

    ___ very well   ___ fairly poorly

    ___ quite well   ___ quite poorly

    ___ fairly well   ___ very poorly

4. Other people in the group listened and understood each other . . .

    ___ very well   ___ fairly poorly

    ___ quite well   ___ quite poorly

    ___ fairly well   ___ very poorly

5. As a group, we were . . .

    ___ extremely open and honest   ___ somewhat controlled
                    and careful

    ___ quite open and honest   ___ quite controlled and careful

    ___ somewhat open and honest   ___ extremely controlled
                    and careful

6. We were . . .

    ___ extremely friendly and   ___ somewhat unfriendly
         courteous   and discourteous

    ___ quite friendly and   ___ quite unfriendly
         courteous   and discourteous

    ___ somewhat friendly and   ___ extremely unfriendly
         courteous   and discourteous

7. We were . . .

___ extremely supportive and positive

___ quite supportive and positive

___ somewhat supportive and positive

___ somewhat critical and negative

___ quite critical and negative

___ extremely critical and negative

8. There exists in this group a . . .

___ very high level of trust

___ quite high level of trust

___ fairly high level of trust

___ fairly low level of trust

___ quite low level of trust

___ very low level of trust

In the future, I think it would be helpful if we would:

If such a postmeeting reaction sheet is used, a group will quickly identify potential and existing problems. Suppose that in a group of ten, four people said that they thought the group members were "somewhat controlled and careful," and six said they were "somewhat honest and open." The group could then discuss possible reasons for the lack of ratings in the range from *quite* to *extremely* open and honest. They could then discuss the ways in which openness and honesty could help group functioning. The group members might also want to look at supportiveness and trust ratings. Are people controlled and careful because they see the group as critical and negative? Because they have feelings of distrust? If the answers are yes, changes in group process are indicated.

Postmeeting reaction sheets may be devoted to task-related issues. The reaction sheet on pages 197 and 198 is an example of a task-related reaction sheet.

The questions are related to the goals for the meeting, the procedures and methods, the kind of task, the pace and length of the meeting, the availability of resources, and overall efficiency and effectiveness. All of these factors either influence how well a group can function or reflect on the individual's assessment of the group's level of functioning. By making the results known to group members, difficulties can be discussed, analyzed, and managed in the future.

These two postmeeting reaction sheets contain suggested items. A group leader can select any of these items and add others. A reaction sheet should be specific to each group. The use of such sheets is usually beneficial. Problems can be identified. Members who attend meetings become aware that their views and feelings are being heard and used. The net result is more effective group functioning. However, sometimes group members cannot cope with the problems that surface. They do not know how to overcome difficulties with procedures, how to manage conflict, or how to listen or participate effectively. The answer is training.

Training Group Members

A group is only as effective as its members. Some organizations and communities spend a lot of time, money, and effort on training leaders, but place little emphasis on training members. Probably the most effective way to influence group process is to provide members with the knowledge, skills, insights, and values needed to work in a team setting.

There are two kinds of training available. One involves sending members to training sessions. The other involves organizational development. Sometimes a combination of both is useful.

If members are sent outside the organization to training sessions, they can attend the type of session that meets their needs most appropriately. Various organizations, associations, universities, and community-education programs offer workshops in listening, assertiveness, problem-solving, and other skills necessary for working effectively in groups.

Organizational development is the process of providing a training program or process for the entire group. Usually, a trainer comes to the groups.

POSTMEETING REACTION SHEET

Directions Reach each item carefully. Respond honestly. The space at the end of the form is provided for your comments, concerns, and suggestions. Do not sign your name to the sheet.

You will receive a summary of results either before or at the next meeting. The summary will be discussed at the beginning of the next meeting. Your observations will be welcomed.

1. Our goals during this meeting were . . .

   ___ very well defined   ___ fairly poorly defined

   ___ quite well defined   ___ quite poorly defined

   ___ fairly well defined   ___ very poorly defined

2. Our procedures and methods for this meeting were . . .

   ___ far too structured   ___ somewhat too unstructured

   ___ quite a bit too structured   ___ quite a bit too unstructured

   ___ somewhat too structured   ___ far too unstructured

3. Our tasks were . . .

   ___ extremely appropriate to our skill and membership

   ___ quite appropriate to our skill and membership

   ___ somewhat appropriate to our skill and membership

   ___ somewhat inappropriate to our skill and membership

   ___ quite inappropriate to our skill and membership

   ___ extremely inappropriate to our skill and membership

4. The pace of the meeting was . . .

____ far too slow   ____ somewhat too fast

____ quite a bit too slow   ____ quite a bit too fast

____ somewhat too slow   ____ far too fast

5. The length of the meeting was . . .

____ far too long   ____ somewhat too short

____ quite a bit too long   ____ quite a bit too short

____ somewhat too long   ____ far too short

6. The information and resources we needed to work on tasks in this group were . . .

____ very readily available   ____ somewhat unavailable

____ quite readily available   ____ quite unavailable

____ somewhat readily available   ____ very unavailable

7. We were . . .

____ extremely efficient   ____ somewhat inefficient

____ quite efficient   ____ quite inefficient

____ somewhat efficient   ____ extremely inefficient

8. We were . . .

____ extremely effective   ____ somewhat ineffective

____ quite effective   ____ quite ineffective

____ somewhat effective   ____ extremely ineffective

9. The group is . . .

____ far too large   ____ somewhat too small

____ quite a bit too large   ____ quite a bit too small

____ somewhat too large   ____ far too small

10. For the work we are expected to be doing, this group is . . .

____ extremely representative   ____ somewhat unrepresentative

____ quite reprsentative   ____ quite unrepresentative

____ somewhat representative   ____ extremely unrepresentative

In the future, we should:

Various kinds of assessments, some similar to the postmeeting reaction sheets, are used to diagnose problems. The trainer assists the group in becoming more aware of its problems. Since the trainers are knowledgeable and experienced, they can provide suggestions for alternative ways of working together. However, an efficient trainer will insist on having the group actually work out changes and improvement so that they can continue to operate effectively on their own. This kind of training is often available through local commercial organizations or consultants and almost always from the faculty of universities and colleges.

SUMMARY

While group processes are not predictable or totally controllable, they can be influenced. The most difficult maneuver is to attempt to influence group process during a meeting. That requires the ability to diagnose what is happening and then make an appropriate comment or intervention. People use two different ways to exert influence in a meeting. One involves hinting, sarcasm, withdrawal, or other indirect techniques. The other requires direct confrontation of the issue or problem.

Group process extends over time and across meetings. Another point of influence occurs between meetings. Most people talk over the important ideas from a meeting with other group members or with outsiders after the meeting. This serves to put the meeting into perspective and give it meaning. Sometimes people get together either as a result of being delegated a task or on their own. They talk about how to make a change (or prevent one) at the next meeting. This is subgrouping between meetings. It also is possible for one or more persons to use the time between meetings to develop ideas, create options, or generate suggestions for the next meeting.

Over the long term, group process can be affected through the use of postmeeting reaction sheets on which members give their opinions about what has happened. The effect is usually positive. The reaction sheets become the basis for opening discussion at the next meeting. Discussion of the group process thus becomes one of the ongoing tasks of the group. In addition, groups can seek training to improve group process. Members may be trained individually or as a group. They may go outside the organization or invite a trainer to come into their facility.

REFLECTING/EXPLORING

1. Observe a small group meeting. Keep a record of attempts to influence group process. Identify each attempt as either direct or indirect. For those which you identify as indirect, describe how you would revise each

one to make it direct. What do you believe might have been the effect on the group process if these attempts had been introduced in direct ways? How could you report your observations to the group?

2. Keep a record of the interactions you have with members of one of your groups between meetings. Also, keep a record of any comments you hear from other members about members they have talked to and what they said. What effect do you think this talk has on the meetings of your group? What purpose does this talk serve for you and for the other members to whom you talked? Would it be useful for this talk to take place during the group meeting? Why? How might you influence the group process in ways that would put this change into effect?

3. Using the sample postmeeting reaction sheet on page 195, design a reaction sheet for one of your groups. Ask the members to complete the form. Then compile the results, write a summary, and give copies to members. Discuss the results at your next meeting. What was the effect on the interpersonal relationships and the group process?

4. Using the sample postmeeting reaction sheet on page 197, prepare a reaction sheet for one of your groups. Ask the members to complete the form. Then compile the results, write a summary, and give copies to members. Discuss the results at your next meeting. What was the effect on task-related issues in the group process?

5. Visit or write community agencies, colleges and universities, and private agencies that offer training programs that might be useful to you and to members of your groups. How might you compile this information and make it available to members of your group or groups?

SECTION FIVE: READING LIST

Information skill approach with relevant theory in group process and dynamics:

Baird, J. E., Jr. and Weinberg, S. B. *Communication: The Essence of Group Synergy.* Dubuque, Iowa: William C. Brown, 1977.

Dessler, G. *Human Behavior: Improving Performance at Work.* Reston, VA: Reston Publishing Company, Inc., 1979.

Fiedler, F. E. and M. M. Chemers. *Leadership and Effective Management.* Glenview, IL: Scott, Foresman, and Co., 1974.

Tubbs, S. L. *A Systems Approach to Small Group Interaction.* Reading, MA: Addison-Wesley, 1978.

Verderber, R. F. *Working Together: Fundamentals of Group Decision Making.* Belmont, CA: Wadsworth Publishing Company, 1982.

FUNCTIONS AND MESSAGES

16

KEY FUNCTIONS IN GROUP WORK

When people form groups and work together, they must function as group members. There are two principal types of functioning involved in group work: task and interpersonal. *Task functions* serve to complete the work of the group. *Interpersonal functions* help members get along together in ways that permit and encourage task effectiveness. In this chapter we will focus on the interpersonal and task functioning of individual group members. We will see how the different functions performed by members can contribute to group effectiveness. The nature of the oral and written messages that group members exchange have an impact on both their task and interpersonal functions. Messages will be the focus of Chapter 17. Then, in Chapter 18, we will examine successful strategies for completing group work. These strategies involve using messages to enhance task and interpersonal functioning. These strategies draw upon the information in all of the chapters you have read up to this point.

We will begin with the functions in group work. This chapter is divided into three sections:

1. Interpersonal functions in group work

2. Task functions in group work

3. Understanding functions in group work

We will begin by introducing you to the group we will use to illustrate functions in group work. In the following example, we have deliberately made the members of a small group work very well together. This was done in order to illustrate interpersonal functions. In real life, the process probably would not be as simple and direct.

Interpersonal Functions in Group Work

The William S. Rafferty Stock Brokerage in Bakerton is a medium-sized company. It has a sales force of twelve people and a bookkeeping staff of four. The business has been in the family for three generations. William S. Rafferty III is now president of the company. Two of his sons and a daughter are salespeople in the company. We will look in on the members of the bookkeeping department. They are having a discussion among themselves in the lunchroom. It is the end of November and all four bookkeepers are working overtime to balance their ledgers before the end of the week.

Marian Billings is the senior bookkeeper. She manages the department. She also runs the control ledger. (The balances from each bookkeeper's ledger must match the balance of the control ledger at the end of each month.) Marian talks about the bookkeeping machines.

MARIAN: (Marian is in her early sixties. She has worked for all three generations of Rafferty's.) You know, if Mr. Rafferty would break loose with some of the profits, we could start replacing these machines! Why, Julia, I'm sure that your machine was an original purchased by old Mr. Rafferty when he opened this company. Julia, don't you think we would put in fewer overtime hours if we had new machines? (Marian is performing a function called *gate opening* by bringing Julia into the conversation.)

JULIA SIMPSON: Marian, I don't know whether we would work fewer hours. I do believe we would have fewer errors. I've noticed that even at the end of the day, my tallies are out of balance more often than not. When I check my tapes on an adding machine, usually they are accurate. I think my bookkeeping machine no longer keeps an accurate tally. I don't trust it. I just expect to put in an extra hour or so each night—and I shudder every time I think of balancing at the end of the month!

MAXINE TYNDALL: You know, I've been having trouble with my machine, too.

MARIAN: Maxine, I don't believe Julia is finished. Julia, what is the problem at the end of the month? (Marian performs the function called *gate closing*. In effect, she tells Maxine to wait her turn and gives a signal to Julia to continue talking. Marian closes the gate to Maxine.)

JULIA: Well, we've each talked about how long it takes us to balance in order to get accurate figures to you, Marian, to match with the control ledger. None of us knows whether we will need to work this Saturday, or maybe even Sunday. And you, Marian, sometimes you work all night on the last day of the month to have the work completed before we start a new month. I don't know how you do it!

MARIAN: I certainly appreciate your concern for me, Julia. And I appreciate how each of you hang in with me through a weekend so I can close the books as close as possible to the last day of the month. Preston, you even stayed last month to help the three of us, even though you balanced. We owe a lot to you for helping us stay ahead of the game this month—and November has been a very heavy month! (Marian is performing the function of *supporting* and *encouraging* with both Julia and Preston.)

PRESTON SCOTT: Marian, I appreciate your compliment. I may not have the luck to balance as easily this month as I did in October. In any case, I'm not going to work overtime. I'm in school now and finals are coming up in December. Marian, I overheard Mr. Rafferty talking with you about our machines. He wants to replace every one of them with computers. You told him our machines have a lot of life left in them. Marian, I think you are frightened of the word *computer.* I think this is why we're not balancing, why we work overtime at night, and why we have such an inhumane push to finish work at the end of every month. It has been difficult for me to say this, Marian. You're like a grandmother to me. I've held it back for two weeks trying to decide whether to talk with you in private or to discuss it when all four of us are together. When you made the comment about the old machines needing to be replaced, well, it just seemed to be the right time. (Preston is performing the function of *confronting* Marian.)

MAXINE: I do *not* believe my ears!

PRESTON: Maxine, I want to hear from Marian, please. (Preston functions as *gate closer* with Maxine.)

MARIAN: Well, Preston, you're right. Mr. Rafferty did offer to buy computers. And that may be fine for you, Preston, but I don't know anything about computers—and I have to run this department!

PRESTON: Marian, computers are little more than glorified bookkeeping machines. The company will send each of us to school for specialized training—and on company time! We'll do the work in half the time!

MARIAN: Yes—and then four bookkeepers won't be needed. I'll be urged to retire early. . . .

MAXINE: Marian, you're a fixture around this place. Why, you were hired by old man Rafferty himself! What are you worrying about?

MARIAN: I'm worrying about you wanting to take over my job, Maxine. *That's* what I'm worrying about.

MAXINE: Why, who would want your job! I've got enough pressure just working with *a* through *h.* I sure don't want responsibility for the whole darn alphabet! Just let someone try to push more on me and I'll . . .

JULIA: (Julia interrupts.) I think it's important that we slow down here. Each of us is under pressure. Preston, you want extra time to get ready for your finals at school. Marian, you're feeling insecure about computers and your job. Maxine, I guess you just want to get your work done and go home. And, as for me, I'm ready to look for a new job if I don't get some relief from a machine that makes my work look sloppy and careless. I'm ready to go back to fight that monster now. But, Marian, will you ask Mr. Rafferty to meet with the four of us on Monday so we can talk about computers or some other solution to this problem? (Julia serves the function of *mediating* the conflict.)

MARIAN: Yes, I will. Thanks, Preston, for opening up this discussion. (Marian *supports* and *encourages*.) I guess I've just been acting like an old dog who doesn't want to learn new tricks.

PRESTON: Well, Marian, with a young pup like me around pulling on your ears, there's not much chance for an old dog to stay old for very long! (Julia, Maxine, and Marian laugh. Preston gives Marian a hug as they all walk back to the bookkeeping area. Preston has performed the function of *releasing tension* and he also has *supported* and *encouraged* Marian.)

Let's take a closer look at the four interpersonal functions. They are

1. Regulating interaction (*gatekeeping*) including (1) opening and (2) gate closing

2. Supporting and encouraging

3. Managing conflict, including (1) mediating and (2) confrontation (bringing issues into the open), and (3) releasing tension

Regulating Interaction

Regulatory interaction is an important function. It is a direct way of controlling who talks to whom. There are two kinds of regulating: (1) Gate opening brings people into the discussion. "Bill, what do you think about the new model?" is an invitation for Bill to speak and an example of gate opening. At the luncheon meeting of the bookkeepers, Marian brought Julia into the discussion and Preston invited Marian to talk. (2) Gate closing is a request for a person to stop talking. It is the opposite of gate opening and often more difficult to practice. A direct form of gate closing might be "Ben, I'd like to hear Mary's view on this topic." This is a message to Ben that he may have been talking too much, preventing Mary from saying much (or anything). A less direct form of gate closing might be "A number of us have talked at length. Do we need to hear from others?" This is a more tactful way of saying "Ben, you've been talking too much." Since it is a more indirect statement, Ben may or may not hear the message as directly meant for him and he may or may not act upon it. In the luncheon meeting, both Marian and Preston used gate closing with Maxine in a direct manner.

Taken together, gate opening and gate closing often are referred to as *gate-keeping.* Their effect is to regulate or control discussion.

Supporting and Encouraging

Perhaps the easiest and most important function to perform is supporting and encouraging. Supporting and encouraging results in increased motivation and cooperation among group members. Yet, opportunities to use support and encouragement in a simple, direct form are often overlooked. It is much more common to hear statements about what was not accomplished, or what needs to be done, than it is to hear statements of appreciation for what has been done. "Cindy, you've been giving us a number of ideas tonight and I want to thank you for that." "We owe a lot to Bill for compiling the information for this meeting." Statements such as these are easy to make, much appreciated, and provide a lift for the person receiving them. The bookkeepers' luncheon meeting included several examples of support and encouragement. If group members give and receive enough support and encouragement, the result will be a positive group atmosphere.

Managing Conflict

Conflict is most successfully managed in those groups where a positive atmosphere exists. Disagreements and differences of opinion exist at some time in every group. Effective answers and careful, open planning sessions require that differences be stated and discussed. The airing of disagreements do cause social and interpersonal stress, however. Emotions may run high. It is important in managing conflicts that two functions be performed by one or more people: (1) confrontation and (2) meditation.

The *confrontation* brings an issue directly into the open. "I feel uncomfortable. I see two factions developing here. I don't want to take sides. Does anyone else feel uncomfortable?" This statement provides the opportunity for an open discussion of the two factions or viewpoints. In the lunchroom discussion, Preston confronted Marian about a topic that involved the working situations for all four bookkeepers. Since Marian had initiated the discussion of machines, Preston chose to reveal contradictory information in the presence of the four persons whose lives were affected.

Once an issue has been brought into the open, it is important for someone to mediate the discussion. "I see the group dividing into two factions. We need a decision but not at the expense of our relationships with each other. Can we reach a settlement? As I see it, the two positions can be described as . . ." Julia served as a mediator for the bookkeepers. She called attention to the stress each person felt and suggested a special meeting with Mr. Rafferty to resolve the issue about the machines. Mediation may cause the discussion to be moved to another time for completion. It may also cause the discussion to continue at the time. Usually people talk about their feelings and their relationships in a discussion of the task involved.

Releasing Tension

When a group works long, hard hours together on a project, tension builds. Tension is an excessively high energy level that must be used before it is released. Sometimes a joke, an ability to laugh at oneself, or the ability to help a group laugh at itself will release the tension. Preston was able to help Marian feel important at the end of the meeting. At the same time, he helped all the bookkeepers laugh at themselves. Laughter is one of the best forms of tension reduction. It is important that someone in the group recognizes when tension is building and knows how to help the group release it in a positive way.

When these four interpersonal functions are performed regularly by various group members, the result is a pleasant working environment. Group members tend to feel motivated, respected, and cooperative. However, interpersonal functions provide only half the picture. Even people who get along well with each other must perform task functions well in order to work together successfully.

Task Functions in Group Work

When they are working together, group members provide each other with information, opinions, and suggestions. These task functions tend to shape the type of information and the way it is exchanged. We will first examine four major procedures groups use in completing their tasks. These include

1. Problem-solving

2. Planning

3. Information processing

4. Decision making using parliamentary procedure

Each of these procedures includes the task functions that must be performed by someone in the group so that the group task can be completed. We will examine the task functions as they are performed in these four group procedures.

Problem Solving

There are five traditional steps involved in problem solving:

1. Defining the problem

2. Setting criteria for evaluating solutions

3. Identifying possible solutions

4. Selecting the most workable solution

5. Describing potential difficulties that may arise after the solution is implemented

Problem-solving procedures will be discussed in more detail in Chapter 19. Each of the steps listed above represents a task function. If one or more group members do not complete each task, necessary parts of the group's work will not be done and the group's problem solving will not be as successful as it could have been.

It is also important that each group member provide information related to the issue or problem. For example, in the bookkeepers' discussion, Marian seemed to define the problem as "How can we convince Mr. Rafferty that he should purchase new bookkeeping machines?" However, after Preston confronted Marian, the problem shifted to "what kind of training program will help us adapt our work to computer processing?" Without Preston's information, the group might have put a great deal of effort into solving a problem that did not exist. In fact, the bookkeepers apparently already have a solution to the problem: Mr. Rafferty is willing to replace the old bookkeeping machines with computers and a training program is included with the purchase. This group may actually be faced with a planning task, not a problem-solving task.

Planning

A group that has decided on a solution, but has not yet implemented it, is faced with a planning task. When the group task is planning, five steps are involved:

1. Defining goals and objectives

2. Listing necessary activities or materials

3. Scheduling activities and deadlines for materials

4. Assigning tasks

5. Budgeting costs

The steps of this planning procedure are described in more detail in Chapter 19. Marian and the other three bookkeepers will need to prepare a work schedule that will permit each of them to stay abreast of daily and monthly bookkeeping needs. At the same time each person must have some training. They need a time period to phase in the computers. On the other hand, it might be possible to bring in a specialist from the computer company. The bookkeeping machines could then be shut down for a day or two so that the new machines can be installed. At the same time, the bookkeepers could receive training together. In any case, the changeover of equipment and skills will require planning. As is true with problem-solving procedures, each planning step is a task function that must be performed by one or more persons in the group in order for planning to be effective.

Information Processing

Some groups are provided with information and then asked to discuss it and report their conclusions to another group. For example, Mr. Rafferty might provide the bookkeepers with brochures about several computers. He might invite salespeople to give demonstrations of their machines. Mr. Rafferty might ask the bookkeepers to recommend a company that will provide a computer appropriate for their needs and an appropriate training program. As head of the department, Marian probably would be in charge of the information-processing task. Any one of the four bookkeepers might perform one or more of the task functions involved in information processing:

1. Acquiring data and information
2. Filing, sorting, and classifying data and information
3. Analyzing and assessing data and information
4. Condensing, summarizing, and abstracting data and information
5. Formulating and writing a report
6. Reporting (orally, in writing, or a combination of both)

The task functions in these six steps are self-explanatory. Whether or not the computers and training program Mr. Rafferty purchases will meet the needs of the bookkeepers will depend, in part, on how well the bookkeepers perform the functions involved in information processing.

Information processing is often a task for community groups. For example, a community group may create a subcommittee and assign it the task of surveying the available open land in the county. Subcommittee members may begin by examining county and township maps. The members would then systematically drive through the countryside to observe areas of open land. Each empty space or open lot would be identified, its location noted, and its size and shape described. The subcommittee would analyze the data they had collected, formulate and write a report, and present the report to the community group. Each step in the information-processing task is a function that must be performed before the next step can be completed logically and successfully.

Decision Making Using Parliamentary Procedure

The bookkeepers are a small, informal group. In fact, the meeting we described occurred at an informal gathering over lunch. This group probably will not use parliamentary procedure for making group decisions. However, in more formal groups, parliamentary procedure is used. There are then a minimum of five task functions that must be performed if the procedure is to be workable. Someone in the group must

1. *Make a motion.* If there is no motion, discussion cannot occur. The motion puts a topic before the group.

2. *Second the motion.* Until someone seconds the motion, it is not officially a topic of discussion.

3. *Amend the motion.* Introducing an amendment to a motion is the only way the wording of the topic under discussion can be revised or changed. (Changes are often necessary as a result of group discussion.)

4. *Vote.* Voting is the procedure used for making an official group decision. No voting means no decisions.

5. *Take minutes.* Minutes are the official record of decisions made by the group. Unless there is a written record, technically no official business has been conducted.

6. *Make rulings.* Someone must be familiar with the rules of parliamentary procedure so they can be used correctly and in a way that facilitates communication. A group leader or the person appointed as parliamentarian is usually responsible for making rulings. It is important for the sake of consistency that only one person in the group perform this function.

Each of these six functions must be performed for parliamentary procedure to be used effectively. A more detailed discussion of parliamentary procedure is provided in Chapter 19.

The use of problem solving, planning, information processing, and parliamentary procedure involves specific task functions that must be performed by one or more members of a group if the group wishes to use these procedures successfully. In addition, relationship functions must be performed by group members in such a way that the resolution of tasks is possible. It is important that a group function successfully at both the relationship and task levels. In the next section, we will examine the usefulness of understanding both relationship and task functions.

Understanding Functions in Group Work

Both interpersonal and task functions are related directly to the kind of work a group is assigned. In any kind of work, the functions being performed by group members determine, and are determined by:

1. The *roles* individuals play within the group

2. The type of group structure

3. The procedures being used in the group

The roles, structure, and procedures are reinforced if they help the group achieve its goals and objectives. The roles, structure, and procedures can be revised or changed completely if a group's work is not being facilitated. Let's examine each of these in turn.

Individual Roles

If a group member functions in the same way regularly, other members come to expect that person to fulfill a specific function. For example, group members may expect a member to provide support or list a large number of ideas when support or ideas are needed by the group. Preston is the person the other three bookkeepers expect will relieve tension when it builds. Marian may be the specialist in providing support and encouragement, even though others might perform this function from time to time.

A group is very fortunate if it includes one or more members who function equally well as interpersonal and task specialists. Usually, some members perform the interpersonal functions regularly while others are more task conscious. We will examine the characteristics of each specialization.

The interpersonal specialist. A person who specializes in interpersonal functions often tries to settle differences between people by stressing their points of agreement and by minimizing their disagreements. Julia did this for the bookkeepers. Another role of the interpersonal specialist is to identify the existence of tension and conflict between people and try to release it: "I sense that we are at a stalemate here. Bob looks a little upset and Jan hasn't said anything in the last half hour. Are we getting to the point where we need to talk about our group and how we work together?" The person who makes such a statement is fulfilling an interpersonal function—conflict management. If a member does this regularly, that individual will be viewed as an interpersonal specialist by group members. Sometimes a specialist in this area performs only one of the four interpersonal functions regularly and effectively. Other specialists may perform more than one function well.

The task specialist. A person who is a task specialist may not function as well in social areas. The task specialist may be the person who typically provides the group with several new ideas just when they seem to be at a loss for suggestions. The same person may be limited in the ability to plan the actions needed to put the ideas into practice in realistic and cost-effective ways. To be effective and efficient a group needs within its membership all the task specializations necessary for completing its work.

It is not necessary or realistic to assume that every group member will function equally well in both the interpersonal and task areas. However, the group members must be able to perform the necessary functions. This is a major reason for considering diversity of skills when organizing a group. It also is the reason for choosing as group leaders individuals who have at least a minimum level of skill in both interpersonal and task areas.

The Type of Group Structure

A group may be organized on the basis of specific functions that must be performed. The land-survey subcommittee was created for the purpose of processing information about open land areas. Sometimes one committee is given the responsibility of obtaining and organizing information while another is assigned the task of analyzing the information. A third group may write the final report. Each of the three groups could be defined on the basis of the functions assigned.

Informal structures grow around functions. Instead of one person serving as an interpersonal specialist, a subgroup of three or four individuals fills this function. A subgroup may form when three or four people notice that they function in common ways. They may also notice that the support and encouragement they give members seems to have positive effects on the group. They may informally and unofficially recognize themselves as a subgroup by scheduling social events at which all group members can relax, become better acquainted, and put the task deadlines into perspective.

Organizational charts reflect the formal structure of groups. For example, if a group uses parliamentary procedures for decision-making purposes, a recording secretary is a necessary position. The secretary records, prepares, and distributes the minutes or records of the meetings. The functions performed by the recording secretary are critical. By examining job descriptions, it is possible to analyze the functions that an organization or community group believe are essential to its existence. In fact, the formal structures of a group usually are designed according to the minimum functions that must be performed. Analyzing the necessary functions in your groups is a way to evaluate the effectiveness of the formal structure.

The Procedures Used in the Group

The ways in which a group must function in order to complete its work determines what procedures might be most successful. This statement applies most obviously to task functions. If a group must solve a problem, someone must help the group focus the problem by defining it. Without a definition, there is little point in listing solutions. In a city commission meeting, the discussion may be confusing and awkward if no one puts a motion on the floor to focus the interaction. The procedures that have developed over time as effective tools for groups have emerged because they serve task functions. Chapters 19 and 20 explain the most used and most practical procedures available for meeting task functions.

Interpersonal functions also define the more subtle procedures that help members of groups relate to each other in useful ways. For example, a group may find that meetings begin and end with a great deal of agreement and support. However, disagreement and conflict occurs in the middle half of the meeting. The support in the initial and final phases of the meeting serves the function of helping people get along with each other. It helps to create a positive atmosphere that promotes the honest discussion of disagreements during the middle of the meeting. Studies of phases in meetings have shown definite shifts in behaviors that tend to fulfill specific functions. These shifts occur from the beginning to the middle and again from the middle to the end of the meeting. Once it becomes clear either from practice or from reviewing research that a particular pattern of functioning promotes group work, the pattern can be deliberately introduced into the group process by the leader or by the members.

Using a Worksheet to Study Functions

We have provided you with a worksheet to use in studying the functions that are performed and those that need to be performed in your groups. This worksheet is on page 215. The analysis should be made by all or by most of the members of your group. The views of one person may be biased. For example, if people lean more toward interpersonal functions, they may think these functions either are not being met or that they are meeting them very well. Others in the group who may be more task oriented may have a far different view.

In completing the worksheet, first consider the types of tasks with which your group usually works. Is it problem solving, planning, information processing, or decision making? Do the group's tasks require the use of parliamentary procedure? List the task or tasks and the task functions (steps) involved in each task. Consult the appropriate section of this chapter for the functions important to each procedure. The major interpersonal functions are listed for you on the worksheet.

Once you have listed the task functions, answer the key question for each function: To what extent are each of the task and interpersonal functions met during the meetings of this group? The worksheet provides you with a scale from 1 to 5 to use in answering this question. Use *1* when the function is not met at all. Use *5* to stand for a function which is met totally.

There is space in the right-hand column to describe both what your group might do to improve the situation and specifically who should be responsible for doing it. Complete the worksheet as a group and you will tend to have a more balanced, overall image of what functions are important in your group and how well those functions are performed. Most groups discover that some functions are not performed adequately or often, while others are managed regularly and effectively.

The way your group uses both oral and written messages will have a definite effect on the successful performance of interpersonal and task functions within your group. Messages will be considered in Chapter 17.

WORKSHEET FOR ANALYZING SMALL-GROUP FUNCTIONS

Task Functions	To what extent is this function met in our group?	What can we do to improve? Who should do it?
	(Circle one number.)*	
1.	1 2 3 4 5	
2.	1 2 3 4 5	
3.	1 2 3 4 5	
4.	1 2 3 4 5	
5.	1 2 3 4 5	
6.	1 2 3 4 5	
7.	1 2 3 4 5	
8.	1 2 3 4 5	
9.	1 2 3 4 5	
10.	1 2 3 4 5	
11.	1 2 3 4 5	
12.	1 2 3 4 5	

Interpersonal Functions

1. Supporting and encouraging	1 2 3 4 5	
2. Confrontation	1 2 3 4 5	
3. Mediation	1 2 3 4 5	
4. Gate opening	1 2 3 4 5	
5. Gate closing	1 2 3 4 5	
6. Releasing tension	1 2 3 4 5	
Other:	1 2 3 4 5	

*1 = Function not met at all. 2 = Function met to small extent. 3 = Function met to moderate extent. 4 = Function met to great extent. 5 = Function is totally met.

In Chapter 18 we will examine strategies you may want to use for completing group work successfully.

SUMMARY

Groups of people who work together perform both interpersonal and task functions. Task functions help the group complete their work. Interpersonal functions help members get along in ways that promote successful work completion.

There are four major interpersonal functions: (1) regulating or controlling interaction through both gate opening and gate closing. These are forms of gatekeeping which serve to direct the flow of communication. (2) Supporting and encouraging serves to motivate members and build a cooperative group atmosphere. (3) Managing conflict includes confrontation and mediation. Confrontation results in bringing issues out in the open so they may be discussed directly. Mediation helps to focus the discussion and settle the conflict. (4) Tension releasing serves to help the group dispose of energy that has built up during the pressures of intense or difficult work.

There are four principal task functions. They are related to the procedures available to groups for use in completing tasks: (1) problem solving, (2) planning, (3) information processing, and (4) decision making using parliamentary procedure. The task functions identified with each of these procedures emerge out of the four procedures.

Both interpersonal and task functions directly affect (1) the roles members take on in a group, (2) the way a group is structured, and (3) the procedures a group uses. By studying the extent to which group functions are fulfilled, members can determine whether additions or deletions in roles, structural factors, and procedures will increase the group's ability to complete its work.

Reflecting/Exploring

1. Participate in or observe a group over two or three meetings. List the names of group members and identify the number of times each member performs one of the interpersonal functions listed on page 206. How would you describe the group atmosphere? To what extent are all of the members involved in creating this atmosphere? What relationships do you see between the interpersonal functions that members perform and the atmosphere?

2. Use the group from activity 1 and repeat the procedure using task functions as your focus. Use the task functions listed on page 208. Are the

types of functions performed appropriate to the procedures the group uses? What functions would you add or delete? What relationships do you see between the interpersonal and task functions in this group? What relationships do you see between the way the task functions are performed and the group atmosphere that exists?

3. Make a list of the interpersonal and task functions you perform in a meeting of a group in which you are a member. How do the functions you perform add to or detract from the work of the group? What changes would you make in the ways you function as a member of the group?

4. Use the worksheet on page 215. Invite the members of one of your groups to discuss the functions performed in the group. Complete the worksheet and identify specific ways the group might improve its meetings by adding or deleting interpersonal and task functions. Describe the effect of the ways group functions are performed on the roles played, the structure, and the procedures used in the group. What changes might be made in the roles, structure, and procedures that would result in more useful interpersonal and task functions being performed in the group?

5. Observe a community group. Complete the worksheet for this group as you observe the group meeting. What suggestions might you make to the group for more effective meetings? What have you learned about the ways you function or could function in your groups by observing this group?

CHAPTER 17

MESSAGES IN GROUPS

If you observe a group of people working together, you will see them use messages to communicate. Sometimes the group members will talk together. They will use oral messages. At other times, members may refer to documents prepared by the group or by other groups for their use. These documents are written messages.

Group members can learn to use messages and the language from which messages are constructed in ways that will improve their interpersonal relations and their work. This chapter is devoted to helping you use messages more effectively. The chapter is divided into five sections. Each section concentrates on one of the following broad, general guidelines to help you use messages more effectively in group work:

1. There should be a mixture of written and oral messages and each should be used appropriately.

2. There should be a balance between abstract and specific statements to provide both general principles and specific applications.

3. Messages should be characterized by immediacy. They should indicate a sense of taking responsibility for the actions described.

4. There should be a mix of descriptive, analytical, evaluative, and prescriptive statements, showing that problems are being considered, decisions are being made, and specific actions are being proposed.

5. There should be metaphors and images which suggest that members view the group as effective and cohesive.

In each section of this chapter, we will explain the importance of one of these guidelines for group messages. We will discuss how your group can follow these message guidelines. We will begin by looking at the characteristics of written and oral messages.

Written and Oral Messages

Guideline 1. There should be a mixture of written and oral messages and each should be used appropriately.

Written and oral messages typically are distinguished from each other on the basis of three contrasting characteristics:

Permanent and ephemeral messages. Written messages are relatively permanent; oral messages are ephemeral. By *ephemeral* we mean that oral messages are spoken and then disappear. Only the memory of what was said remains, unless someone is recording every word as the proceedings in a courtroom are recorded. When there is no permanent record of oral messages, later "legalistic" arguments over what was said are usually kept to a minimum. Written messages are almost at the opposite extreme. They are permanent and can be filed and referred to later. There can be no argument about the words that were used, although arguments may occur about what was meant or intended by the words.

Pace of communication. Written messages slow communication; oral messages can be rapid. Speed is not a major advantage of written communication. Someone must write the words, edit and revise them, and finally, type, duplicate, and circulate the finished message to others. A written message can require from half an hour to as much as a month or more for delivery. In contrast, an oral message may take a few seconds to formulate and deliver. People can talk to each other over the telephone and exchange information quickly in hallways or at work stations. With oral communication there is no need to wait for the words to be put into proper sentence structure, to get signatures, and to transmit the message. Each person simply talks and listens.

Feedback. Written messages imply infrequent and intermittent feedback; oral messages imply immediate and continuous feedback. Feedback to written messages is often nonexistent or very slow in coming. This is particularly true if the response must also be written. A letter or a memo may take a day or two to be delivered, and a delay of several days may occur before replies are received. However, in talking and listening, feedback is continuous. The individuals can ask questions, seek clarification, give their own ideas, and respond to each other rapidly. Consensus can be reached quickly as individuals hear and see each other speak and modify their positions or seek common understanding.

These descriptions of the three main differences between written and oral messages is based on a traditional view of them. In group work, the differences blur because the situation is complex.

Oral and written messages are used in combination in at least three ways.

Oral messages made about written messages. Talk often is based on written messages. There is talk about committee, program, and project reports and proposals. Group members refer to pages and statements in written documents. Minutes of prior meetings are discussed and corrected orally. Planning a meeting requires that people talk together about what items should be included in the official written agendas for meetings. Carefully written messages often provide the stimulus for rapid-fire oral exchanges.

Written messages made about oral messages. The process described above is often reversed. The minutes of a group meeting are the written record of oral messages exchanged among group members. Individuals take notes of what has been said and use them in future meetings. In brainstorming or similar procedures, someone keeps a written list of the ideas presented in an oral form. In negotiations, the parties involved frequently put into writing and sign their understanding of what was agreed upon orally. Oral messages have the advantages of speed and provision for continuous feedback. They can also be converted into written form to provide the additional advantage of a permanent record.

Written messages guide oral messages. Parliamentary procedure, bylaws, constitutions, and agendas are examples of written messages that group members use to guide oral discussion. These written messages are used to make decisions about the order in which topics will be discussed and the order in which people will talk. Without written guidelines, some meetings could end in confusion and frustration.

In these three ways, written and oral messages are alternated in group work. Both types of messages are needed in various combinations.

Abstract and Specific Statements

Language is common to both written and oral messages. The way language is used in constructing messages affects the ways group members work together. One way language affects messages involves the levels of abstraction represented by the language used.

Guideline 2. There should be a balance between abstract and specific statements to provide both general principles and specific applications.

The language in a message is on one of four different levels of abstraction. Here are four statements about political rallies. Each statement represents a different level of abstraction.

Level 4: "Large rallies are an effective way to make a point in this society."

Level 3: "Nuclear disarmament rallies tend to draw lots of people."

Level 2: "Most Greenpeace rallies draw over 10,000 people."

Level 1: "There were 12,000 at the rally."

Below level 1 is the actual experience at the rally described in the first message. No language is required for this experience. It includes the various sensations which occur. A member of a group may attend a rally to support a cause and experience strong personal emotion as well as feeling the tension in the crowd. Only the group member who was present at the actual rally has the particular *experience*. Other members who did not attend must rely on reports of (messages about) the event. The first level of abstraction is reporting the event to others. The group member who attended can report about the number of people who attended, what was said, how people acted and reacted. These messages represent *reports* of the rally. At the second level of abstraction, the individual may begin to generalize about several rallies of the same type held by the same organization—in this case, Greenpeace. At the third level, the individual discusses all rallies about nuclear disarmament regardless of the sponsoring organization. Finally, at the fourth and highest level of abstraction, the member can talk about rallies in general and about their effectiveness as a tool for achieving political ends.

EXAMPLES OF ABSTRACTION LEVELS

Immediate Experience	Level 1	Level 2	Level 3	Level 4
seeing an IBM factory	IBM	computer companies	high-tech businesses	business world
hearing the committee discuss an issue	ad hoc committee on research strategies	ad hoc committees	committees	groups
holding and looking at the book	self-help book on assertiveness	self-help books	books	written materials

By listening to the conversation in a group, you can identify the various abstraction levels. There should be talk of general principles with which everyone can agree. These general principles serve as guides in arriving at decisions. They will usually be stated at a high level of abstraction. On the other hand, specific plans require bringing the level of abstraction down to practical details. "Budgets should be balanced" is an abstract principle stated at level 4. "What can we eliminate from this budget?" or "We can eliminate fees to pay a recording secretary" are quite specific messages stated at level 1. Group work requires that members create messages in both general and specific terms. This involves working with the various levels of abstraction.

The Degree of Immediacy

Another characteristic of messages involves the degree of immediacy represented by the language used. When group members use statements that have a high degree of immediacy, the members accept responsibility for both problems and successes (or failures). "We did not meet the schedule" is more immediate than "That schedule deadline seemed to pass by the group." Greater immediacy allows the group and group members to take on responsibilities and cope with consequences.

> *Guideline 3.* Messages should be characterized by immediacy. They should indicate a sense of taking responsibility for the actions described.

Here are five statements, each representing a different degree of immediacy. They are arranged in order, from most immediate (1) to least immediate (5).

1. "We have a terrific (terrible) group here."

2. "Jim, Fran, Yvonne, and I make a terrific (terrible) group."

3. "I think that the four of us may be a terrific (terrible) group."

4. "I think that the four of us have solved technical problems in terrific (terrible) ways."

5. "I think the four of us have solved the technical problems in equipment maintenance in terrific (terrible) ways."

Notice that the positive or negative nature of the message does not affect the degree of immediacy. In other words, whether the group's work is terrific or terrible does not determine the degree of immediacy.

Immediacy is characterized by four major features.

Verb tense is in the present. One of the reasons that the statement "We have a terrific (terrible) group here" is the most immediate is that the group is discussed in the present tense. The implication is that the quality of the group is an ongoing feature. It has a record of being terrific (or terrible). Less immediate statements describe the group performance in the past tense.

Pronoun choices reflect mutal effort. The use of *we* implies a mutual commitment and involvement that does not exist with the listing of individual names or with the phrase *the four of us.*

Statements are broad and general. The statement "we have a terrific (terrible) group here" is general and all-inclusive. The fifth statement, "I think the four of us have solved the technical problems in equipment maintenance in terrific (terrible) ways," refers specifically to technical problems in equipment maintenance. Problems in this area represent only five percent of the group's work. Therefore, the effect of their being terrific (or terrible) is quite limited. When comments are restricted to a narrow and specific set of activities or events, messages have less immediacy.

Statements use the, Not that. The final feature of immediacy is not illustrated in the five sample statements. This feature involves the choice between the use of *the* rather than *that*. For example, "The table is loaded with the handouts for the meeting," is more immediate than "That table is loaded with those handouts for that meeting." *That* implies distance between the speaker and the object, where *the* suggests proximity. (The speaker is more directly related to the table being described when *the* is used.) If your group's messages include a high degree of immediacy, they will convey a sense of interpersonal cohesiveness and mutual responsibility among group members for the work in which all of you are involved.

Type of Statements

While immediacy is a clue to the way a group meets its responsibilities, the range from descriptive to prescriptive statements is important in terms of the group's impact on other people.

> *Guideline 4.* There should be a mix of descriptive, analytical, evaluative, and prescriptive statements, showing that problems are being considered, decisions are being made, and specific actions are being proposed.

Descriptive messages are most likely to be neutral and easily accepted by others. As statements become first analytical, then evaluative, and finally prescriptive, they will induce emotional reactions in the receivers. People do not want to hear what they did wrong. They want to be told exactly what they need to do. Most of us seek reward and independence, not punishment and control. Evaluative and prescriptive statements often imply punishment and control. The following list includes an example of each type of message:

1. Descriptive: "The deadline *was June 21,* and we *missed* it."

2. Analytical: "The *reason* we missed the deadline was because of some equipment failures and our optimism in setting the deadline."

3. Evaluative: "We were *wrong* to set the deadline when we did; it was a *dumb* mistake."

4. Prescriptive: "We *should* never set deadlines based on overly optimistic estimates."

Descriptive messages. A message that consists of descriptive language explains events, times, dates, names, and places in objective terms. Ideally, newspaper reporters and eyewitnesses in court cases use descriptive language. Since descriptive language refers to ideas in objective terms, large numbers of people can hear the statements and follow the directions, find the object, or agree upon the decision.

Analytical messages. Analytical messages go one step further than descriptive statements. They provide reasons, causes, correlations, and other relationships between events, issues, and people. Any attempt to assign cause implies that a message is analytical. Analytical messages are characterized by reasons or explanations. There are many different analytical schemes. Accounting, engineering, psychology, and management, for example, all have analytical schemes, which are used to explain events. On the financial pages of a newspaper you will find analytical statements included in the explanations of why the stock market is going up or down.

Evaluative messages. An evaluative message goes beyond analysis. These messages contain judgments of a situation. Typically, evaluative messages include words such as *good* or *bad, better* or *worse,* and *above average* or *below average.* Evaluative messages imply some degree of blame or praise.

Prescriptive messages. The prescriptive message sets forth what ought to happen in the future. These statements often include words such as *ought, should, will.* Prescriptive messages provide directions, just as the prescription provided by a doctor tells a patient what kind of medicine to take and how often to take it.

In order to solve problems, plan, process information, and make decisions, group members must use all of the types of language described here.

Metaphors and Images

People often use images and metaphors in their writing or talk. "We are a big, happy family." "I think of this group as individuals connected to our leader like a series of spokes in a wheel." "Well, the ball is in their court now." These statements include the metaphor of the family, the image of a spoked wheel, and the metaphor of a tennis match.

> *Guideline 5.* There should be metaphors and images which suggest that members view the group as effective and cohesive.

Metaphors and images give clues as to how people view their groups, their work, and themselves as group members. Listen for metaphors and images and you will gain insight into the interpersonal relationships among members of your group. "I am just a cog in the big wheel," certainly gives the notion that the speaker feels left out and unimportant. "We treat each other like brothers and sisters," suggests this person has a feeling of closeness with others in the group. (Perhaps the idea of sibling rivalry may be a second meaning in this image.)

A periodic review of how individuals use language both during and between meetings will help you understand how well your group is communicating and how the communication affects the relationships and the group's work. The five guidelines provided in this chapter are included in the following checklist. You can use this checklist to analyze the messages in your group.

A Checklist for Analyzing the Messages in a Group

1. What kinds of written messages are used? (Examples: agendas, minutes, reports, proposals.)

   How are the written and oral messages used together?

2. What levels of abstraction characterize most of the messages used in your group? How much movement exists between the more abstract and general levels and the more specific and concrete levels?

3. How immediate are the messages used by group members? To what extent are there signs in the language that suggest group members are taking responsibility for actions and events?

4. What is the relative frequency of descriptive, analytical, evaluative, and prescriptive messages? Are all four types used?

5. What metaphors and images are used? What do these suggest about the ways group members view their group, other group members, the task, and themselves?

Based on this checklist, what changes can you suggest to improve the use of language and messages in this group?

SUMMARY

Messages are the basic tools for communication among group members. These messages may be oral or written. There are three major differences between written and oral messages. Written messages are permanent, slow, and imply long-term, intermittent feedback. Oral messages tend to be ephemeral, rapid, and imply immediate and continuous feedback. Written and oral messages are used in three combinations in group work. These include (1) written messages made about oral messages, (2) oral messages made about written messages, and (3) written messages that guide oral messages.

Five general guidelines are used to provide more effective communication in a group:

1. There should be a mixture of written and oral messages and each should be used appropriately.

2. There should be a balance between abstract and specific statements to provide both general principles and specific applications.

3. Messages should be characterized by immediacy. They should indicate a sense of taking responsibility for the actions described.

4. There should be a mix of descriptive, analytical, evaluative, and prescriptive statements showing that problems are being considered, decisions are being made, and specific actions are being proposed.

5. There should be metaphors and images which suggest that members view the group as effective and cohesive.

A checklist for these guidelines can be used by a group member to analyze the messages used in the group's communication.

REFLECTING/EXPLORING

1. As you participate in or observe a group, keep a record of (1) written messages made about oral messages, (2) oral messages made about written messages, and (3) written messages used to guide oral messages. What would you describe as the advantages of the oral messages and of the written messages as they were used by this group? What disadvantages of each did you observe? What suggestions might you make to the group?

2. Tape record a group involved in a problem-solving task. Listen for abstract and specific language. Find at least one example of an abstract principle stated without specific application. Then find an example of several specific applications stated without an overall statement of principle. Revise the first statement to include specific applications. Revise the second set of statements to include a possible principle. What is the effect of your additions and changes?

3. Listen to the tape you recorded for activity 2. Make a list of messages that have a high degree of immediacy. Make another list of messages that have a low degree of immediacy. What patterns do you notice among the situations that include messages with high immediacy? With low immediacy? What suggestions might you make to this group?

4. Listen to the tape you recorded in activity 2. List the five steps in problem solving. (See pages 208 and 209 for these steps.) As you listen to the tape, list under each of the problem-solving steps the number of times you hear messages that are primarily (1) descriptive, (2) analytical, (3) evaluative, and (4) prescriptive. What conclusions can you draw about the use of these types of messages in relationship to the problem-solving procedure? How can these conclusions help you improve your use of language for problem-solving tasks?

5. Observe a group, tape record it, and listen to the recording. As you observe or listen, complete the checklist on page 225. What conclusions can you draw about the use of language in this group? What was effective about the use of language? What suggestions might you make to increase the effectiveness of the messages used in this group?

CHAPTER 18

MAKING STRATEGY DECISIONS

If you have a good idea, groups sometimes get in the way. Suppose you know a way of improving service, obtaining funding, or improving a product. In order to implement your idea, a group must approve it. It's not an idea you can put into effect alone. The group may slow down your progress. Remember Marian, the head bookkeeper, in Chapter 16? Perhaps Mr. Rafferty had been trying to put computers in the bookkeeping department for months or even for years. Marian feared them. And the idea did not get past her to the other bookkeepers until Preston overheard a conversation between Mr. Rafferty and Marian and chose to confront Marian in front of the other bookkeepers. A few members of your group, like Marian, may fear your idea. Some group members may not like it. Others may agree with it, but may have to be convinced that it will not be too expensive. Working through a group can be discouraging. It also can be exciting and challenging if you know how to plan strategies successfully.

In this chapter, we will provide information for group members who want to plan strategies for completing group tasks. These plans will help you improve your chances of being successful. Your own strategies will be built upon your understanding of group functions and messages in groups. In fact, your strategy decisions will also involve your knowledge of group structure, of people in groups, and of group process. We will approach this chapter by examining five steps in making strategy decisions. These steps will form the sections of the chapter. They include:

1. Setting the goal

2. Using the group structure

3. Using information about people, which includes predicting the responses of key people, and developing reactions to the responses

4. Developing a strategy based on group process

5. Designing the message

We will start at the beginning with the first strategy decision.

Strategy Decision 1: Setting the Goal

Setting the goal means writing out what it is that you want to accomplish. A social worker might want to change the method used in assigning case loads in a human-services agency. A fireman might have an idea for a better way to clean equipment. A citizen may devise a method for improving traffic flow in a local neighborhood. Each must think through the goal before proceeding with action.

Let's assume Mrs. Wise, a citizen, wants to improve the flow of traffic in a neighborhood. This goal statement could be revised. It is quite broad. Mrs. Wise might ask herself, What must be done to achieve this goal? Perhaps the specific objective is to reduce the *amount* of traffic in front of the Northwood Elementary School. Maybe Mrs. Wise wants to reduce the *speed* of traffic on Deerfield Avenue. Notice that the wording of the two specific objectives fits within the general goal of improving traffic flow. Each statement will result in a very different discussion and solution. They are both worded at a lower level of abstraction than the original statement because they include specific descriptions of the concern and the location: amount of traffic by the school, or speed of traffic on Deerfield. The information in either of these statements would help the group focus its discussion in the general direction of Mrs. Wise's concern.

Let's assume that Mrs. Wise would prefer to be even more specific because she has a definite way in mind of decreasing the speed of traffic at a specific point on Deerfield Avenue. Actually, her plan is to have a stoplight erected at the corner of Deerfield and Doe Trail. (Mrs. Wise lives at the intersection of these two streets.) Suppose she introduces her goal of putting a stoplight at the corner to the city planning commission. She may have more difficulty resolving the problems of the speed of traffic on Deerfield Avenue than she would have if she introduced the problem and invited the group to help her solve it. In fact, there may be other ways of reducing the speed of traffic on Deerfield. Even if Mrs. Wise's idea does emerge as the most effective method, the city planners have expertise, experience, and believe that they have useful ideas. If Mrs. Wise communicates her belief that her idea is the right and only solution, she may fail in her attempt to reduce the speed of traffic.

The key to effective strategy decisions in setting goals is this: Describe the *problem* to be solved specifically. Avoid presenting a single specific solution at the same time. Describing a problem and presenting a solution at the same time can create problems for several reasons. The most obvious is that the planning committee, in the case of Mrs. White, may reject the idea of a traffic light and, along with it, throw out the problem. The goal is to get the traffic flow modified, not necessarily or only to get a traffic light put up. A second potential difficulty is that when people are presented with a ready-made solution, they have little or no involvement in its success.

Better to let others wrestle with the problem, develop solutions of their own, and then select the best one. They are more likely to develop a real understanding of the problem and have a commitment to the solution. Chapter 19 offers more suggestions about how to word a problem. These suggestions will help you set goals successfully.

Once you have a goal statement, it is time to make the second strategy decision, using the group structure.

Strategy Decision 2: Using the Group Structure

In Chapter 8, we introduced the idea that a group is a number of individuals and subgroups linked together in complex ways. Your knowledge of individuals, subgroups, and how they are linked will help you develop strategies for achieving positive group action. Once Mrs. Wise has clarified her goal, she needs to ask herself three questions about the group structure in the city planning committee:

1. What coalitions, interest groups, or other types of subgroups exist?

2. Who are the key people (opinion leaders) in the subgroups?

3. Who are the key people (liaisons or linkers) who build bridges between the subgroups?

You can apply these questions to a work group in an organization or to a community group.

In dealing with the problem of traffic flow, Mrs. Wise could have identified at least three coalitions or interest groups. First, the other persons in the neighborhood who would like to see changes in the traffic pattern in the neighborhood. These people are a coalition of neighbors with common interests and could appear before the planning committee. Second, the traffic and urban planners on the staff of the city government. Such people have expertise and opinions about such matters as traffic flow and stoplights. They will probably be heard by the planning committee. Very probably a third subgroup, a negative one, is made up of those persons who want to hold down city expenditures. After all, stoplights cost money to buy, install, and maintain.

You will increase your chances for success in persuading a group to react positively to your proposals if you direct your messages to key people. If key people are persuaded, they will influence others to agree. One of the reasons key people are called opinion leaders is that their attitudes and viewpoints carry weight with others. In addition, someone who acts as a bridge between two or more subgroups has influence in both groups. If liaisons and linkers are favorably inclined toward a suggestion, they will mediate and explain the suggestion to both factions. They will assist others in understanding and accepting the suggestion.

It is important for you to identify subgroups in order to locate liaisons and linkers. Subgroups are also useful for another reason. It is better to have an idea accepted by a large or powerful subgroup than by a small, isolated fringe group. You may have to make a decision about which subgroups to concentrate on. You will need to focus your time, energy, and efforts. Eventually, all ideas presented to a group must be agreed upon by consensus, voting, or some other method of polling total group opinion. Knowing where the power lies will help you focus your energies and save time in enlisting the aid of influential people. The result will be that you will use group structure in ways that increase your chances for successfully presenting your proposal.

As you draw upon your understanding of group structure, it becomes important to make use of your information about people.

Strategy Decision 3: Using Information about People

It is important to understand people, especially their motivations and personal styles. Each of us approaches people in different ways depending on their personalities, styles, or needs. We begin to learn this in infancy. Mom is approached one way, Dad another.

An understanding of motivation and personal style is a key issue in understanding and influencing people. Here is an example. Bob, a member of a steering committee, is very goal oriented. Bob likes efficiency; he is time conscious. Bob wants to get ahead. However, Hal is quite different from Bob. He enjoys talking to people. He wants to be liked by the members of the steering committee as well as by people in general.

A person who presents an idea to Bob and Hal in exactly the same way will discover that one of them likes it and the other does not. Bob can be approached successfully by quickly introducing the problem and then suggesting a way of solving it. The solution must result in greater effectiveness or productivity. It would help if it allowed Bob to appear in a good light. The message to Bob might begin like this: "I need just a minute of your time. We have a problem with . . . More people can get good service if we . . . We need you as part of the team that supports this idea so that we can benefit from it."

The same approach to Hal would be received negatively. The initial conversation with Hal might not even deal with the problem or solution. It would begin with a discussion about mutual friends, or talking about a hobby and common interests. After a comfortable conversational period, the topic could be changed to the problem. A possible approach to Hal might be: "I have checked with several other people, and they all seem to think we have a problem here. It would be nice to have you as a member of the group supporting us." This kind of message appeals to Hal's need to be a member of the team, to be included in the group.

Effective members of the group are able communicators who change their approach to people intuitively and without really thinking about it. They seem to be able to sense the other person's style and needs. They adapt to them easily. It might be helpful for Mrs. Wise to attend a few city planning meetings before she introduces her concern about the speed of traffic on Deerfield Avenue. By observing members of the city planning committee, she might learn their styles and decide how best to approach them.

This brings us to two important issues involved in using information about people:

1. It is important to predict the responses of key people.

2. It is equally important to develop reactions to those responses.

Predicting the Responses of Key People

The purpose behind identifying the motivations and styles of people is to predict their responses to ideas or suggestions. It is not necessary to do this for all members of a large group. Five to eight key people can be identified and their responses can be predicted.

One problem is to determine in general the possible responses to a proposal, issue, or suggestion. There are two key features to be considered in the possible responses:

1. Will the suggestion or idea be *understood?*

2. Will the suggestion or idea be accepted and agreed to?

Even though people may respond with enthusiasm, criticism, apathy, rebuttal, or countersuggestions, the only crucial responses to your proposal are understanding and acceptance. If the basic issues are understanding or misunderstanding, and acceptance or rejection, there are four possible combinations: understanding and acceptance, understanding and rejection, misunderstanding and acceptance, and misunderstanding and rejection.

Possible responses are slightly more complex than a simple classification of all responses as accepting or rejecting and understanding or misunderstanding. There are degrees of acceptance and understanding. A useful analysis can be made by listing (1) key persons by name, (2) the degree of understanding or misunderstanding, and (3) the degree of acceptance or rejection. The sample form on page 233 may be used in analyzing the degree of understanding or misunderstanding and the degree of acceptance or rejection among key people in the group.

The key persons are listed in column one. The extent to which each may understand or misunderstand as well as the degree to which each may accept or reject the proposal are noted in columns two and three.

Why try to predict responses? Simply because that is the best way to look ahead for trouble spots and for support. People waging political campaigns have found this out. One standard political strategy is to find the yes votes and get them to the polls. In other words, predict who will support your position and encourage them to do so. Marketing experts know the same is true of getting people to try a new product. If a few key people in an area begin using a product, they will spread the word and others will begin buying it. The trick is to predict who will use the product and talk to others about it.

ANALYZING UNDERSTANDING OF ACCEPTANCE

List Key Person by Name	Degree of Understanding or Misunderstanding (as Percent)	Degree of Acceptance or Rejection (as Percent)
1.		
2.		
3.		
4.		
5.		
6.		

In dealing with a group, whether it is a commission, a committee, or a board of directors, it is wise to have some idea ahead of time about who will resist your proposal. In that way, you can be ready to deal with obstacles put in your path. It is a little like finding out from the highway patrol or an auto club that there is a detour in the road ahead. You will be prepared for it and can, if you must, choose an alternate route.

Most of us assume that other people will understand our ideas if we explain them well. For very simple suggestions, this may be true. However, in the committees, councils, and boards that are a part of our complex, everyday lives, programs and projects are complicated. It often takes lengthy discussion and explanation before people even partially understand what is being proposed. Therefore, an individual group member can have a level of understanding ranging from 100 percent (total understanding) through 0 percent (no understanding) to –100 percent (total misunderstanding). In the latter case, the person actually has an idea opposed to that suggested by the initiator. A similar range may exist for acceptance. Some people will have acceptance at the 100 percent level (total acceptance) while others are neutral (the 0 percent level). Still others will be at a –100 percent level (total rejection). For the key people, the degree of understanding and acceptance must be estimated. These estimates are based on the nature of the idea being proposed and an estimate of how it will probably be viewed by the key persons in terms of their motivations and styles.

Developing reactions to the responses of key people. An accurate prediction of how someone will respond is only useful if it permits further action. This further action is a reaction to the response. You can plan reactions by using the four-way classification system of responses just described. We will now expand this system by adding the ways that you can react to the responses of others. The following table shows this expanded classification system:

COUNTING REACTIONS AND RESPONSES

Responses of the Key Person	Preferred Reaction to the Response	Next Preferred Reaction to the Response
Understanding and acceptance	Expressing appreciation, soliciting support in discussions with others	No reaction
Understanding and rejection	Providing more information or persuasive arguments; willingness to negotiate	Attempting to nullify any overt opposition
Misunderstanding and rejection	Providing more information to reach understanding, hoping that understanding will lead to acceptance	Attempting to nullify any overt opposition
Misunderstanding and acceptance	Providing more information in order to reach understanding, while expressing appreciation for support	Expressing appreciation and hoping that misunderstanding does not get in the way later

Let's begin with the simplest reaction. Suppose the key person responds with understanding and accepts the suggestion. The preferred reaction is to express appreciation for support. "Thanks, Al, I appreciate your support in this matter. If I can do something for you, let me know." If the other person understands but rejects the idea you have proposed, your first reaction should be to provide more information and additional arguments. This should be done in a way that is likely to increase acceptance and not in a way that will harden the key person's present position. Sometimes this means being willing to negotiate. If the person persists in opposing the idea, the next best approach is to minimize the opposition. It is important to keep that person from convincing others to reject the suggestion.

Somewhat more complex is the situation in which the key person misunderstands and rejects at the same time. The first reaction ought to be to help the individual understand the idea. Such understanding may lead to acceptance (since the rejection may be based on misunderstanding). Of course, there is also the risk that understanding will lead to even stronger opposition.

The final situation is the most confusing in some ways. Suppose that other group members misunderstand but accept and agree. The first impulse probably is to take advantage of the agreement even if it is based on misunderstanding. There is danger here, however. The person may agree with the suggestion, vote for it, and then discover later what is really involved. A supporter can be turned into an enemy in this way. The person may feel cheated or foolish. Usually it is preferable to help the person understand your idea, even if understanding brings with it the risk of rejection.

The four possible combinations of understanding and acceptance can provide you with a framework for thinking about your possible reactions. The next step is to devise strategy based on your understanding of group process. This means devising a plan and a sequence of actions.

Strategy Decision 4: Using Group Process

In Chapters 13 and 14, we divided group process according to the time it occurred: during meetings and between meetings. This division suggests the choices which must be made in developing a strategy. Option one is to introduce a suggestion in a meeting. The second choice involves approaching key people between meetings to solicit support, to ask for suggestions to improve your idea, and to assess possible opposition.

Sometimes it is best to put the idea before a group directly. This is especially true in groups where discussions between meetings may result in negative reactions. If an idea is to be introduced at a meeting, a timing decision must be made. When in the course of the meeting should an idea be presented? In some very structured meetings, new ideas must be put forth in the segment reserved for this purpose. However, there is considerable latitude in less formally structured meetings. In many groups, the first suggestion made in a meeting does not usually get accepted. The group wants to hear two or three ideas before adopting one. Being very excited and suggesting an idea at the opening of a meeting may well result in defeat.

One useful time to make a suggestion is when a group is at a stalemate over two other ideas. If the new suggestion allows the group to get around the obstacle without hurting anyone too badly (and allowing some people to save face), it is likely to be accepted. An alert group member will sense the appropriate time to introduce an idea.

Sometimes it is useful to pave the way for introducing an idea at a meeting by approaching key people between meetings. Then the questions become, Who should be approached and in what order? Generally, groups operated on a very formal basis require that ideas be presented to the leadership before being introudced in a group meeting. In formal groups, the leader develops the agenda for meetings. An idea must be understood and accepted by the group leader before it will be brought to the members.

Less-formal groups permit discussion between meetings. In this case, the issue becomes one of choosing which leaders to approach and in what sequence. Most people decide to tell their friends or the members of their subgroup first. This solicits support. Sometimes it results in minor changes to the suggestion to make it more acceptable. Many individuals stop at this point and wait to confront the opposition at the meeting. However, by approaching the opposition, as well as persons who are neutral, before a meeting, it is possible to hear opposing opinions or arguments. In some cases, you can modify your proposal to make it stronger or more acceptable to group members who oppose it.

General strategy, then, in making a proposal to a group involves a choice between bringing the proposal to a meeting and asking for preliminary approval before the meeting. In bringing the proposal directly to the meeting, the question becomes one of deciding at what point the idea should be introduced in order to enhance the chances of positive action. If you choose to seek support before a meeting, you must choose whether to approach the leadership or the members first. If you choose the members, which ones should be sought out first? Once these choices have been made, and your strategy acted upon, you must design a message.

Strategy Decision 5: Designing the Message

Once decisions have been made about the goal or objective, about the key people, about possible reactions and responses, and about the group process, the final strategic step is to develop a message. That message must make sense to the other people in the group. It must be acceptable and useful to them.

First, assess the kind of task involved and the functions which must be fulfilled by the message. Consider this example: Maxine wants to make a change in the curriculum at St. Jude Elementary School, a private school at which she teaches. She wants the change because some students are not able to perform some arithmetic operations accurately by the time they reach the fifth grade. These are operations they should have mastered in the lower grades. The task is to improve the learning of arithmetic operations in the third and fourth grades (and maybe even in the first and second grades). The functions which must be performed are similar to those in a group problem-solving situation: defining the problem, developing criteria for a solution, identifying possible solutions, and selecting the most workable solution. Maxine must decide which of these functions she intends to fulfill in her proposal.

At a minimum, she must define the problem as she views it. Then the group can devote its efforts to further definition, to criteria, to possible solutions, and to the best solution. Maxine could go further, however. She might define the problem, set up what she thinks are the criteria, and suggest three or four possible solutions. She could let the group select the most workable solution. On the other hand, Maxine could even do the analysis and recommend the best solution.

The more Maxine does, the less the group will do. There will be less group participation if Maxine performs all the functions. This could result in criticism or rejection of her proposal. Also, if her solution is accepted, it could result in low motivation among group members. This would hinder her in implementing the solution.

Maxine must decide how much her message will include, how much she will leave to the discretion of the group. In addition, she must decide what kind of language to use in her message. This is a matter of studying the people who will receive the message. She must understand (1) their opinions on the topic and (2) the group culture. Let's examine each of these considerations.

People and Their Opinions

If the majority of the group members, and particularly the key members, are likely to be in favor of the message, Maxine can use much stronger and more emotional language. She can be highly evaluative and prescriptive if others share her attitudes. In the case of an attempted curriculum change, it is unlikely that everyone will share her ideas. Some teachers will not want to change. This usually means that the message must be descriptive, analytical, and free from evaluation. The statement, "The children are not learning what they are supposed to in the lower grades" will almost certainly raise opposition among the teachers in the lower grades. This statement will be seen as an attack on them. However, a descriptive statement can be made: "In my sixth-grade class, thirty percent of the students are not able to do long division if the numbers have more than three digits." This is a statement describing a situation. The statement can be verified. If the students should be able to do the division problems, Maxine has stated a problem which needs attention. It is now more likely to be seen as a mutual problem to be solved, not as an attack on the teachers in the lower grades.

Group Culture

The second factor to be considered is the group culture. Every group develops its own way of managing problems and issues. Each group has a language of its own. This can be heard in its use of metaphors. Some groups are like efficient engines with well-oiled parts. Others are more like families. Still others may be seen as combat infantry squads. Your message should use the metaphorical language that makes sense to the group. If Maxine's teaching staff see themselves as a family, her best approach might be to use a phrase like, "We all need to pull together, as we have in the past, to get beyond this rocky place in the road." However, if her group sees itself as a machine, the best beginning might be "In order to be as efficient as possible and not waste energy, we need to. . . ."

It is important that you hear a group's language. The group members, and leaders, need to listen to the phrases used in group meetings and between members outside of meetings. They provide clues as to how to phrase statements in ways that will appeal to group members.

Group norms and culture also dictate the extent to which a message should be direct, or phrased in ways that avoid the main issue. Some groups have great difficulty in confronting issues directly. In such a group, to bring up a problem directly might result in failure. Some groups thrive on confrontation and directness. In either case, the message should be appropriate to the way the group functions.

Cultural norms will also dictate the level and kind of abstraction appropriate for a message. The person making a proposal or seeking an answer must take this factor into account. Sometimes an abstract statement is better: "Long division is an important math skill." Then the group can work its way to more concrete statements. Sometimes the specific statement can be made immediately: "Thirty percent of the students in my afternoon class cannot complete long division problems accurately." Decisions about the degree of abstraction should be based on listening to and sensing the preferences of the group involved.

The group member and the leader need to listen to the language the group members use in messages. Designing a message involves listening. It involves thinking about the functions to be fulfilled and the group culture in which the message will be heard. Both of these factors influence the effectiveness of the message.

SUMMARY

Completing work successfully in a group requires making strategy decisions. The first step is to set a goal about what needs to be completed. A knowledge of group structure will provide an analysis of the key persons in the group as well as information about interest groups or other subgroups which may exist. Based on this information, it is possible to predict the responses of these key individuals to the suggestion or proposal you will present. Responses can be classified according to the degrees of agreement and understanding. Once possible responses have been determined, it is possible to prepare your reactions. Your reactions may range from "Thank you for understanding and accepting," to "Let me explain it in more detail."

Analyzing group process will be helpful to you in deciding whether to introduce your idea during a meeting or between meetings. A related choice is whether to approach the leader or the members first. Once these basic strategy decisions are made, you can design a message which takes into account the functions of the group and the group culture and norms. When strategy decisions have been made carefully, the usual result is a message that has maximum success.

REFLECTING/EXPLORING

1. Observe a meeting of a group in an organization or in the community. Note the points in the discussion where ideas are not received positively by the group. Review the five strategy decisions. What advice might you give the individuals whose ideas were not accepted?

2. Review the five strategy decisions as you think about the most recent experience you have had in presenting an idea to a group. Was the presentation positively received? Which of the five strategy decisions did you use? If your presentation was rejected, what might you do to improve in making and following through on the five strategy decisions?

3. Observe a problem-solving discussion. After the problem has been defined, criteria have been identified, and several possible solutions have been named, predict the responses of key people. Use the discussion of possible responses on page 232, and the sample form on page 233. Develop what you believe might be effective reactions to the responses of the key people. Use the table on page 234. When the discussion is finished, check the accuracy of your predictions.

4. Observe a meeting of your city commission. Obtain the agenda for the meeting before the meeting. Select one agenda item and use this chapter to guide you in making decisions in the five strategy categories that would help you succeed if you actually were presenting this agenda item to the city commission. After the meeting, review how successful your choices might have been. Think about what you would change and how you would change it.

5. Using your family or a group of close friends, plan how you will present a proposal to them that you believe will receive opposition. Follow this chapter in making your strategy decisions. Then present the plan or idea and evaluate how effectively you made the decisions.

SECTION SIX: READING LIST

Information about group functions and messages in groups:

Farb, P. *Word Play: What Happens When People Talk.* New York: Alfred A. Knopf, 1974.

Frank, A. D. *Communicating on the Job.* Glenview, IL: Scott, Foresman and Company, 1982.

Gouran, D. S. *Making Decisions in Groups: Choices and Consequences.* Glenview, IL: Scott, Foresman and Company, 1982.

Hunt, G. T. *Communication Skills in the Organization.* Englewood Cliffs, N. J.: Prentice-Hall, Inc., 1980.

PROCEDURES AND LEADERSHIP

19

ORGANIZING
PROCEDURES

Every group uses procedures to complete its work. Sometimes the procedures that are used are not planned—they just "happen." However, even when there is no planning, a series of events occur: something is done first, something else is done second, and so forth. When procedures are not planned, there may be repetition of efforts. Or time may be spent in discussing issues or topics that do not apply to the desired end product. In any event, a sequence of events occurs. This sequence could even be charted on paper so that a group could observe its procedures.

We believe it is important to understand the direction in which your group wishes to move. This direction is usually toward a goal or a completed product of an objective, describable nature. Next, we believe it is important to know how to determine the most effective and efficient method or procedure to follow in reaching the goal or solution, or in completing the product. The purpose of these next three chapters is to assist you in making these determinations.

Some groups adapt their procedures from a traditional, time-proven source: parliamentary procedure. Other groups develop procedures in creative ways that work especially well for their particular group or for a specific task assigned to their group. In this chapter, we will help you understand three kinds of procedures frequently used by groups: (1) an agenda-guided discussion, (2) a problem- or item-list procedure, and (3) simplified parliamentary procedure. We will also discuss the use of problem-solving methods and basic planning procedures in this chapter. In Chapter 20, we will discuss specialized procedures that are available to you. Finally, in Chapter 21, we will explore the role of the leader and the characteristics of leadership. It is leadership that is needed if a group is going to define its task clearly and select a procedure for achieving that task successfully.

In this chapter, we will introduce you to three kinds of group procedures. These are procedures for organizing your regular meetings. We call these *basic procedures* because they form the most fundamental first step toward an intentionally organized approach. Next, we will help you understand procedures that are especially useful if your group is assigned a problem-solving or a planning task. Finally, we will provide you with a set of procedures for planning in a group setting. This chapter, then, includes:

1. Three basic procedures for organizing a group meeting: the agenda-guided discussion, the problem or item list, and simplified parliamentary procedure

2. A five-step problem-solving procedure

3. A five-step planning procedure

Organizing a Group Meeting

There are three basic procedures to use in organizing a meeting. You can use them to provide an organization or system for the work of your group no matter what the goal of your group is. These three methods are a first step away from no organization or system at all. They are a step away from the group meeting that is characterized by informal talk that has no direction. Adopting one of these three basic procedures is a very important step for a group to take. Because they provide a basic system for organizing talk, these procedures will help a group put order into discussion topics. They will help a group learn to function in an organized fashion. We will discuss the following three basic procedures, from the least to the most formal:

1. Agenda-guided discussion

2. Problem or item list

3. Simplified parliamentary procedure

Let's begin with the least-formal procedure, the agenda-guided discussion.

The Agenda-guided Discussion

An agenda is simply the topics to be discussed at a meeting. A meeting guided by an agenda follows a list of the important topics for discussion. These topics are normally listed in the order of importance or in the order in which tasks must be completed in order to finish the work. This is the least formal of the procedures we will present here. It is suitable for task forces or work teams that must complete projects or maintain programs. It is particularly useful for teams of professionals or highly skilled technical personnel. An example of an agenda for a small research team of fine persons is shown here:

C.M.S. IMAGE RESEARCH TEAM. MEETING: NOON, TUESDAY, 15 JANUARY.

Agenda

1. *Replacement for Bobbie?* Suggestions? Do we need a replacement?

2. *Questionnaire.* We have budgeted $80 for printing the questionnaire.

Should we use our print shop or go outside for estimates? Does anyone have a printing contact where we can get inexpensive but quality work?

3. *Statistical analyses.* We have not yet discussed the kinds of statistics we will use to process the questionnaire data. A plan is needed. We must decide what we want. We must make plans for computer time, data entry, and processing.

4. *Editing and phrasing the research purpose and goals.* We have postponed final decisions for three months. We need to decide the final language for purpose and goals. Who will take on this task and report to us on suggestions for final wording?

5. *Other.* Anything else you think needs to be discussed by the team before we distribute the questionnaires.

Consider the first item on the agenda: Replacement for Bobbie? The item is worded casually. There is little explanation. Members of the team are expected to know that Bobbie has left. The current problem is whether or not the team needs a replacement for her, and, if so, who? This will be discussed at the team meeting. A decision will be made about whether or not a replacement is needed. Then the group will proceed to the next item on the agenda. This mode of operation continues until all of the items on the agenda are completed. It is one step more formal than a casual discussion or a social gathering. Structure for the meeting is provided by the agenda. Sometimes a group will rearrange the order of the agenda at the meeting. There may or may not be a logical relationship between one item and another.

To help you understand what occurs in an agenda-guided discussion, the "minutes" for the C.M.S. Image Research Team are presented here:

CMS IMAGE RESEARCH TEAM. MINUTES FOR THE MEETING OF 15 JANUARY

1. No replacement for Bobbie needed. Carl will assume computer responsibilities for the present. Cheryl will develop a data-entry format once we have finished the questionnaire format.

2. Bill will obtain an estimate from Thrifty Printing.

3. We agreed on the following statistical analyses:

   a. Compute mean, median, and mode on each item in Sections I and II.

   b. Examine distribution of ratings to identify items where mean, median, and mode may not truly represent the variety of opinions (compute variance, standard deviation).

   c. Perform factor analysis to see if the resulting factor structure can be used for developing recommendations for image programs.

   d. Use demographic variables to determine if there are major differences among respondents based on demographic characteristics. (Note: variables are yet to be determined.)

4. Cheryl agreed to write a proposed statement of the research purpose and goals and circulate it to team members before our next meeting.

5. No other items of business.

Next meeting: Conference Room. 29 January at 1:00 P.M.

See you there! Be on time!

Jim

These are relatively informal notes and agreements. The minutes (record) of a meeting may be written with varying degrees of formality. They include the topics discussed, action taken, and responsibilities assigned to various committee members with due dates noted. When these specifics are put in writing, the group can refer to the minutes at the next meeting and follow up on its progress. Minutes usually end with the time and location of the next meeting. For many groups, an agenda-guided discussion procedure creates the only form of organization needed for the group to work successfully. As indicated earlier, groups that succeed with this simple form of organization usually include highly technical personnel or professional people who work well together and who understand most of the parts of the task to be accomplished. If there is less similarity among group members, less mutual understanding of the total task, or a high degree of subgrouping, a more formal procedure may be useful.

The Problem or Item List

A more formal procedure than the agenda-guided discussion is used in many business organizations when a project is to be accomplished by several subgroups or work units. A list of possible problems that must be solved in order to finish a task is the first requirement. A meeting is held at which a list is made of all of these items. Each item is numbered sequentially, based on the order in which it must be completed. This list guides the group and the discussion at group meetings for the rest of the project. The following meeting agenda forms part of the problem list of a coordinating group in an industrial organization. The agenda is for a meeting midway through a project called Project MBX.

PROJECT MBX COORDINATING COMMITTEE MEETING: 12 OCTOBER

Agenda
Items 1 through 23: Resolved.

24. *Gearbox Retrofit.* Supplier of the gearbox is behind schedule. We may have to change our schedule to accommodate the supplier. *Responsibility:* Drive-train design group.

25. Resolved.

26. Resolved.

27. *Performance Testing.* Several test fixtures are showing signs of wear. One dynamometer calibration has been questioned by the customer. *Responsibility:* Performance test group.

28. Resolved.

29. *Weld Failures.* Structural testing of the MBX has resulted in 12 failures of welds. There apparently is no pattern to the failures. They are occurring in different locations and the welds have been made by different machines and operators. *Responsibility:* Manufacturing.

30. *NEW ITEM: Mod II Design.* MBX Model II design is forty percent complete with initial drawings going to manufacturing and quality control this week. A final production schedule needs to be established. *Responsibility:* MBX Model II Project group.

Since the Project MBX is ongoing, the list now consists of items 24 through 30 (with the exception of 25, 26, and 28 which have been resolved). There are four active problem areas: 24, 27, 29, and 30. Item 30 is a new item added for this meeting. Note that the agenda indicates which group has the primary responsibility for the unresolved items.

At the meeting of the coordinating committee, the project manager or team leader will start the discussion by asking for a report from the leader of the drive-train design group. If the gearbox retrofix problem has been resolved, item 24 will be dropped from the agenda. In the agenda for the next meeting, item 24 will not appear. Items 25 and 26 will also be dropped since they have been resolved in past meetings. It is possible that a new item 31 might be added.

As we indicated earlier, this kind of procedure is common in business and industrial settings. However, it can be used in any group that must monitor a project or program from its beginning through completion. It is especially useful when a number of work units or subgroups involved and the work of these groups must be coordinated in order to complete the program or project successfully.

While the problem- or item-list procedure is more formal than the agenda-guided discussion, there is a still more formal basic procedure: simplified parliamentary procedure.

Simplified Parliamentary Procedure

The most formal of the three basic meeting formats is parliamentary procedure. Parliamentary procedure can be used in a very strict form. It can also be used in a simplified version. Many groups simplify parliamentary procedure by following these five steps:

1. Someone asks that an item of business be discussed. (This is called *making a motion.*)

2. Another person must agree that the item needs to be discussed before the item of business is put before the group. (This is called *seconding the motion.*)

3. Once the motion is seconded, the item is *on the floor*. This means the topic can be discussed. In most simplified versions of parliamentary procedure, suggestions are made and discussed informally. Individuals speak in turn and may not be called upon by the leader before they talk.

4. If changes in the original motion are extensive, someone makes a motion to amend the original motion. Another person must second the motion to amend. If the motion is seconded, it is read aloud and voted on. Usually it passes because the group has reached consensus or agreement that the change should be made in the wording. In simplified parliamentary procedure, formal amendments to the motion are usually not made. The person who made the original motion (called the *main motion*) informally accepts the suggestion for a change in the wording. (This is called a *friendly amendment.*) A friendly amendment provides a revision without following the formal process of making, seconding, and voting on the motion to amend. It is used most often in small groups when there is agreement and when parliamentary procedure is being used mainly to provide an official record of decisions.

5. The motion as amended is voted on. If the motion has not been amended, or if an amendment was made and does not receive support, the original or main motion is voted upon.

Some groups do not structure their discussion formally by using agendas and parliamentary procedure. After discussing an issue informally, these groups may put the group consensus into a formal motion. Then a second is asked for and the motion is voted on. The vote makes the motion a matter of record.

Other groups follow a more formal version of parliamentary procedure. They also use an agenda that has a standardized format. It is called the *order of business.* The business for a specific meeting is simply filled in on the standard format. Here is an example of the order of business and the specific agenda for a meeting of a public commission:

COMMISSION ON RENOVATED HOUSING
MEETING OF 21 APRIL

Agenda

1. Call to order

2. Minutes of the last meeting

3. Reports of standing committees

    a. Committee on financial liaison

    b. Committee on historical districts

    c. Committee on Elm Street project

4. Old business

    a. Development of a planning process for local neighborhoods

    b. Listing of cooperating financial institutions

5. New business

    a. Publicity and public relations need of the commission

    b. Other new business from the floor

6. Announcements

    a. Historical homes tour

    b. Next meeting

7. Adjournment

These items are the standard parts of the formal order of business. Under item 2, minutes of the previous meeting are normally approved. This is especially true of formal groups that have legal standing (boards of trustees, public commissions). The next step involves a series of reports from committees that exist on an ongoing basis. They are called *standing committees.* In some groups, reports from officers are listed in this section. After committee reports, old business is discussed one item at a time. Action is taken on each item before moving to the next. New business is the last major part of a formal agenda. The meeting usually concludes with announcements and a formal adjournment.

A number of clearly written handbooks exist that are devoted to parliamentary procedure. You will find several listed in the reading list of this section. The purpose in using the formal rules of parliamentary procedure is to ensure that all members have a fair and equal opportunity to express their views. Either the group leader or the person appointed as parliamentarian must understand the rules. Formal parliamentary procedure is often used in large public meetings such as meetings of a city commission. The use of these rules provide for orderliness and fairness. They make actions taken by the group a matter of official record.

Sometimes a group is faced with work that involves problem solving or planning. Agenda-guided procedures, item-list procedures, and simplified parliamentary procedure may be helpful. However, there also are specific procedures that can be used for problem solving and planning. These will be considered in the next two sections of this chapter. We will consider the problem-solving procedures first.

Problem-solving Procedures

There are ways to approach a problem that will increase the chances of reaching a workable solution. However, no method can guarantee success. There are five steps in the basic problem-solving procedure:

1. Defining the problem

2. Setting criteria for evaluating solutions

3. Identifying possible solutions

4. Selecting the most workable solution

5. Describing potential difficulties that may arise after the solution is implemented

Defining the Problem

How a group defines the problem usually determines the outcome of a problem-solving session. We will illustrate this principle with two examples.

Problem 1. First, a committee in a local school district was assigned the problem of how to remove the leaves from the lawns at three schools that were located in heavily wooded areas. Each fall, the school district spent $10,000 raking, transporting, and disposing of leaves. The committee listed possible solutions. For example, some or all of the leaves could be burned, but there were problems of air pollution and fire hazard. The district could buy some modern equipment to blow the leaves into rows and then vacuum them. Several other solutions were proposed to solve the problem of leaf removal.

Then someone said, "What if the problem is not removing the leaves? Instead, let's look at them as a resource rather than a waste. Is there some way we could *use* all of these leaves?" In other words, the problem may not be one of disposal, but of use. This resulted in a barrage of suggestions. One member voiced the possibility of mulching flower beds and shrubs with the leaves. Another suggested a compost heap which could be used to demonstrate some facts about science and agriculture to students. The way you define the problem will directly affect the type of solutions that are proposed.

Problem 2. Another classic example was given by Russell Ackoff in his book, *The Art of Problem Solving.* Here is an explanation of the problem. A new office building had been erected and was fully occupied. Within a few months, there were several complaints about slow elevators. Both clients and workers were complaining. The building manager consulted elevator specialists. One suggested installing a computer-controlled elevator system which would respond to demands at peak hours in more efficient ways. This would cost an estimated $10,000. Another consultant suggested installing extra elevators on one end of the building—at a cost of over $40,000. The owners of the building rejected both ideas.

The building manager called in an acquaintance who was renowned for his problem-solving skills. The man spent a morning in the building and then went to the building manager. He said, "I think I can solve your problem for about $1,000." "How?" asked the building manager. "Quite simply. The problem is not the elevators. You need to install mirrors on each floor right next to the elevator doors so people can adjust their clothing and check their appearance. You also need to post a copy of the front page of the morning newspaper and the front page of the sports section of the paper. Put them next to each elevator." The idea was used. Complaints dropped to almost none. The problem was not slow elevators. It was people with nothing to do while they were waiting.

Clearly, a group must define the problem in a way that will result in the most effective solution. This involves creativity. It is difficult to prescribe a standard way to work creatively. However, one rule is that a group always should look for the problem behind the problem: leaves as a resource rather than waste, the boredom of people rather than the response time of elevators. It is important to look for the problem behind the obvious problem.

Evaluating Solutions

A second important step in problem solving is describing the criteria against which solutions will be evaluated. The group must specify whether time, money, or some other factors are important in deciding whether the final solution is workable. These criteria may be based on technical considerations that are provided by experts. They may be based on the needs of interest groups (those needs may be described by the representatives of the interest groups). In part, the criteria will depend on how the problem is defined. A discussion of criteria usually will lead to a discussion of possible solutions. The two are intimately connected.

Identifying Possible Solutions

As a basic rule, the more possible solutions that can be identified, the greater the possibility of finding one that will work. A chemical company was faced with the problem of removing a powdered fungicide from bags into the mixing tank of water on a tractor. It was important to prevent the powder from floating in the air because it might be inhaled by the farmer driving the tractor. The chemical was potentially dangerous. In a period of slightly less than a week, the project team had identified over 100 ways to move the chemical from the bag and into the water without pouring it. One of the more obvious ways was to use a water-soluble bag and throw the whole bag into the tank. Unfortunately, water-soluble bags fall apart in rain or when highly humid conditions prevail!

A variety of solutions provides a wide range of choices. It also increases the chances of finding one outstanding answer. In addition, if more solutions exist, there is a better opportunity to find several solutions that might be combined into one superior method.

Selecting the Most Workable Solution

Once the solutions and the criteria for evaluating them are determined, each solution can be tested against the criteria. By definition, the answer that best meets all of the needs and demands listed in the criteria will be the best solution. Sometimes one solution emerges clearly as the most workable. At other times, two or three solutions all seem to be appropriate. If this occurs, additional criteria must be defined, or the group may decide to choose one solution based on a hunch or a feeling for the problem. The latter approach is less rational, but sometimes results in a good solution. Group members may have lived with the problem long enough that they have a feeling for what will work, but cannot seem to put it into words or state their feelings as criteria.

To get the potentially dangerous chemical from the bag to the mixing tank (the problem discussed earlier) the engineering team finally picked an unusual and little-known solution. Water flowing past an opening in a tube or pipe actually can create suction if everything is designed properly. The engineers decided to suck the chemical out of the bag using the energy from the water flowing in and out of the mixing tank of the tractor.

Predicting Problems

After a solution has been selected, the group is well-advised to spend time imagining how it will work. The group must think through the implications of their solution. Sometimes there are problems which can be predicted and avoided ahead of time. Experienced problem solvers know that every solution brings one or more further problems with it. What are they? Can they be predicted and prevented or circumvented? The group needs to consider this issue.

Once a group completes a problem-solving sequence, they must implement their solution. This usually involves creating a schedule, deciding on a budget, and assigning tasks. It takes planning to implement most solutions. Procedures that a group can use for planning are discussed in the next section.

Planning Procedures

It takes deliberate planning for a group to develop a work schedule, a budget, and the assignment of the tasks involved in implementing a solution. Furthermore, team members are most likely to understand and accept their assignment, their budget limitations, and their due dates if they have been involved in the planning process. Therefore, we will provide you with a simple set of procedures to use for planning in a group setting.

There are five steps in the basic planning procedure:

1. Defining goals and objectives

2. Listing necessary activities or materials

3. Scheduling activities and deadlines for materials

4. Assigning tasks

5. Budgeting costs

Defining Goals and Objectives

The first step is to define the intended outcome. That usually means stating goals and objectives. Goals are broadly stated intentions: "we need to finish the publicity project." Objectives are specific statements often worded in measurable terms: "we need to mail one thousand brochures." A plan is directed toward a goal or objective. Sometimes a plan is centered around a group of related goals and objectives. The members of a group must define these. The group may wish to write statements of goals and objectives in a meeting of the whole. Sometimes this task is assigned to an individual or a subgroup.

Listing Necessary Activities or Materials

Once the goals and objectives are identified, the next step is to convert them into a detailed list of what must be done or obtained in order to accomplish the project. For example, if a group is going to prepare a four-page, two-color publicity brochure, the following activities would be listed:

1. A logo must be designed.

2. A title or theme for the brochure must be created.

3. Written copy must be prepared.

4. A design for the brochure must be created.

5. Pictures or illustrations must be drawn.

In addition to these activities, materials must be made available. There must be paper on which to print the brochure. Arrangements must be made to set type and print the five hundred brochures. Every planning process requires that the planners specify in detail what is needed to finish the task or project. Something will be missing when it is needed if a list of activities and materials is not prepared.

Scheduling Activities and Deadlines

The next logical step is to develop a schedule. This is simply a chart that shows when the various activities must be completed or when materials must be available. Wise planners usually work back from deadlines. That is, they start with the completion date for the whole project. Suppose the brochures in our example must be mailed by 15 February. The planner must know how long it will take to print the brochures once the final copy is delivered to the printer. If this takes two weeks, the material must be ready for printing at least two weeks before the due date for mailing. Obviously, copy cannot be created instantaneously. Therefore, the planner must estimate the length of time it will take to design, write, edit, typeset, proofread, and correct the copy and to take and develop pictures. For each activity that must be completed, a time period is noted.

A simple but effective schedule chart is shown below.

BROCHURE SCHEDULE

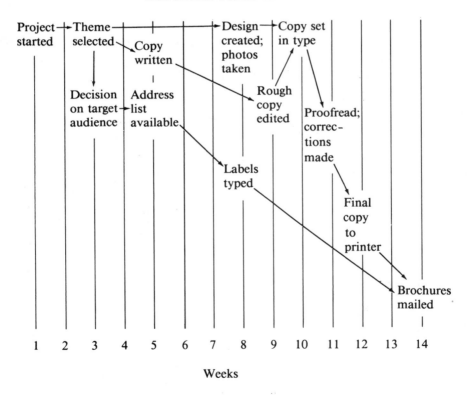

Weeks

Starting with the mailing date for the brochures, the schedule shows that 14 weeks will be needed to complete the various tasks: selecting a theme, deciding on a target audience, writing copy, compiling the address list, creating the design and taking photographs, typing labels, editing the rough copy, typesetting final copy, proofreading, correcting, and printing.

Assigning Tasks

Another important document is based on the schedule chart: the task-assignment chart. Here is an example.

BROCHURE TASK-ASSIGNMENT CHART

Activity	Due Date	Assigned to	Comments
Theme selection	3 weeks after start	Publicity committee	
Decision on target audience	3 weeks after start	Whole commission	
Copy written	5 weeks after start	Rebecca Stone	
Address list available	5 weeks after start	George Northhouse	
Design created; photos taken	8 weeks after start	Jan Cary	
Labels typed	8 weeks after start	Typing service	
Rough copy rewritten and edited	9 weeks after start	Bill MaGuire	
Copy set in type	10 weeks after start	Wordgraphics Inc.	
Proofreading and correcting	11 weeks after start	Ted Green	
Final copy to printer	12 weeks after start	Whole Earth Printing Co.	
Brochures mailed	14 weeks after start	Mailing service	

The scheduled activities are listed together with due dates and the name of the person or group responsible for each activity. Tasks can be assigned, or sometimes people volunteer for assignments. In either case, the people responsible for each task know what they are expected to do and when they must complete their tasks.

The assignment chart can be an effective tool in group meetings. Here is a task-assignment chart as it might look halfway through a project.

BROCHURE TASK-ASSIGNMENT CHART

Activity	Due Date	Assigned to	Comments
Theme selection	3 weeks	Publicity committee	done
Decision on target audience	3 weeks	Whole commission	done
Copy written	5 weeks	Rebecca Stone	done—3 days late
Address list available	5 weeks	George Northhouse	We were one week late on this. Lack of cooperation from national headquarters.
Design created; photos taken	8 weeks	Jon Cary	started
Labels typed	8 weeks	Typing service	Typing service notified of delay in address list— may be able to do job in one week
Rough copy rewritten and edited	9 weeks	Bill McGuire	started
Copy set in type	10 weeks	Wordgraphics	waiting for copy
Proofreading and correcting	11 weeks	Ted Green	waiting for copy
Final copy to printer	12 weeks	Whole Earth Printing, Co.	waiting for copy
Brochures mailed	14 weeks	Mailing service	probable delay of one week due to problem with address list

The assignment chart can be used to assess progress and to identify problems so that solutions can be proposed quickly. At each meeting, the task-assignment chart should be reviewed. People can give progress reports on their assigned tasks. The chart becomes an agenda for the meeting and a way of keeping a record ("minutes") of the meeting. It also serves as a general communication tool that provides everyone with a current understanding of the status of the project.

Budgeting Costs

The final step in the planning process is to develop a budget that shows both the predicted and the actual costs. Each activity and every set of materials that will cost something must be built into the budget. In our example of the publicity brochure, the following items would normally involve costs: buying the address list, typing labels, designing the brochure and taking photographs, typesetting, and printing. In addition, the editor might be an outsider who must be paid for the service. The budget would look like this:

PUBLICITY BROCHURE BUDGET

Item	Estimated Cost	Actual cost
Address list	$ 35.00	
Typing labels	75.00	
Editing	50.00	
Design	150.00	
Typesetting	100.00	
Printing	250.00	
Total	$660.00	

As work on the project progresses, actual costs can be entered in the right-hand column so that everyone knows whether the project is being completed within the budgeted amount. Suppose that the delay in obtaining the address list for the brochure results in the typing service having to hire additional typists, use higher-paid but faster typists, or pay overtime. The cost for typing might increase to $100 and the total project would increase to $685—$25 over the original estimate. If this increase in cost is noted at the time it occurs, adjustments might be possible elsewhere in the budget. In that case, the project can be brought in within the $660 allocated.

Taken together, the five steps involved in planning produce a set of documents that can be used in meetings as the agenda and as a way to assess progress toward project completion. By keeping these documents current, the team keeps itself informed and ensures maximum involvement for each person assigned to a task. Planning procedures, problem-solving procedures, and the three methods of organizing a meeting can be used by a group to function successfully on a meeting-by-meeting basis.

In the next chapter, we will provide you with some special techniques to meet specific challenges within your meetings. Then, in Chapter 21, we will present the leadership functions that will help make these procedures work for you.

SUMMARY

All groups use procedures in conducting meetings. The simplest and least formal method is the agenda-guided discussion. This procedure is appropriate for small groups of professionals or for technical experts. In some cases, a problem- or item-list procedure is used. This is particularly helpful in coordinating large projects or programs. Groups also can use a simplified form of parliamentary procedure for conducting an orderly meeting in a somewhat formal way.

When a group meeting is focused on a problem-solving task, a standard form of problem solving is useful. The standard format involves five steps: (1) defining the problem, (2) setting criteria for evaluating solutions, (3) identifying possible solutions, (4) selecting the most workable solution, and (5) describing potential difficulties that may arise after the solution is implemented.

Planning is another important function in most groups. Once a solution is identified, implementing it usually involves planning. A procedure is available for planning. It, too, involves five steps: (1) setting goals and objectives, (2) creating an activities or materials list, (3) scheduling, (4) assigning tasks, and (5) budgeting costs. If these planning steps are followed by a group, all members will be aware of and understand the overall plan.

REFLECTING/EXPLORING

1. Analyze an announcement of the next meeting of one of your groups. If it is only an announcement of the meeting time and place, create what you think might be an effective agenda or problem list for the meeting. If an agenda or problem list is included with the announcement, add items that you believe should be included. Use the agenda or item list to make notes on each topic so that you are prepared for the meeting. How does your preparation prior to a meeting affect your participation in the meeting?

2. Observe or participate in a meeting in which parliamentary procedure is used. Use the simplified format on pages 247 and 248 to guide you. Record any questions you have about the use of parliamentary procedure. Obtain one of the handbooks listed in the reading list for this section.

3. Use the five steps in the problem-solving procedure. For a group that you observe or one in which you participate, follow these steps to outline a problem that will be the topic of the group meeting. Each member can use these steps prior to the meeting to prepare by recording individual

responses to the issue raised in each step. Take your homework to the meeting. How does this preparation affect your involvement as either a group member or an observer?

4. Repeat activity 3. This time, focus on the five-step planning procedure described on page 253. Outline your individual responses to each step prior to the meeting so that you will be prepared to share your viewpoints with the group.

5. Agencies of city governments often conduct problem-solving and planning sessions in private meetings and announce the results in public meetings. Use the procedures you have worked with in activities 3 and 4 to analyze one or more decisions of your city commission. At a meeting of the city commission, raise the points that will help you understand the full process the commission used in private meetings. For example: "I understand that you are recommending this approach. I would be interested in knowing the criteria you used to arrive at this solution. I'd also like to know two other possible solutions that were in competition with this one prior to your final decision."

CHAPTER 20

PRODUCTIVE COMMUNICATION

The procedures discussed in Chapter 19 are primarily intended to help group members and leaders organize their tasks. By using these procedures, tasks can be completed very efficiently and effectively. The resources of time, energy, and materials will be conserved and the end product will fit the needs of the group.

This chapter introduces three additional procedures for helping group members and leaders work together successfully. These three procedures are designed to promote productive communication in a group setting. The three procedures include (1) brainstorming, (2) the nominal group technique, and (3) the delphi method.

Each of these procedures has certain characteristics that make it especially useful in a particular situation. *Brainstorming* is a method of identifying ideas. It can be used in combination with the problem-solving technique, for example, to generate a large number of possible criteria against which to evaluate solutions. It can also be used to provide a long list of possible solutions. The *nominal group technique* is a set of rules that is useful in directing group interaction into productive channels. The *delphi method,* another set of rules, is designed for problem solving. One attractive feature of this method is that it can be used to complete group tasks without the necessity of bringing the participants together in a face-to-face meeting.

The rules of each procedure should be followed consistently and systematically. Doing so results in a meeting that seems relatively formal. In some groups, the rules are followed strictly one time and modified, simplified, or discarded at other times. The judgment of the leader and the typical ways group members interact are factors to consider in deciding how closely to stay within the rules as we have described them.

The chapter is divided into three sections. Each section will be devoted to one of these three procedures or sets of rules. Remember that they are designed to promote communication within your group.

Brainstorming

The purpose of brainstorming is to generate as many creative and innovative ideas as possible. Alex Osborn, who developed this procedure, set forth the following general rules for brainstorming:

1. Criticism is ruled out. Both positive and negative evaluation of ideas must be withheld during the brainstorming session.

2. "Free-wheeling" is encouraged. The wilder the idea, the better—it is easier to tame down than to think up an idea.

3. Quantity is encouraged. The greater the number of ideas, the greater the likelihood that several ideas will be workable.

4. Combinations of ideas are encouraged. The participants may combine two or more stated ideas in still another idea.

5. "Hitchhiking" is encouraged. This involves suggesting an idea similar to, or triggered by, someone else's idea.

During the brainstorming session, one person records all the ideas so that everyone can see them. A chalkboard, pieces of paper, or an overhead projector may be used.

The brainstorming session is over when all of the available ideas appear to be recorded. Usually a long silent pause will occur, indicating that group participants have exhausted their sources of ideas. At this point, twenty to forty ideas may have been listed in as little as twenty minutes. Here is a partial list of ideas suggested by a group of people who were asked to brainstorm about better bathtubs:

"padded tubs . . ."

"an automatic bath-oil dispenser . . ."

"a soap dispenser built into the water flow . . ."

"perfumed water . . ."

"an underwater audio system . . ."

"an underwater light system . . ."

"a built-in telephone . . ."

"a built-in television set . . ."

"a television monitor that watches the kids . . ."

"a built-in electric heater . . ."

"a built-in whirlpool . . ."

"a built-in martini dispenser . . ."

"an agitator to massage . . ."

"an automatic body dryer . . ."

"an automatic self-cleaner for the tub . . ."

"an automatic self-cleaner for the person . . ."

"an automatic back scrubber . . ."

Notice how some of these ideas seem to play off the previous idea, while others are different from the preceding thought. You may find yourself laughing at some of the ideas. Brainstorming often stimulates wildly funny alternatives. It can be fun to participate. Those who feel insecure or foolish about participating may find themselves joining in the brainstorming process when the focus is on quantity rather than quality, and on ideas rather than people. On the other hand, it may be difficult to use this technique if someone is present who is likely to frown on wild ideas or on having fun while conducting serious business.

In the past, brainstorming was used only in face-to-face group meetings. However, it can be used at great distances as well. One person may begin by writing down a series of ideas and then giving or sending them to another person who continues the process by adding to the list. The process continues until everyone involved has had an opportunity to make suggestions.

Note that brainstorming is an informal procedure, yet it gives shape to a meeting. It is not intended to be formal. In fact, formality may limit creativity and innovation. A major advantage of brainstorming is that ideas are not associated with the persons presenting them. This facilitates candid evaluation of ideas. A major difficulty with brainstorming is that it produces ideas without screening them. Effective solutions to problems usually have been screened, tested, and evaluated. Brainstorming does not provide for this. For this reason, brainstorming is often used as the first step in an overall problem-solving process.

The Nominal Group Technique

The rules of the nominal group technique were deliberately designed to overcome problems that occur in group interaction. The net effect of using this method is reduced interaction. It may be productive to limit face-to-face communication for a variety of reasons. For example, one participant may have an undue amount of influence over others. The influential person may be a high-ranking official or someone with a great deal of expertise. In another situation, one or more people may have strong vested interests, emotionally or politically, that result in avoiding rather than tackling the main issue. Such problems may be managed by using the nominal group technique. The steps involved are:

1. Each person writes down ideas, options, or solutions privately without discussing them with others. (This can be done before the group meeting.)

2. The results of step 1 are presented to the group by each person in a procedure known as the *round robin*. Each person presents his or her ideas in sequence. There is no discussion. The ideas are written down on a chalkboard or large sheet of paper so that everyone can see them.

3. After all the ideas are out, anyone may ask another person for clarification of an idea or proposal. However, at this point, there is no evaluation, no discussion, and no debate for the purpose of arriving at a sense of agreement or disagreement.

4. Each person ranks the various proposed solutions privately. The results are tallied to determine the relative support for each idea.

When these rules are followed strictly, this technique is quite effective. Notice that discussion is minimized and, in contrast to brainstorming, group members do the idea generating and idea ranking in private.

As an example of the way the nominal group technique works, consider the following simplified example from a real situation. A group of four professionals were involved in project management. Each person was responsible for two to five separate projects. Each project required a monthly progress report. Over the past six months, the reports had been late and, in some cases, inadequate. Rather than try to fix blame, the four people decided to use the nominal group technique to come up with a solution. Here, in edited form, is what happened in the round robin:

TED: I think we should use a standard format for the progress reports. Then all we would have to do is sort of fill in the blanks each month. The format would be able to handle all of our projects.

SARA: My idea is to have one person do all of the progress reports. Select the person who is best at it and willing to do it.

AL: I think it would be best if Ginny [the secretary] would simply give us a copy of the last progress report on each project ten days before the current one was due. Then we could use it as a model for the current one. That would eliminate the need for us to dig them out of the file each month.

DEE: A simple solution would be to have Ginny draft the progress report based on past samples for each project. Then we could fill in details and she could type of the final version of each report for our signatures.

Step 1 is complete when each person has presented one idea. The second step is clarification.

AL: Ted, I don't understand your standard format idea. How would you do that?

TED: The way I see it, we all have to report dollars expended, dollars left, person-hours expended by category, and milestones achieved for each project. Well, we could create a format that would include the dollar amount columns and person-hours plus a section for milestones. Then it would require only filling in the blanks, instead of starting from scratch.

AL: But it seems to me that wouldn't work.

DEE: Al, we're not supposed to discuss or evaluate. Just listen and try to understand.

In step 3, the group members rank the four ideas. Here are the results:

1. The idea proposed by Ted: 2,3,3,4

2. The idea proposed by Sara: 3,4,4,4

3. The idea proposed by Al: 1,2,2,3

4. The idea proposed by Dee: 1,1,1,2

The idea presented by Dee was clearly ranked above all the others. But the idea offered by Al received some support. Therefore, the group decided to combine the two ideas: Have Ginny run a copy of last month's report and draft the current month's report based on the last one.

A variation of the nominal group technique is sometimes used, resulting in this six-step procedure:

1. Each person writes down ideas in private.

2. Ideas are presented in the round robin.

3. Clarification is sought and provided.

4. Ideas which are similar, or actually overlap, can be combined to reduce the number of possibilities. But no ideas can be eliminated. Ideas can be combined only with the agreement of their presenters.

5. Each person ranks the ideas privately.

6. The averaged rankings for the ideas are circulated to group members who then rerank them based on the averages. (This is called the *delphi method* and will be discussed next.)

The major differences here include the possibility of combining ideas and the ranking of them at the end.

In contrast to brainstorming, the nominal group technique is quite formal. It requires the leader and members to adhere to the procedure without deviation. By cutting down on discussion and interaction, informal exchanges are eliminated. All the steps are directed to arriving at a solution or answer. Any discussion defeats the purpose of the technique by allowing social and interpersonal factors to influence the presentation and evaluation of ideas.

The nominal group technique affects groups in three ways:

1. Meetings can be relatively short because people can list their ideas before the group meeting. They also rank ideas in private after the meeting.

2. Members must do their homework in order for the technique to be used effectively. Group members must be familiar with the problem and with the implications of proposed solutions. While information about the problem and solutions emerges in group discussion, the nominal group technique assumes a level of understanding that requires premeeting preparation by members.

3. The group arrives at more useful solutions than they would without the technique. This is caused in large part by the thorough involvement of group members.

Even though the use of this technique controls the discussion by eliminating informal talk, the quality of the solutions that result often seem worth the formality that is imposed on communication.

The Delphi Method

This method eliminates the need to have a group meet face-to-face at all. The interactions between members are conducted in writing and by routing information among them. Here are the five steps in this procedure:

1. A problem statement is sent to each participant, who writes down possible solutions, ideas, and suggestions. These are then forwarded to one person, who collects information from all of the participants.

2. The collected list of ideas is reproduced and sent to all the participants. They combine and integrate the ideas in a way that seems to make sense, and return the results to the central collection point.

3. The proposals are synthesized and integrated into one list by the person conducting the process. The list is then sent to all the participants.

4. The participants place in rank order, or rate, the proposed solutions and return them to the central collection point.

5. The averaged rankings or ratings are sent out to the participants for reranking or rerating, and the list is sent back to the central collection point once again. This procedure is repeated until convergence occurs in the ranking or ratings. The solution with the greatest support emerges as the clear choice of the participants.

Obviously, the person who collects and distributes the information has a high degree of control over the process and must be trusted by the participants. This is important, particularly if the outcome is crucial in the lives of the participants.

As an example, here is a simple problem for which four solutions were suggested. The problem was how to make sure that everyone in a work unit had equal access to the services of the secretary and the typist. There had been some inequities in the past. The four proposed solutions were

1. To have the typist devote three hours to each person in the group each week

2. To have the secretary keep a record of how much each person was using the typist's services to make sure that there was relative equality

3. To use a visual schedule-assignment board in the office showing who had requested typing services each week

4. To have the work-unit supervisor approve all requests for typing services to ensure equality

The ideas were routed to the group members who provided the following rankings:

Ideas	Individual Rankings	Average Rankings
1	2,3,3,4,4,4,4	3.43
2	1,1,2,3,3,3,4	2.43
3	1,1,1,1,2,3,3	1.71
4	1,2,2,2,2,4,4	2.43

These rankings were distributed and the rerankings were as follows:

Ideas	Individual Rankings	Average Rankings
1	4,4,4,4,4,4,4	4.00
2	2,2,2,2,3,3,3	2.43
3	1,1,1,1,2,2,2	1.43
4	1,1,1,3,3,3,3	2.14

The process was repeated one more time with the following result:

Ideas	Individual Rankings	Average Rankings
1	4,4,4,4,4,4,4	4.00
2	2,2,3,3,3,3,3	2.71
3	1,1,1,1,1,1,2	1.14
4	1,2,2,2,2,3,3	2.14

Solution 3—using a visual schedule-assignment board—received increasing support. Six of the seven group members ranked it first in the final round. Solutions 1 and 2 lost ground, while solution 4 remained relatively the same (the second choice) in the overall rankings.

A major advantage of the delphi method is that it requires written solutions. Written solutions usually are of higher quality than ideas verbalized spontaneously in a face-to-face meeting. In addition, this method avoids proposals suffering the effects of social conformity, at least initially, since no one knows whose ideas are being assessed. The politics of cliques and subgroups are avoided.

SUMMARY

The three procedures described in this chapter—brainstorming, the nominal group technique, and the dephi method—have special applications. They are examples of high technology in group work. Instead of simply allowing the group process to wander at the whim of individual members or under the direction of group politics, the rules inherent in these methods shape the ways in which people communicate. In effect, use of these methods tend to reduce the amount of evaluative statements, extended presentations, and rebuttals.

There are advantages and disadvantages in using each of these methods:

COMPARING COMMUNICATION PROCEDURES

Method	Emotional Involvement of Members	Quality Decision Outcome	Major Advantage
1. Brainstorming	Very high	Moderate to low	Creativity
2. Nominal group technique	Moderate	Moderate to high	Blend of quality and efficiency
3. Delphi method	Very low	Moderate to high	Efficiency

Brainstorming is highly involving. Its use often produces a great deal of enthusiasm. However, it does not include the necessary steps of evaluating and selecting the most workable ideas. In this sense, brainstorming is an incomplete procedure because it only identifies ideas.

The dephi method is almost at the other extreme. Participants are quite distant from each other and from any ideas except their own. Little enthusiasm or involvement results. In its minimal form, the delphi method provides only statistical summaries for what may be very critical issues in people's lives. On the other hand, the delphi method eliminates the need for long meetings and for bringing members together in the same room at the same time. Direct confrontation and conflict are avoided. However, conflict may still occur informally in the hallways and at work stations.

The nominal group technique is an attempt to achieve a balance between emotional involvement in and the technical quality of decisions. Participants meet and present their ideas orally. There is an opportunity to explain and clarify, but not to criticize or defend. Ratings or rankings permit people to voice opinions in private without being subjected to peer pressures or to the influence of superiors. The restricted amount of interaction in the nominal group technique may leave some people dissatisfied.

These procedures are effective with particular problems in group work. They affect group work by altering the ways members communicate with each other. They are not universally applicable. A leader must choose carefully, assessing both the advantages and disadvantages. In the next chapter, we will discuss group leadership.

REFLECTING/EXPLORING

1. Analyze the proceedings of a group over a period of three meetings. Use either a group in which you are a participant or a group you can observe. Make written notes at those points in the meetings when you believe one of the three procedures described in this chapter might be useful. Identify the advantages and disadvantages you see in using each of the methods. Use the table on page 267 to guide you in making these decisions.

2. Brainstorming can be added to the procedures a group uses without changing the habitual pattern of the group drastically. The next time your group is attempting to list a large variety of ideas, introduce the brainstorming technique. How does brainstorming affect the group process?

3. Often problems are most difficult to solve when they involve individuals with whom we have strong emotional ties. Use the delphi method to resolve an issue that arises within your family unit. You may wish to involve an outsider to conduct the procedure. Discuss with your family how the use of this method affects your decision making. Also discuss personal emotional reactions to using the method.

4. Repeat activity 3. This time use the nominal group technique and a new issue. Discuss reactions following the use of this procedure.

5. Review the discussions that followed activities 3 and 4. What have you learned about using these techniques that can help you decide when to use them in the organizational and community groups of which you are a member? Examine the advantages and disadvantages shown in the table on page 267. What changes would you make in this table based on your actual experience within your family unit?

CHAPTER 21

LEADERSHIP

In our view, leadership is a very practical, down-to-earth matter. Some writers have, for example, looked at leadership styles. There are authoritarian or democratic leaders, task-oriented or person-oriented leaders. These are abstract labels which refer to complex patterns of behavior. They do not describe what a leader has to do.

Sam Perkins was appointed the leader of a committee in a bank. The committee's task was to develop ways to find out more about customer needs and desires by getting information from branch managers and tellers. In Sam's four-year experience, he had never been the leader of a committee in the bank. Now he had to get ten or twelve people together, from branch managers and tellers to marketing and product-development specialists, to work on a project. Sam's first question to himself was not What style should I adopt? Rather, it was What do I need to do to get the first meeting off the ground? He knew that they had to have a place to meet, some chairs and a table, an agenda, and so on. Was that all? And what was involved in the "so on"?

We have divided this chapter into three sections to help Sam and you:

1. Leadership decisions for the group

2. Leader activities for a meeting

3. Long-term leader activities

We believe this chapter will help you understand the ways in which a leader functions to provide the group with direction that results in successful meetings and task accomplishment.

Leadership Decisions for the Group

The leader must make a series of decisions about a meeting. These include:

1. Tasks and goals for the meeting

2. Membership and attendance

3. Time and length of meeting

4. Location and facilities

5. Arrangements and equipment

6. Documents and materials

7. Methods and procedures

These seven decisions are normally made for every meeting. Often it may seem as though all decisions must be made at once since they are interrelated. We will discuss each one separately.

Tasks and Goals

This is a key decision and one that is frequently overlooked. Ask yourself, at the end of this meeting, what should we have accomplished?

Notice that defining tasks and goals is different from setting an agenda. In the listing of agenda items, there is a title describing a topic. An agenda does not tell group members what ought to result from completing the discussion of its items. For example, an agenda item might be *publicity*. The task could be to develop a publicity campaign, to create a plan for the campaign, to review efforts and approve them, to design a pamphlet or poster, or any other specific publicity task.

The leader is responsible for providing a preliminary definition of the goal or task. In some groups, members may want to discuss the definition at length. However, the leader must provide a working draft or statement. The advantage of clearly defined goals and tasks is that both the leader and members can decide whether they have completed their work at the end of a meeting. Without goals, there are no criteria for completion.

Membership and Attendance

The leader is responsible for deciding who should attend a meeting. This is especially true if members are not determined by a membership list for a standing committee or by the bylaws or constitution of a group. It will be helpful to remember the principle about group size that we discussed in Chapter 19: Use the smallest group possible that includes the necessary expertise or representation to manage the task. A Proctor and Gamble executive has said that their policy was to include as few people as possible in the decision-making process. It is a useful rule.

Some people go to meetings to avoid doing other work or to have something to do. Others may go who want to be seen in attendance because status is associated with being a participant. Their presence is a sign that they are "in" on the key issues in the organization or community. But if you follow the rule, small is best, the members who are in attendance will be there because they are highly involved in the outcome and want to work. They will be likely to attend every meeting of the group.

Time and Length of the Meeting

Some groups have traditional meeting times. Work schedules and other factors may influence when a group meets. If choices can be made, the leader should weigh various factors. For example,

1. When are members likely to feel most energetic?
2. When are interruptions least likely to occur?
3. When are people most likely to have the information needed at the meeting?

The length of the meeting is as important as the time it is scheduled. Members may become bored if a meeting is long. If a meeting is short, some people may not have the opportunity to participate, or a decision may be rushed. The length of time required for a meeting will depend on the goals and tasks, in part. The decision also involves the amount of time needed to permit members to discuss and reason together in order to reach consensus or agreement. Avoid meetings of the same length no matter what topic or task is involved. A group that always meets for an hour should consider meeting for longer periods when the task warrants longer meetings. They might also have some meetings that last only fifteen minutes. Variety is helpful for its own sake. However, it is important that variety be introduced to meet differing goals, tasks, and members' needs.

Location and Facilities

Many meetings are held wherever it is convenient. Members of a community group may invite the group to their houses for meetings. A corporate committee may go to the first available conference room. Although convenience is a factor, there are other criteria of greater importance in selecting a location. Here are three major concerns:

1. Room size is critical. Too few people in a large room leads to less interaction and a feeling of formality and distance. People will tend to spread out in the large space. On the other hand, too many people in a small room can result in discomfort. Ideally, the room should be full but not packed.

2. The room should include necessary equipment. If people must take notes or work with a pile of papers, they need tables or some flat surface on which to work. If the group is to engage in formal conversation for the purposes of resolving differences in opinion, comfortable seating with no tables may be more useful.

3. Lighting and room colors can be important. Bright lighting and plain decor may be helpful for getting work done. Yet to enhance discussion and interaction, softer lighting and attractive decorations on the walls may be a wiser choice.

If choices such as these are available, the leader should make them.

Arrangements and Equipment

Some leaders overlook the possibility of using furniture arrangements to provide both variety and a setting that will promote communication in ways that are useful for achieving the task or goal. Long meetings require more comfortable seating and more space so that people can change posture. Chairs should be arranged in a small circle for informal meetings. If people must get up and sit down or move often during a meeting, they will need space in which to do it.

Equipment availability also is important. Easels, chalkboards, and projectors may be very helpful in problem-solving or planning meetings. Almost any meeting will be enhanced by the presence of a chalkboard or an easel equipped with large paper. The leader or a member can write lists, proposals, motions, or other items so that every person can see them and know what is being discussed. If someone is making a presentation, flip charts or an overhead projector might be useful. The extra effort it may take to provide special arrangements or equipment will improve the effectiveness and efficiency of a group meeting.

Documents and Materials

Group members should be provided any documents, pamphlets, photographs, drawings, or other materials necessary for completing the work outlined for the meeting. What kinds of printed or reproduced information are members likely to need in order to participate in the discussion, arrive at a decision, or develop a workable solution to a problem? It is the leader's role to answer this question prior to each meeting.

Methods and Procedures

Finally, it is the leader's responsibility to determine what procedures should be used in any meeting. Reviewing the information provided in Chapters 19 and 20 will be helpful. The selection of procedures should be based on the task to be accomplished as well as on the motivation and skills of the group members. A basic choice is between formal and informal ways of proceeding. For simple tasks, or in groups where members need structure, the more formal methods may be most useful. When tasks are complex, or when members are highly professionalized or technically skilled, informal procedures may work best. The leader must make these decisions prior to the meeting and be ready to suggest the best ways of working together to the group members.

There is a large number of items to consider in conducting a meeting. Each of them provides part of the answer to the question, What do I do at the first meeting? A leader's consideration of these items can be arranged in terms of premeeting, meeting, or postmeeting activities. The next section of this chapter will help you use this type of organization.

Leader Activities

It is not possible for a leader to do everything at once. The activities that are his or her responsibility can be organized in three ways: premeeting, meeting, and postmeeting activities. Leader activities can be arranged according to these three categories.

Premeeting Activities

At a minimum, there are four activities a leader must complete prior to a meeting. We will discuss each one.

Make arrangements for a meeting place. In an organization, this involves reserving a conference room for a specific time and date. In a community group, there may be a need to arrange with a member to host the meeting in his or her home. Sometimes a community center is available for meetings. In addition, public meeting rooms are often provided by agencies such as the YMCA or YWCA, or by banks and shopping centers. A commission or board usually meets in a public room at a city hall, county building, or a school. The leader is responsible for these arrangements.

Issue an announcement of the meeting. Public bodies must publicize their meetings in local newspapers or by posting notices one or two weeks before each meeting so that citizens may attend. A business committee meeting may be announced through a memo or by telephone. Informal community groups or religious groups often use the telephone or a written bulletin to remind members of meetings. A leader may have a choice as to the method of announcing the meeting, but it is the leader's role to do it.

Prepare the agenda. Sometimes an agenda is included with the announcement of a meeting. This is often a requirement for public bodies and governing boards. When the agenda is prepared after the announcement of the meeting, the leader may either circulate it before the meeting or give it to members at the beginning of the meeting. In either case, the leader is responsible for preparing the agenda before the meeting. Information in Chapter 19 should be helpful to the leader. Use the agenda-guided format or the problem–item list if the group functions informally. Use the traditional form of agenda associated with parliamentary procedure if the group uses more formal procedures.

Bring necessary materials to the meeting. The leader is responsible for providing members with whatever handouts, documents, and other kinds of written information necessary for full participation in the meeting. If these materials are distributed before a meeting, the leader is wise to bring extra copies to the meeting for those members who do not have copies with them.

Premeeting activities include arranging for the meeting place, announcing the meeting time and place, preparing the agenda, and providing necessary written documents to persons in attendance. These are the minimum activities. It sometimes is helpful for leaders to make a list of premeeting activities and simply check each one off as it is completed. When a leader is thorough in completing premeeting activities, the activities that occur during a meeting flow more smoothly.

Meeting Activities

The leader is responsible for a series of activities during a meeting, from the beginning of the meeting to its end. There is a minimum of five activities for which the leader must take responsibility.

Opening the meeting. Once members arrive at the meeting place, the leader should begin the meeting on time. Opening remarks may range from a brief greeting to remarks that set the tone for the remainder of the meeting. Courtesy suggests that the opening of a meeting should include at least two elements: (1) A friendly greeting and welcome, including a statement of appreciation for coming. People appreciate having their faithfulness recognized. (2) Information about the tasks or goals of the meeting. It is amazing how many meetings begin without an explanation of what is expected or what needs to be accomplished. If asked, a leader often will say, "It's obvious what we have to do," or "Everyone knows." It may be obvious to the leader but often not to the members or to persons in attendance at the meeting. (Sometimes, the leader who believes the purpose of the meeting is obvious cannot give a simple description of meeting objectives.) Opening the meeting can be accomplished in a very brief time.

Setting the tone for the meeting. What occurs in the first few minutes of a meeting sets the tone for the rest of the meeting. This may be one of the reasons clergymen start their meetings with a brief prayer or meditation. A religious meeting is expected to begin with religious thoughts. A business meeting is sometimes started by stating the first agenda item. The message is, Let's get down to business. In contrast, a meeting that begins with a round of sharing What's new in your life? sets an atmosphere in which people and their personal lives are important to the group's work.

Describing the procedures for the group's work. Once the meeting has started, the leader is looked to for procedure. Members may want a voice in selecting a procedure, but the leader is expected to provide methods and options for conducting the meeting. The leader should be ready to suggest that a vote be taken or that the nominal group technique might be useful or that the group should brainstorm some ideas for a new program. The work that a leader has done prior to the meeting will be helpful at this point.

Maintaining control. During the main section of the meeting, the leader functions in a variety of ways. Informal groups often include the leader as a working member who provides ideas, asks questions, and helps make decisions. Formal group procedures require that the leader function separately from the group members. The leader must recognize members so they can speak, run the meeting according to rules of parliamentary procedure, and delegate tasks to individuals or subgroups. Whether the meeting is conducted in an informal or formal way, group members expect the leader to maintain control. The leader is responsible for ensuring that the group will meet its goals in the time provided.

Dealing with conflict. Sometimes a leader has to step in when a dispute or conflict arises. Members cannot always get themselves out of such situations. A leader must understand that there are two kinds of conflict (although they sometimes get tangled up). Some differences are over ideas (content). These are called *substantive conflicts.* They can be handled through such procedures as problem solving, the nominal group, or voting.

There also are personality clashes, differences which become emotional and are based on deep disagreements on values or principles. When such disputes break out, it is the responsibility of the leader to act as a mediator. Various actions may be called for. A common first step is a cooling-off period. This means delaying a decision and giving people a chance to get over the immediate anger. Once that has happened, the conflict needs to be approached directly. A good second step is to find out what is at stake for both parties. How important is this issue? Is it a matter of winning or losing, of saving face? If possible, all parties should be made aware of what is at stake. Finally, there should be a search for creative ways to allow everyone to gain something. This can take a lot of time and work, but it is well worth it. The alternative is to have people continue to be angry. Perhaps they will even leave the group.

Closing the meeting. The leader is responsible for ending the meeting. One leadership activity is often overlooked: assessing the meeting. Before a meeting is ended, it is important that each member be involved in discussing how well the group functioned during the meeting. They should suggest any changes that need to be made before the next meeting. The leader must guide the group in self-assessment. In many cases, it may be desirable to use a postmeeting reaction form. The leader compiles the results after the meeting, providing copies to group members before or at the beginning of the next meeting, and using the results in planning the next meeting. Only through self-assessment can a group consciously improve its performance. When the meeting is finished, the leader turns to the postmeeting activities.

Postmeeting Activities.

There are specific activities a leader should complete before beginning the process of planning the next meeting:

Preparing minutes or a record of the meeting. The leader may ask a recording secretary or a member to take notes for the meeting. Ultimately it is the responsibility of the group leader to ensure that minutes are typed, reproduced, and distributed to members. In small, informal groups, the leader may type an distribute the minutes or the record of the meeting.

Following up on persons assigned tasks during the meeting. One effective way to make the next meeting successful is to follow up on assignments given to individuals at the last meeting. If more information is needed from a member or someone has been asked to bring a proposal to the group, the leader should check with the people involved. By checking, the leader lets the individuals know their work is important. The leader also ensures that the person remembers the assignment. When leaders initiate this procedure, it gives them and the members involved an opportunity to discuss the particular assignments.

Compiling data from postmeeting reaction sheets. If the members evaluate the effectiveness of their meeting after it is finished, the leader must compile the results and distribute them. The leader may choose to distribute the information to the members either before the next meeting or at its beginning. In either case, the leader should compile the results soon after a meeting so that he or she has the information to use in the next premeeting phase.

Once postmeeting activities are completed, the cycle begins again with premeeting activities for the next meeting. When a leader works with a group over a long period of time, further activities may be useful.

Long-Term Leader Activities

A leader may become aware of group needs if he or she works with a group for a year or longer. Group needs include problems that inhibit the members from working effectively together. Group members may want an opportunity to create closer personal ties or simply to engage in recreation together. The leader does well to break the routine of weekly or monthly work meetings and help the group determine a time and place for interpersonal needs or recreation.

Many groups find that a retreat is useful. Group members leave the work or group setting for a day or for a weekend. An organizational group may go to a resort. A community group might go camping. In either case, the needs for recreation and closer personal ties can be met. Retreats also may serve training purposes. Group members can acquire new skills in informal, nonthreatening surroundings.

Suggestions for group activities outside the routine meeting situation may come from group members or they may be suggested by the leader. The leader is responsible for identifying such needs if they are not directly stated by members. The leader must determine how and when to meet these needs, just as he or she must guide the group through regularly scheduled meetings.

SUMMARY

The leadership of a group entails making decisions about a range of items that affect the group's functioning: goals and tasks; membership and attendance at meetings; the time of meeting and its length; location; facilities and arrangements; the methods to be used in working on tasks; and any documents or information needed by the group. The effective leader thinks about these issues rather than just relying on past rituals and social norms.

For each meeting, the leader engages in premeeting, meeting, and postmeeting activities. The premeeting activities include making arrangements, sending out an announcement, setting and distributing an agenda, and getting documents or information ready for distribution at the meeting. Once the members have gathered, the leader is responsible for opening the meeting, setting procedures, maintaining control, and seeing that some kind of assessment is done. Then, upon completion, the leader should get the minutes or the record of the meeting to the members, follow up on tasks assigned to individual members or subgroups, and analyze and distribute assessment data on the meeting to members.

Over the long term, the leader is also responsible for aiding the group by setting up retreats or recreation sessions and creating opportunities for training members or the group as a whole.

REFLECTING/EXPLORING

1. If you are the leader of a group, review the seven leadership decisions for the group. How effectively do you perform these functions? If you are a group member, how effectively do you believe these functions are performed by your group leader? As a member, what can you do to help the leader of your group perform more effectively?

2. Make a tape recording of a group meeting in which you are a participant. After the meeting, replay the tape. How could the leadership functions be improved during your group meeting? How might you share this information with your group? Be sure to include ways that the leader and members might both contribute to improving the ways the leadership functions are performed.

3. Discuss in your group the kinds of premeeting and postmeeting activities the leader of your group performs. Talk about ways that your group can improve the quality and efficiency of your meeting by following through on postmeeting activities and by preplanning. How can both the leader and the members participate in increasing the effectiveness of the leader's between-meeting activities?

4. Discuss in your group the needs that exist for recreational, interpersonal, or training meetings outside of the routine meetings. If needs do exist for an outside meeting or retreat, discuss how these needs might best be met.

5. Attend a meeting of your city commission. How do you think leadership functions could be improved? Based on your observations, what guesses would you make about the thoroughness of postmeeting and premeeting work? As a citizen, how can you voice your ideas about improving the leadership functions?

SECTION SEVEN: READING LIST

Information on the rules of parliamentary procedure:

Stech, E. and S. A. Ratliffe. *Working in Groups.* Lincolnwood, IL: National Textbook Company, 1976.

Sturgis, A. *Sturgis Standard Code of Parliamentary Procedure.* New York: McGraw-Hill Book Company, 1966.

Roberts, H. M. *Robert's Rules of Order.* Rev. ed. Glenview, IL: Scott, Foresman and Company, 1970.

Information on brainstorming, the nominal group, and the delphi method:

Baird, J. E., Jr. *Positive Personnel Practices: Quality Circles.* Prospect Heights, IL: Waveland Press, 1982. Two separate manuals exist: *Leader's Manual. Participant's Manual.*

Debecq, A. L. "The Effectiveness of Nominal, Delphi, and Interacting Group Decision Making Processes," *Academy of Management Journal,* 17. April, 1974.

Huseman, R. C. "The Role of the Nominal Group in Small-Group Communication," in R. C. Huseman, D. M. Logue, and D. L. Freshley. *Readings in Interpersonal and Organizational Communication.* 2nd ed. Boston: Holbrook, 1973.

Linestone, H. A. and Turoff, M. *The Delphi Method: Techniques and Applications.* Reading, MA: Addison-Wesley, 1975.

Osborn, A. F. *Applied Imagination: Principles and Procedures of Creative Problem-Solving.* 3rd rev. ed. New York: Charles Scribner's Sons, 1957.

Ulschak, F. L., L. Nathanson, and P. G. Gillan. *Small-Group Problem Solving: An Aid to Organizational Effectiveness.* Reading, MA: Addison-Wesley, 1981.

SECTION **8**

SETTINGS

22

WORK GROUPS

There are ten people on the 7:20 A.M. bus. Its route extends from the suburb of Arcadia to the downtown area. The passengers include a salesman, a travel agent, a lawyer, a nurse, a busboy, a bank teller, a social worker, an advertising account executive, a custodian, and a personnel records clerk. The passengers are on their way to work. There are major differences between their work groups.

The salesman, George, happens to be working in town this week. He has decided to take the bus to work as a change of pace. His work unit consists of fourteen salespeople. Each is assigned a sales territory. A sales supervisor oversees the entire sales force. More often than not, the sales people are on the road. It is a rare day that all of them are in the office at the same time. In fact, this only happens when a sales meeting has been called by the supervisor.

The travel agent, Marcie, will arrive at an office she shares with six other agents. Each person has a desk, a telephone, and a reservations computer terminal. Two of the travel agents own and manage the agency.

Sandra, the lawyer, will go to a suite of downtown legal offices that are occupied by the five partners and nine associates in the law firm. One partner is the managing partner. In effect, though, each partner manages his or her own law practice within the larger firm. Sandra is an associate. She works for Anne Landry, one of the partners.

As the bus nears the downtown area, Fred, the busboy, gets off and walks into Alex's. This is a small, popular restaurant with a heavy breakfast business. Fred will work with one other busboy, four waitresses, two cooks, and Alex, the owner–manager.

Jean is a nurse. She gets off at the same stop as Fred, but goes in the opposite direction, toward a large, modern hospital. Jean's work group consists of two other registered nurses, several licensed practical nurses, and two orderlies, all of whom work in the pediatric unit of the hospital. Jean is the nurse in charge.

The bank teller, Harry, gets off at the main intersection of the downtown area. He will go to work in the home office of the largest bank in town. His work group consists of sixteen tellers working under the supervision of a chief teller. Their place of work is the lobby of the downtown branch.

Jerry also gets off the bus in the downtown area. He walks to his job as a social worker in an agency for the elderly. The agency has over fifty social workers, aides, and other personnel. There are three other social workers in Jerry's work group. They specialize in finding housing and medical assistance for the indigent aged of the community.

Kelly is an account executive in a small advertising agency. She is the vice president of the agency as well. Two account executives work under her direct supervision. In addition to Kelly and the two account executives, the agency includes a president, three more account executives, and a secretary who supervises a pool of typists (which varies in size depending on current workload). The typists are hired as temporaries.

The custodian, Martin, also works downtown. Actually, he works in the same bank as Harry. There is a crew of four custodians in the bank building during the day. They rarely see each other except during breaks and the lunch hour.

Roberta, the records clerk, will join twenty-two other clerks in the personnel office at the headquarters of a major industrial firm located in the city.

Each of these ten people goes to a different kind of work unit. They differ in size, location, structure, and purpose. However, most work groups also have factors in common. These factors permit a comparison of work groups with other types of groups.

In the remaining chapters, we will describe the characteristics of four types of groups: (1) committees, (2) negotiating teams, (3) policy and governing boards, and (4) teleconference groups. In this chapter we will consider work groups. We will explore

1. Characteristics of work groups

2. Problems of coordination and control in work groups and ways to solve them

3. Staff meetings as a part of the work group process

4. Quality circles as a way of improving both quality and productivity

We will begin with the characteristics of work groups.

Characteristics of Work Groups

Work groups can be compared by answering five basic questions:

1. Is the unifying basis for group functioning a common task, common skills, or a combination of both?

2. Is the work group embedded in an organization or does it exist separately?

3. Do members work together or are they dispersed?

4. Is the leadership style authoritarian or participatory?

5. Is the work flow independent or interdependent?

The similarities and differences among work groups can be reviewed by answering these five questions.

Is the unifying basis common tasks or skills? Most work groups occur within organizations. Some groups are created to accomplish a common *task* or goal, such as serving food to customers in a restaurant or producing automobile parts in a factory. The task is identified and defined by someone outside the group at a higher level. The task still serves to unify the group. People may also be grouped because of similar *skills* and expertise. Accountants may be in one group, lawyers in another. When people share a task, skills, or both, they are apt to share a group culture and language.

Members of most work groups are paid for their work. This is not universal, however. There are work units consisting of volunteers. In many hospitals, volunteers work in the gift shop or distribute mail, magazines, and flowers to patients. Volunteers who share common tasks or skills are a work group even though they are not paid for the work they do. While almost every work group is based on a common task or set of skills, there remain four other factors which charcterize such groups. Answering each question about work groups will help you become aware of the differences between them. Adjusting to these differences is one way of increasing the possibility of effective work.

Is the work group embedded in an organization? Some groups exist in isolation. For example, the barbers in a neighborhood barbershop or the ten employees of a small manufacturing company are work groups which exist independently. There is no larger parent organization with which each is affiliated. Other groups are embedded in larger organizations. The local grocery store may be one of a national chain of stores.

The major difference between an independent and an embedded group is that the embedded group must follow the policies and procedures of the parent organization and must coordinate its activities with other work units. For example, the headquarters of a chain of grocery stores may dictate the policies all store managers must follow in preparing weekly advertisements for the local newspapers. Each of the store managers within a given area may work together to coordinate their special sales. When a work unit is independent, the manager sets policies and procedures within it. The owner of the barbership decides how his shop will be managed.

Do members work together or are they dispersed? Most work groups exist in a building that includes adjoining offices for members. They see each other frequently and can speak to each other easily.

In some work units, members do not work together in the same physical location. The members of these groups are dispersed. For example, each shift of police officers in a town or in a precinct within a city is a work group. The officers report to one commanding officer. They have similar skills and duties. However, they do not see each other very often because they are assigned either individually or in pairs to specific sections of the community. They may be together for coffee breaks or outside the shift but not while they work. A similar situation exists with sales people like George. George does most of his work in several communities throughout the county. Other people on the same sales force also have assigned territories within the county. As members of a work group, they meet only when a sales meeting is called.

Is the leadership style authoritarian or participatory? The leadership style in work groups ranges from authoritarian (strict and highly structured) to participatory (permissive and loosely structured). A work group that consists of professionals such as lawyers, accountants, doctors, or teachers usually does not require a high degree of direct supervision. Professionals have extensive training. They know what to do and they do it. Professionals often work most successfully under a participatory style of leadership. Work groups that consist of less professionalized personnel work effectively with a more highly structured form of leadership. Fred, the bus boy, or Roberta, the personnel records clerk, might experience a more authoritarian style of leadership in their work units than does Sandra, the lawyer.

Is the work flow independent or interdependent? All work units manage the flow of group tasks. Tasks may be managed along a range from an independent manner to an interdependent one. In independent work, each person completes his or her own task alone and then goes on to the next. Fred clears one table of dishes and then starts on another. Clearly, bussing dishes does not involve the work of anyone other than Fred. Teachers working in separate classrooms provide another example of independent work flow. Lawyers who supervise their own cases is another example.

Interdependent work flow is more complex. Work flow is interdependent (1) on assembly lines, (2) when work flows back and forth among work unit members, or (3) when the task involves the total work unit as a team. On an assembly line, each person performs the same task many times. When one person completes the task, the product moves to the next person. Products continue to move on the assembly line as each worker completes the assigned task. The assembly line only moves as fast as the slowest worker or the most time-consuming task. Sometimes the sequential flow of the assembly line is eliminated, but the product or job moves back and forth among the workers. Perhaps the most complex form of interdependent work involves the total work unit as a team. In this case, every person must be present in order to complete the task. A medical team involving a doctor, a nurse, a physical therapist, and other specialists deciding on treatment for a patient is an example of a complex form of interdependent work flow.

Groups differ widely in how they manage work flow. The type of flow that works well in one group might not work in another. Work flow, leadership style, the physical location of members of a work unit, and the independence of a work group are characteristics of work groups that are interrelated. The basic unifying factors of work groups are the type of task and the skills or expertise that workers have in common, or a combination of both. Understanding the tasks and skills demanded of a group assists work groups in deciding specifically how to handle the other four variables.

Coordination and Control

The basic problems to be solved in any work group involve coordination and control. The problems can be approached in these how-to questions:

1. How can work be finished on time to meet the specifications of clients or customers?

2. How can a task be divided so that group members can work together toward the common goal?

The answers to these questions depend on work-group characteristics: work flow, leadership style, and the work location.

There are three ways for work groups to manage problems of coordination and control. These include

1. Using written documents and supervisory control in combination

2. Holding meetings and creating committees

3. Encouraging one-to-one contacts between employees

These solutions are actually methods of communication. They all exist to some extent in every group. It is the relative emphasis on each method that differs among groups.

Documents and Supervisory Control

Written documents include schedules, plans, procedures, budgets, and policies. When information is put in writing, everyone has access to it. If there is doubt about what needs to be done or who is responsible for a task, workers can refer to the documents. The leader or supervisor is responsible for preparing and distributing the documents. The supervisor is expected to help members of the work group use the documents. Work-group members must follow the written procedures, instructions, or guidelines.

Most work groups use some written documents and supervisory control. They may use work schedules, assignment sheets, job descriptions, standard operating procedures (SOPs), or procedural manuals. A significant part of a manager's job may be writing, enforcing, and revising written documents. The process is continuous.

The use of written documents and supervisory control is the most formal of the three basic methods of coordination. Decision making, or control, is centralized in the supervisor. The criteria for supervisory decisions are available in written form.

Holding Meetings and Creating Committees

The use of meetings and committees is a less formal, less centralized, method of coordination and control than written documents with supervisory enforcement. Meetings may be a useful alternative when the personnel or the task of a work group do not lend themselves to the more formal method of coordination. For example, professionals usually expect to meet together to share ideas. They prefer a participatory leadership style which permits their involvement in deciding how a task will be completed. Explicit manuals, rigid schedules, and written operating procedures may not be appreciated in a law firm or in a family counseling agency. In addition, a task that involves inventing a new method or creating new strategies may require meetings and committees. In such a situation, coordination by written procedures and control by strict supervision could be fatal.

If a work group is assigned a task that requires creativity, meetings and committees may be a useful method of coordination and control. New products and services may be more successfully developed if a subgroup of people with the needed skills meets frequently to brainstorm, build on each other's ideas, and generate enthusiasm. Progress toward task completion is likely to emerge from their conversations.

Informal Contacts between Employees

The third technique for maintaining coordination and control is the least formal. It requires workers to check with each other occasionally. A telephone call from an employee in one department to an employee in another department is an example. When one person walks over to the desk of another for a brief chat about a technical problem, one-to-one contact has been made.

In effect, these are very brief, unscheduled meetings between two or perhaps three people for the purpose of asking about the status of a task. Workers also solicit ideas about how to solve a problem during the "meetings." Rather than waiting for a large, scheduled meeting, going to the supervisor, or referring to written documents, people talk directly to each other.

Only a very few highly rigid work groups do not permit this kind of contact. Employees may be seen in almost any work situation talking to each other about the job. In groups with complex tasks or with professional members, these informal contacts occur regularly.

Actually, all work units combine the three methods. One group may rely mainly on written documents and supplement them with one-to-one contacts between employees. Another group may find that meetings and one-to-one contacts are the most effective means of coordination and control. Still another group may use documents, a few large meetings, and very few one-to-one contacts. Work groups tend to emphasize one method. They rarely eliminate any method entirely.

Staff Meetings

There are two major forms of communication in work groups. One of them, the staff meeting, is a tradition in such fields as human services and education. A much newer development is the quality circle. We will consider the staff meeting in this section. Quality circles will be the focus of the next section.

In professional settings, the staff meeting is used as a way to encourage participation among employees. Policies and procedures which directly affect the workers are developed in staff meetings. Some work groups have weekly staff meetings in which current and ongoing problems are discussed. Other groups have occasional staff meetings as conditions demand.

Staff meetings almost always are led by the supervisor or manager of the work group. That person arranges a time and place, prepares an agenda, and provides equipment or refreshments. The supervisor normally provides written materials—handouts, data, reprints, or diagrams—that assist the discussion. In most cases, staff meetings are held during normal working hours and last an hour or two.

The most useful topics for staff meetings include items which permit workers to use their expertise or to express their self-interests. Items that require consensus and commitment among workers are also useful topics. For example, by allowing group members to decide policies and procedures, the leader ensures that the final decisions will have the commitment of the people who participated and agreed to the statements. It is important to reach consensus so that most of the work-unit members find the policies and procedures acceptable.

A common use of staff meetings is to disseminate information. The supervisor makes announcements and informs employees of policy or schedule changes, new procedures, meetings, and other activities. Members of the work group have the opportunity to ask questions and clarify information items. Common problems can also be discussed. Technical problems, new developments in methods or strategies, and procedures for standard situations or conditions of work can be discussed and clarified.

In some organizations, the staff meeting is set aside occasionally so that managers from higher levels in the organization or experts outside the organization can address the staff. This may be for the purpose of indoctrinating or training staff members. Group members often have the opportunity to respond to presentations and provide feedback.

The staff meeting is an opportunity for the members of a work unit to meet in open forum. During normal working hours, people meet each other in small groups or one-to-one. Members of a dispersed group may not meet each other at all. In the staff meeting, all members of the work unit meet face-to-face.

Quality Circles

Quality circles began in the United States, moved to Japan, and then returned. An American professor of management developed the idea of worker involvement. Managers of industrial companies in the United States did not use the idea initially. However, some Japanese managers instituted methods for involving workers in the improvement of quality and productivity. The technique they used was the quality circle. Because of their success in Japan, quality circles have been reimported to the United States.

The key to quality circles is the willingness of workers to volunteer to be involved in them. The membership, of course, changes over time. Some workers may start with the quality circle and then drop out. Others may not join initially and may choose to participate later. There is no coercion. In fact, if no one wants to join, there is no quality circle within that work unit.

The group structure of a quality circle includes the work-unit supervisor as leader, the employees as members, and an outside quality-circle consultant available to the group. The supervisor is the leader because the group discusses ways to improve productivity and quality in the task of the work group. Ultimately, the supervisor will be responsible for evaluating and implementing the suggestions.

The structure of a quality circle and its relation to its work unit is shown in the diagram on page 291. Typically, a quality circle consists of four to ten members who meet during regular working hours with pay. In other words, they are expected to work during group meetings. The group selects the problems to be discussed. It meets in a room away from the regular work area. The process involves defining a problem or problems, collecting information and technical data, seeking ways to improve work methods, and developing a proposal. The group is responsible for making the proposal—for presenting it both orally and in writing to the managers affected. The managers agree to provide the quality circle with the information necessary for solving the problems. They also agree to hear the proposals and give them serious consideration.

The quality-circle consultant or advisor assists the group leader and the members in discussing problems. The advisor can help by providing techniques in problem solving and by suggesting ways the group might function. The advisor normally is a member of a special staff group responsible for implementing the work of the quality circles. Thus, the advisor is not a member of the work group or one of the managers who will make decisions about the proposals.

Most successful quality-circle programs include a training phase. There are two minimum requirements: (1) supervisors must be trained as group

CROSS MEMBERSHIPS IN WORK UNIT AND QUALITY CIRCLE

The Work Unit

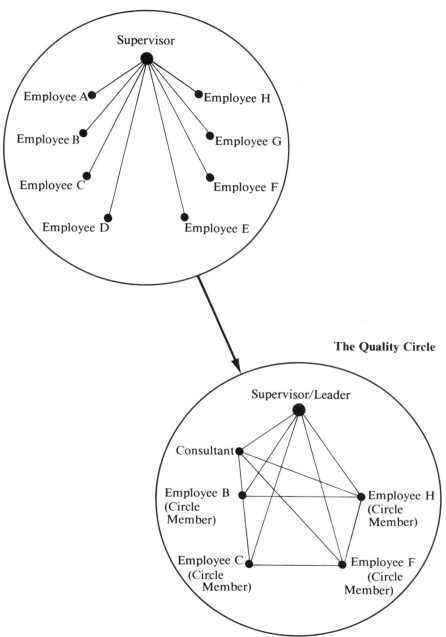

leaders, and (2) workers must be trained in group methods. The training for supervisors helps them learn how to assist members in group problem solving. The skills for employee participation usually differ from usual methods of employee functioning in industrial work settings. Members of quality circles participate by making suggestions, listening to the ideas of others, and working together to reach group consensus on a single solution. Many workers have no previous training in these group skills.

Quality circles are subgroups of the work unit. They are formed for the purpose of improving the effectiveness and efficiency of that work unit through using the expertise of the employees. Where they have been seriously tried, quality circles have been beneficial for both managers and workers. Higher quality and increased productivity pleases managers. Workers have a sense of involvement and participation and fewer problems associated with ineffective procedures and poor materials.

Employee and manager cooperation is needed before quality circles can succeed. Some managers use quality circles in an attempt to pacify workers without really giving them a voice. Occasionally, employees see the quality circle as an opportunity to receive pay and rest for a few hours each week. But when managers and employees cooperate seriously in using quality circles properly, both quality and productivity increase.

SUMMARY

In this section, we will devote a chapter to each of five types of groups: work groups, committees, negotiating teams, policy and governing boards, and teleconferences. In this chapter, we have examined work groups.

Work groups can be compared by describing five basic characteristics: (1) The unifying basis for group functioning is a common task, common skills, or a combination of both. (2) Some groups are embedded within a parent organization while others exist separately. (3) In some work groups, members work together in a specific location. In others, members may be dispersed. (4) Leadership in work groups may be authoritarian or participatory. (5) The work may be done by individuals completing whole tasks, or it may be interdependent. There are groups in which each member performs one specific task (an assembly line), groups in which work is passed back and forth among members, or groups in which the presence of all members is necessary for task completion.

The problems faced by most work groups involve issues of coordination and control. Coordination and control can be focused in two questions: (1) How can work be finished on time to meet the specifications of clients or customers? (2) How can the task be divided so that each person can work together toward the common goal? Methods of communication provide solutions to problems of coordination and control. These include (1) using a combination of written documents and supervisory control, (2) holding meetings and creating committees, and (3) encouraging one-to-one contacts between employees. While work units may emphasize the use of one method over the other two, rarely is any method completely eliminated from a work group.

Two major forms of communication are used in work groups. (1) The staff meeting is a traditional way of involving employees in their work while providing a place for managers to disseminate information and to indoctrinate and train employees. (2) The quality circle is a more recently developed method of communication in work groups. It actually is a work-unit subgroup that consists of volunteers who meet regularly with their supervisor to discuss problems within the unit. They have a consultant available who is a specialist in quality-circle communication. Most successful quality circles provide group-communication training for both the supervisor and members. The purpose of the group is to involve employees in decisions that affect their work. When managers and employees cooperate, both quality and productivity can increase.

REFLECTING/EXPLORING

1. Using the five characteristics of work groups, evaluate at least three different work groups with which you are familiar. How do they differ and how are they similar? How do these characteristics affect the work of the groups?

2. Apply the five characteristics of work groups to your work group. How would you describe your group in terms of each characteristic? In what ways might you change your work group to increase the effectiveness of the group? How do these ways differ from changes you might make to meet your personal needs as a worker or a manager of the group?

3. What problems of coordination and control typically occur in your work group? Of the three methods identified for managing such problems, which are typically used in your work group? What changes might you make the increase the effectiveness of your group?

4. For what purposes are staff meetings used in your work group? In what ways do you believe staff meetings might be improved? If your work group does not use staff meetings, in what ways might they be useful?

5. Consult the books listed in the reading list in this section that discuss quality circles. Consult your local library for periodicals that include recent articles about quality circles. What information in these materials provides you with useful ideas that you might implement in your work group?

23

COMMITTEES

Committees come in many sizes. Their purposes vary greatly. The work of committees may affect numbers of people.

At one extreme is the House Committee on Foreign Affairs in the Congress of the United States. This committee is composed of members of congress. The chairperson is usually the highest-ranking majority member, either Democrat or Republican. Within the committee there exists a series of subcommittees, each of which focuses on a specific area of the world. For example, there is a subcommittee on Africa. The House Committee on Foreign Affairs has as part of its structure a staff of persons who conduct research, write reports, and assist the committee members. This committee is large. The work of the committee is important to Congress, to the citizens of the United States, and to foreign countries throughout the world.

At the opposite extreme in terms of both size and impact is the two-person committee that is planning a garage sale to be held by the homeowners on Alps Drive in Tehachapi, California.

Many activities and much of the work of businesses, government agencies, educational systems, hospitals, associations, and other organizations occurs in committees. This chapter is devoted to this type of group. We will examine the nature of committees by focusing on five topics:

1. Two kinds of committees exist: standing committees and ad hoc committees (task forces).

2. Committees exist in both organizations and communities.

3. Committee personnel may be members who represent other groups, members who are technical experts, and nonvoting members who are consultants.

4. Committee structure has common elements: leaders, subcommittees, and staff positions.

5. Group process in committees is characterized by relatively infrequent meetings, frequent turnover of members, and formal, task-oriented meetings.

The information in this chapter will help you understand how committees differ from other groups. Based on this understanding, you will be able to work in and with committees more successfully. Let's begin by exploring the two types of committees that exist.

Two Kinds of Committees

In spite of the many variations that exist among committees, they can be classified by placing them in two major categories. The feature that distinguishes one category from the other is whether a committee is permanent or temporary. One category is the permanent or standing committee. The ad hoc committee (task force) constitutes the second category.

Standing Committees

When committees are permanent, they are referred to as *standing committees.* The House Committee on Foreign Affairs is a standing committee. Most associations function according to a written constitution and bylaws. Standing committees are identified in these documents. Finance, membership, and program committees are typical examples. Their duties are continuous. Their members meet regularly. Many of their tasks are repetitive because convention programs, budgets, and plans for recruiting members are regularly occurring concerns.

Ad Hoc Committees (Task Forces)

Ad hoc committees are temporary committees. An ad hoc committee may also be called a *task force* to indicate that it has been assigned a specific task. Task forces exist until their tasks are finished. If parliamentary procedure is used, temporary committees are discharged when their reports are received or approved by the larger groups that created the committees.

The board of a school district may appoint a task force of parents, teachers, and administrators to make recommendations on computer usage in the elementary schools. Once the recommendations are made, there is no longer a reason for the committee. This committee would be classed as a task force rather than a standing committee. Probably the committee of two that planned the neighborhood garage sale in Tehachapi was also a temporary committee. Both temporary and permanent committees are widely used.

Committees in Organizations and Communities

Democracy is valued highly in the United States. Most citizens want to participate in decisions that affect them. One indirect method of participation is through representatives. A major reason committees exist is to provide representation for a wider membership. (Committees provide opportunities for *direct* participation only for their own members and leaders.) Committees provide representation in both organizations and communities.

Committees in Organizations

Organizational committees are almost always designed to include members from departments or units within the larger organization that will be affected by the committee's work. Committee membership thus cuts across department lines, as well as lines of authority, in order to promote coordination and to manage conflict among the units of the organization.

A common problem in most business organizations is pricing. We will use as an example of committees in organizations a company pricing committee. The structure of the committee is diagrammed on page 297. The reoccurring question for this committee is: What shall we charge for our products or services? Lower prices mean more sales and more income over the short run. However, quality may have to be sacrificed and customers lost over the long term. In this particular industry, jobs are bid to a variety of customers. Some want very high quality and are willing to pay for it. Others want quick delivery and, although they say they want quality, do not inspect the delivered items very carefully. For several years, the pricing decision was made by one person: the manager of the estimating department. She was subject to frequent complaints from production, shipping, marketing, and sales.

It was decided that a committee should be formed to determine what procedure to use in setting prices. The committee is to describe strategies to be used in decision making. The committee on pricing strategies is not to set actual prices, quotes, or estimates. This is the task of the estimating department. However, the committee on pricing discusses a series of issues that affect pricing:

1. How can we tell which customers should get a low bid so that they will give us more business in the future?

2. What kinds of requests for estimates do we get that could result in trouble?

3. Which customers have complained about prices in the past?

4. On which kinds of jobs do we make the largest profit?

5. On which jobs do we have the smallest profit margin?

By answering these questions, the committee on pricing strategies can develop methods to identify the most effective estimates.

Creating the pricing committee is actually a method of managing conflict within this organization. The committee is a setting where differences between the sales and marketing departments and the production and ship-

FORMATION OF A COMPANY PRICING COMMITTEE

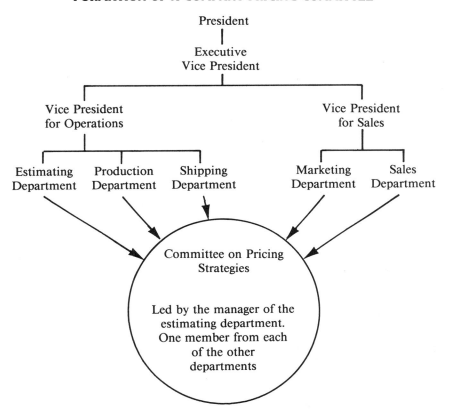

ping departments can be expressed and negotiated. Sometimes the management of the conflict involves political maneuvering, as each subgroup attempts to control or affect the group's outcome. Even though such a committee may be created primarily to permit the maneuvering among factions to occur so that the conflict can be worked out, these committees may be viewed as inefficient and time-consuming. However, the recommendations or decisions that result from the committee's work will be supported by the departments involved in making them. While the level of efficiency may be low, conflict-managing committees are effective because the work of the committee increases coordination among the departments in the organization. This coordination has both immediate and long-term benefits for both working conditions and relationships.

Committees in Communities

Committees which exist in communities also provide a means of representation. They draw members from various interest groups or from geographical areas within the community. We will describe the story of one committee created by a local school board.

Based on the recommendation of the superintendent of schools, a local school board instituted a major energy-saving program. The program included installing insulation in the schools; using clock thermostats that automatically set the temperature down in the late afternoon and up in the morning; and replacing the heating equipment with newer, more efficient models. Another change involved reducing the window area in a number of schools by installing smaller windows. This was intended to reduce heat loss through the window surfaces and result in a savings of five to ten percent per school. The alternative—a type of storm windows—would cost more and result in more heat loss.

Over the summer, the windows in one school were replaced. By August, there was a storm of protest. The smaller windows changed the appearance of the school so dramatically that long-time residents, parents, and architects complained. The superintendent created a committee to review the plans for window alterations in the energy-conservation program. The committee was created at the request of the school board. The committee was told that the heat loss through the windows must be reduced and asked that options other than smaller windows be recommended to the board.

The committee consisted of two parents whose children attended two of the affected schools, two citizens who had complained about the appearance of the smaller windows, an architect who donated her time, two teachers from the affected schools, and the school district assistant superintendent for facilities and plant operations. The assistant superintendent was chairperson of the committee.

Notice that the membership of the committee was drawn from elements of the community affected by the change. They were given a specific task: achieve the greatest reduction of heat loss through the windows without changing the appearance of the architecture noticeably. Once again, such a committee cannot be expected to be very efficient. It takes time to learn about the problems and issues. It takes more time to study alternative solutions. And it takes even more time to reach a consensus on the best solution. However, when a recommendation is made, it will represent the best thinking of a diverse group of individuals. It will therefore be supported.

The committee met for four months and developed two ways to reduce heat loss in addition to reducing the size of the windows. One solution meant installing insulated glass windows in two-thirds of the spaces and closing off the remaining windows entirely. This plan would cost approximately $30,000 more than the smaller windows. The second option was to install new, experimental solar-heated window boxes at a cost of $120,000 more than the smaller windows. The school board was willing to spend an additional $30,000, and the committee's first recommendation was accepted.

You may be familiar with the saying, A camel is a horse designed by a committee. This is a reference to the inefficiency often associated with committee work. However, where democracy is highly valued, representation overrides efficiency. Committees in both organizations and communities provide for participation in work and issues. The involvement often results in an improved quality of life and more effective working conditions and relationships.

Committee Personnel

If a major reason for using committees is to provide representation and participation, it follows that decisions about committee membership are very important. Membership may be of three types:

1. Representative membership

2. Technical membership

3. Nonvoting membership

Representative Membership

A committee gives people from different departments in an organization or different segments of a community an opportunity to meet together and arrive at answers to common problems. Thus, committee membership is frequently based on representation by units, divisions, agencies, and departments. Representation also involves political issues. Members may form a coalition which can strongly influence the committee's process. The committee on pricing strategies could easily have divided into two coalitions: (1) representatives of the production and shipping departments, and (2) representatives of the marketing and sales departments. Because of the likelihood that coalitions may form, the rules for committee membership are a source of conflict in and of themselves. A general guideline for membership is to include the minimum number of people needed to represent the concerns of all the persons affected by the committee's work.

Technical Membership

Committees must also complete work. They must make recommendations to the authority that created the committee. This often requires an understanding of the technical problems involved in the committee's task. For this reason, some committees include one or more persons who have special expertise, but may not directly represent an affected group. In the task force appointed by the school superintendent, the architect could advise the committee on ways to reduce heat loss without making the windows smaller. The architect served as a technical advisor at the same time as she served as a member of the committee.

Consultants and Nonvoting Members

Sometimes members of committees want or need technical expertise, but it is inappropriate for the expert to vote on issues or take part in reaching consensus. A committee may also invite an expert to the meetings in the capacity of a consultant. The consultant gives advice and helps the group with technical matters, but is not involved in the actual decision-making process. If the expert is needed on a continuing basis, he or she may be included in the committee as a nonvoting member.

An expert has special credibility and influence among the members of a committee. When the expert serves as a consultant or in the capacity of a nonvoting member, this influence is put into perspective. The common notion of a committee is that it is a group of peers or colleagues of equal status solving problems and making decisions. In organizations and communities, however, it is not unusual to find committees in which there are wide differences in the status of members. A committee in a local government might include the assistant city manager, the city clerk, a data processing specialist from the computer department, and a supervisor from the treasurer's office. The assistant city manager and the city clerk have much more influence within the government hierarchy than do the supervisor or the specialist. They must work together on a common problem and minimize the issues of differences in status.

Structure of Committees

Committees are structured in various ways. Committee structures vary in both size and complexity. There are three common elements. These include

1. Leadership

2. Subcommittees

3. Staff

Leadership

Even the smallest committee has a chairperson. Someone must be responsible for the work of the committee. In some cases, the leader is elected by the committee members after the committee is formed. In other cases, the leader may be appointed by a higher authority or elected from the parent group. In an association, a common strategy involves electing the chairpersons of standing committees from the general membership. Then the chairpersons invite people to serve on their committees. When continuity of leadership is desired, a chairperson and a vice-chairperson may be named. The vice chairperson succeeds the chairperson in the second year.

Some committees are small organizations in themselves. Committees of the United States Congress or their equivalents in state assemblies or legislatures are examples. There usually is a chairperson, a vice-chairperson, a legal counsel, and the chairpersons of various subcommittees. There may also be one or more ad hoc committees (task forces) at work at any specific time. Thus, the entire leadership system may consist of as many as ten or more people for a committee that has a total membership of thirty or more individuals.

Leading a committee is a unique challenge. There are differences between leading a committee and supervising a work unit. The major difference involves the power of the positions. A manager or supervisor evaluates employees, suggests promotions and raises in pay, disciplines employees, and may even take over the tasks of a subordinate. The supervisor has coercive power because he or she controls the rewards and punishments. A committee chairperson is in an entirely different situation. The members of a committee may be drawn from a variety of work units in an organization, or from many segments of a community. The leader must be persuasive. There is no way to provide rewards except through praise. The source of motivation lies within the members themselves.

The effective leader of a committee must be acutely aware of the motivations and interests of the members. Why is Fred on this committee? What does it mean to him? Why did Shirley decide to volunteer? What viewpoint is she representing? The answers to questions such as these provide a chairperson with the information needed to focus the energies of members toward completing tasks.

Assigning work in a committee usually is the result of a combination of volunteering by a member and a request from a leader. Rarely can tasks be assigned as they would be in a work unit. Instead, people must be given the opportunity to volunteer. Mismatches between people and tasks may result. These mismatches are one of the difficulties with committee work. Where committee chairpersons have the opportunity to do so, they should create committees that include motivated people who have the necessary expertise.

Subcommittees

Large committees with complex assignments use subcommittees as a way to divide the task into more manageable components. For example, in one organization that was considering the purchase of a new computer system, a committee was formed under the direction of the data services manager. The committee consisted of twelve persons from various departments and units. At the first meeting, the committee was divided into three subcommittees: hardware, software, and user acceptance. The hardware subcommittee was given the responsibility for studying the various kinds of machines available, their limits, and their special features. The software subcommittee was to investigate the range of programs already available for various machines. They were to study those programs which would apply to the specific situation in their organization. Finally, the user acceptance subcommittee was given the responsibility for determining what programs potential users wanted. They also were to investigate users, needs for keyboard terminals. Each subcommittee was to report to the total committee at monthly meetings. Each subcommittee would meet as often as twice a week.

Subcommittees not only make complex tasks more manageable in large committees. They also provide the opportunity for a committee to work simultaneously on different parts of a task. The use of subcommittees often helps a committee become more efficient. Time and energy can be saved through their efforts.

Staff

The last characteristic of committee structure is the staff. Very large standing committees may have permanent staffs. Congressional committees are examples. People are hired to conduct research, provide legal guidance, and perform other needed functions. A legislative committee on the environment might have at least one scientist on the staff to advise the committee members and to manage public relation issues. Staffs, subcommittees, and the role of the leader or chairperson of a committee distinguish committees from work units and other types of groups.

Group Process in Committees

The characteristics of committees extend beyond their personnel and structure. The group process is also specific to committees. The committee structure influences group process in three areas:

1. Frequency of meetings

2. Turnover of members

3. Formal, task-oriented focus of meetings

The Frequency of Meetings

In work groups, members usually work together on a regular basis. (An exception occurs when members are dispersed.) Most coworkers talk to each other daily. Committees are different. Standing committees may meet as often as once a week but more commonly they meet once a month or less frequently. Task forces may meet several times a week, once a week, or as little as once a month over a period of a year. (When their project is completed, of course, the task force no longer exists.)

Because committees meet rather infrequently and for shorter periods of time compared to work groups, there is less opportunity for people to know each other well. In fact, a task force may find itself at the end of its task before the members know much about each other at all. As a result, group process in committees probably depends more on the initial surface impressions people have of each other and the status they hold in the organization or community. A doctor on a local neighborhood committee may command respect simply by virtue of profession and degree. A member of a corporate planning staff on the same neighborhood committee may derive status from having been associated with long-range planning efforts.

Turnover of Members

To add to the complication of infrequent meetings, there is frequent membership turnover on committees. The local chapters of some professional associations have committees whose entire membership changes annually. Standing committees typically rotate membership so that each year there is a change in one fourth to one third of the members.

Since membership changes often, committee process tends to remain in flux. Research scientists create groups for the purpose of an experiment. The group has no prior history. Scientists refer to them as *zero history groups*. They compare these groups of people with long-term groups in society. However, most committees are actually a combination of zero history and long-term groups. There is little or no history for new members. For the members who have served on the committee for a year or two, there is some history. Therefore, people must constantly learn about each other. This learning process is never ending as new people become committee members while others leave.

Formal, Task-oriented Focus of Meetings.

Since committee members have little opportunity to learn much about each other and to observe each other working, committee meetings may be relatively formal and task oriented. Most committees rely on some form of parliamentary procedure, although it may be simplified. Examples of committee agendas and minutes are provided in Chapter 21. The tendency for committees to use formal procedures probably stems from the infrequency of meetings and the high degree of turnover in personnel.

SUMMARY

The focus of this chapter has been the features of committees and the ways in which committees differ from work groups. Committees can vary greatly in size and importance. A common distinction is made between standing (permanent) committees and the temporary committees usually referred to as ad hoc committees or task forces.

Committees are found in organizations and communities. In each case, they are formed to represent varied viewpoints and to include technical expertise. This often leads to conflict and disagreement and, therefore, to some inefficiencies. However, discussion among committee members who hold differing views also leads to common understandings and a broad commitment to decisions that they make.

The members of committees can be strictly representative of the interest groups or factions concerned with the task of the committee. They can also include members with the technical expertise required to solve specific problems. In addition, some committees invite consultants or include non-voting members who have special expertise. A feature of some committees is that the members have widely different status in the organization or community. A single committee may include the very influential person at a high level of authority and employees or citizens who have little influence.

Committee structure usually involves an appointed or elected leader who sometimes is assisted by a vice-chairperson. Subcommittees and staffs of persons hired to perform such tasks as research or legal consultation are common in large committees or in standing committees whose tasks are complicated. The leadership of a committee differs from the supervision of work groups. Leaders must rely on persuasive power to motivate members; supervisors have coercive power.

The infrequency of meetings in committees and a high turnover in membership often prevents people from knowing each other well. As a result, the committee tends to be more formal and task oriented than the work group. Even though committees are often viewed as ineffective and inefficient, they are important in organizations and communities as methods for involving people in making the decisions and resolving the problems that affect their work and lives.

REFLECTING/EXPLORING

1. Review the five topics of this chapter. Choose at least three committees with which you are familiar. How do they differ and how are they similar with respect to each of these five topics? In what ways do you believe these committees might change in order to be more successful?

2. Apply the five topics to one of the committees of which you are a member. Describe your group in terms of each topic. In what ways might you change the nature of your committee to increase its effectiveness? What features would you retain?

3. Compare the committee you used in activity 2 with the work group you used in activity 2 in Chapter 22. What conclusions can you draw about the difference between a work group and a committee based on this comparison?

4. Ask the librarian in your local library to assist you in obtaining government publications that include descriptions and organizational charts of the structure of the Congress of the United States. Review the five topics of this chapter as you examine the characteristics of the large, complex committee structure of Congress. What conclusions can you draw about the difference between Congressional committees and the one you described in activity 2?

5. Obtain information about your city government's committee structure. Analyze your city government according to the five topics in this chapter. In what ways can you become involved in this structure to influence the decisions that affect your life?

CHAPTER 24

NEGOTIATING TEAMS

Travel with us to five widely separated locations. At each stop, we will witness a small portion of a meeting between negotiating teams.

A small town in Georgia, 25 August: At 8:00 A.M., the negotiating teams representing the local school board and the teachers' union meet in the high-school cafeteria. The teachers' contract will expire at midnight on 31 August. Bargaining has continued over the entire summer.

EVELYN MCINTYRE (chief negotiator for the teachers): Dr. Robinson, we spent the weekend studying the proposals you submitted. This morning we would like to discuss the layoff article you proposed.

FRED ROBINSON (associate superintendent and chief negotiator for the school district): Evelyn, we want to talk about salaries. That is the real issue we need to settle. There is no sense in talking about the other provisions of the contract until we settle on salaries.

A motel meeting room in suburban New York, 25 August: At 8:00 A.M., the negotiating teams for HiTech Enterprises and G.C.B. Industries are meeting to work out a possible merger between the two corporations.

CHARLIE HANDER (president of HiTech): Bill, we think we can reach an agreement on this merger. The problem is the way you are evaluating our net worth and per-share value. We have arrived at a much higher figure. Our shareholders deserve a better break than your original offer.

BILL MUSSELMAN (chief executive officer of G.C.B.): Well, Charlie, we thought that was a fair offer. Our finance department examined your books and then had Tice Accounting run a separate analysis. Why don't we talk about how you arrived at your figures? Let's compare notes. Maybe we can come to an agreement today.

A medium-sized city in Montana, 25 August: At 8:00 A.M., the negotiating teams representing the city and the county governments convene in a conference room in the city hall. The topic is the city airport. The city wants the county to assume operating responsibilities for the airport because it serves residents of the outlying areas of the county as well as the city. Several large industrial plants are located in the county beyond the city limits. Their employees constitute almost twenty percent of airport usage on a daily basis.

SANDRA RENSTROM (assistant city manager): We have reviewed the results of last week's session. It seems that we have settled the legal details on the changeover. Our notes indicate that we have also worked through most of the changeover problems with the physical plant and personnel. Now, what is left?

DAVE HESS (county administrator): There is one big problem. The county commission just will not support a total changeover in one year. We don't have the votes for that. Several commissioners believe the city should contribute a part of the operating expenses for the next three years. The city contribution would be based on a decreasing percentage each year for three years.

SANDRA RENSTROM: The city council wants to get out from under the operating expenses. But we might be able to convince them that the city should pay off another $200,000 of the capital debt as a condition of the changeover. Would this satisfy the county commissioners? What do you think, Dave?

A large city in Europe, 25 August: At 8:00 A.M., the negotiating teams for two African countries meet in a large hotel ballroom. The parties consist of twenty persons from each country. They are seated on either side of a long table. The subject is the negotiation of loans and food exchanges between the two countries.

AMBASSADOR FROM COUNTRY A: My distinguished colleague, I am pleased to see you again today. Our efforts of yesterday have born fruit. We see many things in the same way. What shall we discuss this morning?

AMBASSADOR FROM COUNTRY B: My very distinguished colleague, your words are encouraging. We, too, feel that our efforts have been rewarded. We have talked to our prime minister last night and he has authorized us to suggest. . . .

A school district conducts labor negotiations, two corporations bargain about a merger, city and county commissions discuss the changeover in the control of an airport, and representatives of two nations consider exchanges of money and food. When *negotiation* is heard, many people think only of labor–management bargaining over wages and other working conditions. Yet negotiations occur continually in communities, within organizations, and among companies, agencies, corporations, and countries.

Many negotiations are conducted by teams. These negotiating teams are the groups on which this chapter will focus. We will discuss three topics with respect to negotiating teams. These include:

1. The characteristic structure and process of negotiating teams.

2. Adversary and mutual-interest types of negotiation.

3. The influence of mutual-interest negotiations on the structure of negotiating teams.

We will examine each of these topics, beginning with the structure and process of negotiating teams.

Structure and Process of Negotiating Teams

A negotiating team may have as few as two or three or as many as forty or fifty members. Team size often depends on the number and complexity of the issues being negotiated. In spite of size differences, most negotiating teams have similar charcteristics in team structure and group process. Let's examine team structure first and then group process.

The Structure of Negotiating Teams

The most common structural pattern in negotiating teams is one chief negotiator who serves as chairperson for a team. The diagram below illustrates the structure of a typical negotiating team:

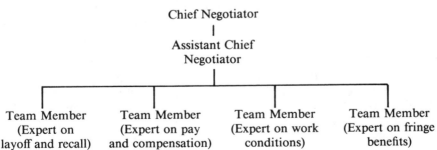

NEGOTIATING TEAM STRUCTURE

Chief Negotiator

Assistant Chief
Negotiator

| Team Member (Expert on layoff and recall) | Team Member (Expert on pay and compensation) | Team Member (Expert on work conditions) | Team Member (Expert on fringe benefits) |

An assistant chief negotiator may be a coleader of the team on a continuing basis or a team member who serves as team leader in the absence of the chief negotiator. Centralized leadership is typical of the structure of negotiating teams.

In a negotiating session, the chief negotiator usually speaks for the team. Other team members may consult with the chief negotiator, but they rarely talk directly with anyone on the other team. If they do communicate with the opposing team, members restrict their comments to carefully worded responses or proposals. The negotiations are conducted by the two chief negotiators.

Team members are selected for one of two reasons: (1) they represent a constituency, or (2) they are technical experts in the subject to be negotiated. On many teams, members are both representatives and experts. The team members for a union frequently represent constituencies (senior members, specialties, trades, or some other interest group). These same union negotiators also develop special expertise in specific areas of the contract. Team structure for a large union may be very complex. It may include economists, accountants, and other technical specialists.

The negotiating team itself may represent a larger department or unit charged with developing bargaining positions and contract language. The following diagram shows an organizational chart for union and management negotiating teams in a corporation. In a union, the negotiating team must be responsive to the bargaining council. The council is under the direction of union officers. The final step in accountability is the union membership. On the opposing side, the management team consists of experts from several areas of the organization. The management team reports to labor-relations or personnel-department executives. These executives are in turn held accountable by the board of directors of the corporation.

The Negotiating Process

A typical negotiating situation involves the exchange of proposals and counter-proposals between teams. The team receiving a proposal studies it and presents a counterproposal. Usually, decisions about proposals and counterproposals are made in private team meetings. Each team determines its positions and the strategies it will use in persuading the other team. When teams meet, the chief negotiators talk to each other rather formally and always within the limits agreed upon by the team in private sessions. If one team presents a radically new or different suggestion, the other team requests a recess. During the recess, team members discuss the new proposal. The team expert in the area of the new proposal advises the rest of the team. They agree on a position and prepare a presentation for the other team.

The negotiating process is relatively formal. It consists of cautious movement back and forth between adversaries who do not trust each other. This traditional negotiation also involves various public-relations strategies. These include news releases and media interviews. Their purpose is to gain the support of various publics.

NEGOTIATING TEAMS

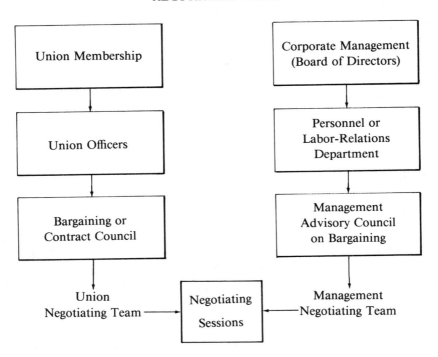

Adversarial and Mutual-Interest Negotiation

A standard view of negotiation is one in which two parties bargain and compromise their way to an agreement. Each team begins with proposals that include extreme requests because both teams understand that the process involves compromise. In essence, the two teams are adversaries. This traditional type of negotiation is called *adversary negotiation*. Fundamental problems inherent in the adversarial form of negotiation have spurred the recent development of *mutual-interest negotiation*. Let's explore adversarial negotiation first. Then we will describe the mutual interest approach.

Adversarial Negotiation

Here is a decription of a typical adversarial negotiating situation.

Cott Corporation has contracted with Banner Supply to provide 10,000 parts at a price of $4.65 each. The price was based on drawings and specifications provided by Cott. After sixty days of tooling design and initial production managers at Banner Supply realized they could not produce the parts for $4.65. Instead, it would require a per-piece cost of $5.15 to make even a slim profit. Banner approached the purchasing department of Cott Corporation to request an increase in price.

This is a typical industrial situation. Each side has vested interests. Cott Corporation wants the 10,000 parts and wants them at the required level of quality and as inexpensively as possible. Banner Supply wants the business to make a profit. The contract is worth $46,500 to them. However, they stand to lose approximately $5,000 on it. Banner's managers would like to break even at least. They would prefer to make a profit.

In adversarial negotiation, the two sides establish their positions. Here is Cott's position: You, Banner, signed a contract to provide 10,000 parts at $4.65 each in 120 days. The contract is legal. We intend to enforce it. Here is Banner's position: Yes, we signed the contract, but as it stands, we will lose money. If we cancel now, we will lose about $3,500. If we deliver the full 10,000 parts, we will lose $5,000. We want to raise the price to $5.15 so that we can break even. If you do not agree to raising the price, we will stop manufacturing the parts. You will receive no supplies from us. We will scrap the 500 parts we have manufactured to date.

The negotiators meet in a small conference room at the headquarters for Cott Corporation on Monday morning. Each team outlines a position. Banner opens. Cott responds. Then the bargaining begins. Their talk focuses on price. Cott wants to see the pricing figures that support the estimate of $5.15. They argue with the methods used to obtain and analyze the data. Banner justifies its pricing analysis. The representative from purchasing on the Cott team proposes to increase the price to $4.90. (Cott paid $4.90 to another supplier last quarter. Of course, Cott will not reveal this information to Banner.) Banner states that they will still lose $2,500. Cott reminds Banner that they will already have lost $3,500 if they cancel now. After two hours of talk, Banner agrees to a price of $4.90. Cott is satisfied because they obtain the parts at the same price they paid last quarter.

This is adversarial negotiation. It has been called *win-lose bargaining.* Banner has lost and Cott came out even. Cott is not a big winner, but certainly they have not lost. Probably each team has negative feelings toward the other team.

These negative feelings that arise in the win-lose circumstances of adversarial bargaining are the main problem with this type of negotiation. Nevertheless, this is the most common form of negotiation. In labor disputes, management offers a salary increases of 2 percent and the employees ask for 16 percent. A senior employee in the organization predicts that the final settlement will be between 7 and 9 percent. Her reasoning? Subtract 2 percent from 16 percent for 14 percent. Divide 14 percent in half as a result of the bargaining process. The result is 7 percent. On the other hand, add 2 percent and 16 percent for 18 percent. Half of this is 9 percent. (Actually, the final settlement was for 7.5 percent!)

We expect teams to begin at extremes: One team begins at an unrealistically high level. The other team opens bargaining at a level that seems ridiculously low. Both parties develop strategies in private and then meet to move toward compromise. It may be that a 7.5 percent increase is considerably higher than the union expected to receive and considerably lower than the management expected to offer. However, neither side may know the other side is pleased with the final figure until after negotiations are completed.

Mutual-Interest Negotiation

Adversarial bargaining emphasizes the differences between teams. However, both parties have mutual interests. In the conflict over pricing between Cott Corporation and Banner Supply, it is to the benefit of both companies to have the parts manufactured by Banner. If Banner backs out of the contract, Cott must order parts from another supplier with a possible delay in the delivery date and a higher price. Banner will lose the entire order and probably eliminate opportunities for additional orders from Cott in the future.

In mutual-interest bargaining, instead of proposing extreme positions, the teams identify their common concerns. The negotiation process then becomes a means for arriving at a solution that satisfies all or most of the interests of both teams. In other words, negotiation becomes a mutual problem-solving process rather than a situation characterized by hidden strategies and negative feelings. While adversarial bargaining is a win-lose proposition, mutual-interest negotiation has been characterized as a win-win situation.

In the pricing conflict between Cott and Banner, it is in Cott's interest to receive the parts on time and at the lowest possible price. It is in Banner's interest to complete the contract and not lose money. The question becomes, how can the interests of both Cott and Banner be met?

It would seem initially that both interests cannot be met equally. If Cott agrees to a price of $5.15 so that Banner can break even, the price is above what Cott has paid in the past. On the other hand, a price of less than $5.15 results in a profit loss for Banner.

There is a solution. An astute purchasing agent at Cott might have suggested the solution if a manager from Banner did not. Cott will need more parts in the future. In fact, they will need another order as soon as the next quarter. Cott could give Banner a contract for another 10,000 parts to be delivered three months after the initial order. In this way, Banner could spread the costs of fixed expenses, tooling, for example, over a larger number of units. There would also be an additional cost savings. Management and employees at Banner will learn how to make the parts in less-expensive ways over a period of time. Cott and Banner could agree to a price below $4.90, but still high enough so that Banner could make a profit on the second order. A price of $4.75 or $4.80 for 20,000 parts, instead of $4.90 for 10,000 parts, would solve the problem.

If this type of solution had been proposed, the net result would be that the interests of both parties would have been met. Instead of negative feelings, a positive relationship would have resulted. Team members would have felt pleased about themselves, each other, and their working relationships. These positive relationships usually result in two groups working cooperatively to develop the most inexpensive methods for producing high-quality products. Positive relationships are the major benefit of mutual-interest negotiations.

Benefits of Mutual-Interest Negotiations

If mutual-interest bargaining comes into common use, the basic structure of negotiation teams will probably change. The differences between the processes inherent in the mutual-interest and adversarial forms of negotiation will force changes in team structure. Instead of exchanges restricted to chief negotiators, mutual-interest bargaining sessions will be more like traditional problem-solving discussions in which every person is encouraged to participate. It will be necessary for both teams to state their interests openly and explore options honestly.

The chief negotiator will be expected to maintain a wide perspective, while individual members become involved in the minute details of their personal interests, expertise, or representation. The leader of the team will need to understand the abilities of team members to participate in problem-solving discussions. It may be less important for the team leader to have expertise in every area being negotiated. The role of the chief negotiator may be closer to that of an athletic coach. The leader will devise a game plan, see that team members are prepared, and make some decisions during the game. The actual playing of the game will be left to team members.

The role of the team member will change, too. In adversarial bargaining, the members function as advisors to the chief negotiator. They warn the leader of risks, look for loopholes, and offer technical information. The mutual-interest team member will talk with members from the other team. All of the expertise required for adversarial negotiations will still be required. In addition, team members will have to think quickly. They will need the skill of brainstorming, the willingness to explore unusual ideas, and the desire to agree to the most workable solutions that meet the interests represented by both teams.

There are decided advantages to mutual-interest negotiation. There is less mistrust and anger between parties. The process is characterized by openness and cooperation. As mutual-interest bargaining becomes widespread, the bargaining teams will acquire a new look. This in turn means new skills in communication for both chief negotiators and team members.

SUMMARY

Negotiations occur in a variety of settings, not just in labor–management disputes. The presence of agreements and contracts makes negotiating teams necessary. The typical negotiation process involves a team led by a chief negotiator who acts as spokesperson for the team. Team members brief the spokesperson by providing views that represent concerned groups, by offering technical expertise, and by advising on strategies and bargaining positions.

Recently, a method of negotiating has been developed which differs from the traditional adversarial bargaining. The new technique emphasizes the mutual interests of teams. Problem-solving methods are used. If a shift to mutual-interest bargaining occurs in the negotiation process, changes must also occur in the team structure. The chief negotiator will become more like a committee chairperson and less like a spokesperson. The chief negotiator also will become more concerned with the motives and competence of team members and less involved with the technical aspects of the issues under negotiation. Team members will become involved directly in discussions with members of the other team.

REFLECTING/EXPLORING

1. Review articles in your local newspaper that describe negotiations occurring between groups in your community. Identify statements which you believe reflect an adversarial form of negotiating. Then list statements which suggest that mutual-interest negotiations are occurring. To what degree do you believe the newspaper articles are unbiased news

reports? To what extent do you believe the articles are strategic attempts to obtain support for the interests of one of the teams?

2. Talk with a friend who has participated in negotiations or who works in an organization and has been affected by negotiations. Compare this person's descriptions of the negotiation process with the adversarial and mutual-interest processes described in this chapter.

3. Attend a meeting of your local school board that occurs during contract negotiations. Ask questions that help you understand the positions of the chief negotiators for the district and for the teachers. How will their decision affect you and other citizens?

4. Attend meetings of your local city commission when bids are let for construction, maintenance, or other work to be carried out by private businesses. Understanding the negotiation process, what questions might you ask to determine whether that process has resulted in the least expensive cost for the highest quality of work?

5. Contact the offices of your local representatives to state and national government. Ask them to provide you with written documents that will enable you to study the negotiation process as it occurs in the state and national governments or between the government of the United states and other countries. Compare several negotiation situations. What conclusions can you draw?

25

POLICY AND
GOVERNING BOARDS

In the city of Goodrich, a list of the major policy and governing boards includes:

The city commission

The board of trustees of Goodrich College

The board of education

The board of directors of Goodrich Chemical Company

The elders of the presbytery

The council of the United Church

The vestry of the Episcopal Church

The board of trustees of Family and Children's Services of Goodrich

The mental health board of the county of Goodrich

The executive board of the Parent-Teacher Association

The executive committee of the teacher's union

The county commission

The board of the YMCA-YWCA

These boards and commissions are typical of policy and governing boards.

The work of policy and governing boards is to set policies and then oversee their implementation. A policy is a rule or guideline established for an organization. For example, both governments and businesses have vacation policies. A typical vacation policy prescribes which employees earn vacation time, how many days they may take, and when the vacation time may be used. One of the common issues with vacation policy is whether vacation time can be carried over from one year to the next. Most companies insist that all vacation time earned in one year be taken in that year. Otherwise employees could accumulate four to six weeks of vacation time and use it all at once.

Let's listen in on the board of directors of the Colfax Company. The board is meeting to discuss their vacation policy. The vice-president for personnel has just presented the policy. It prescribes which employees earn vacation time, how many days they may take, and when vacation time can be used. These are the usual key points in such a policy. The policy stipulates that every employee earns two weeks of vacation each year, that accumulation begins on the date of hire and extends for one calendar year, that each person is eligible for one week of vacation after six months and two weeks after twelve months, and that the vacation must be taken within six months of the time it is earned. If Jerry is hired on 1 July, he is eligible for one week of vacation on 1 January and for two weeks on the following 1 July. He must take the two weeks before the next 1 January or he loses some of it.

DIRECTOR SMITH: Under this policy, can an employee "borrow ahead" on vacation time? For example, could Jerry take two weeks in December?

VICE-PRESIDENT: No. He would have to wait until 1 January. Even though he would only be eligible for one week. If he wanted two weeks, he would have to wait until July.

DIRECTOR KARLINS: That means the employees actually accumulate the time in one week increments, right?

VICE PRESIDENT: Not really. They accumulate some of it every two weeks. That is the pay period. It works out to .54 days of vacation earned every pay period. We have to do that in case they leave. We pay them for accumulated vacation time if they haven't taken it.

DIRECTOR SMITH: So someone could actually take one day of vacation at the end of the first month?

VICE-PRESIDENT: Right.
(Here the directors and the vice-president are clarifying their understanding of the policy.)

DIRECTOR KARLINS: I prefer the system where vacation is earned in a calendar year from 1 January to the following 31 December. It eliminates having to keep track of all this for each employee's working year. Each January all employees start off at zero days and you let them take two weeks any time in the next twelve months.

VICE-PRESIDENT: The problem with that is that the employee may take two weeks in July and quit in September. That person has gotten about four days of vacation that weren't earned.
(Here the Board is discussing an alternative to their policy. This conversation went on for a while and then the following discussion occurred.)

DIRECTOR SMITH: I would like to see the policy written so that it makes clear that vacation shall be taken in such a way that no work unit is below the staffing needed to accomplish its work. If everyone takes off in one work unit for the same two weeks in August we wouldn't have any inspectors, for example.

DIRECTOR CARLINO: I think it should be even more specific. It should say that you cannot have two employees on vacation from the same work unit or section at the same time. That would eliminate the problem entirely.

PRESIDENT: Wait a minute. If we do that we are getting into operations and not policy. We are telling managers how to schedule vacations during the year. We should let them work that out with their employees.
(The president has jumped in because the board has crossed the line from developing policy into the area of day-to-day supervision and operations.)

In practice, policy making often overlaps the actual operations. If the written policy does not apply specifically to a situation, managers create policy as they supervise operations. The interpretations managers place on the written policy create rules and practices that may not have been intended by the policy makers. In addition, many policy makers intentionally insert themselves in day-to-day operations. A city commission may not agree with the way the mayor or city manager has assigned merit raises. The commissioners may override the decision, or request that it be changed. The commissioners become managers by stepping into operations.

This chapter is about the groups who make policies and oversee their implementation. In discussing policy and governing boards, we will examine four topics:

1. Boards may be either public or private.

2. The structure of boards is formal.

3. Group processes in boards tend to be formal and political.

4. Boards are bound by legal and formal requirements that affect meetings, agendas, minutes, and the election or appointment of members and leaders.

Public or Private Boards

Policy-setting boards can be divided into two types: public and private. This is a crucial distinction. There are laws about the operations of public boards. Such boards are usually established by law. In some states there are laws specifying the operating procedures of public boards. These specifications may include a rule that all public boards must hold open meetings, for example. Anyone may attend an open meeting, including members of the press. If a public board operates under such a law, there are few situations in which it may go into executive session and exclude the public and press.

Private boards either create their own rules or rules are created by the total membership. They establish their own bylaws and function according to a constitution or other written documents adopted by the organization. Their meetings may be open or closed. The actions of such boards are not regulated by law.

Both public and private boards have an important similarity: They are legally responsible for their actions. Public boards may make a decision that binds the local government to contracts or commits it to specific actions. When a county commission acts on a zoning case, the decision has legal force. If the commissioners decide that prefabricated houses cannot be erected in Estes Park, Colorado, no one can build a home of this type in that location. Private boards are also legally responsible for their actions. If the board of directors of a corporation declares a dividend, the treasurer must pay the dividend to all stockholders. If the board of a church accepts the bid of a contractor to build an addition on the sanctuary, the contract is legally binding. The legal responsibility of boards has a definite effect on their behavior and their communication.

Another feature of public and private boards involves their membership. Often there is duplication of membership on the boards of a community. The president of the local bank, who serves on the bank's board of directors, may also be on the board of one or more local industries. At the same time, he or she may serve as a member of the board of a church or other community organization. Such community service promotes the banking business. The community organization benefits, too. When a banker is on a board, expertise about and access to financial services may be enhanced. The result of such duplicate membership on boards is a small community network of very powerful people. They serve on numerous boards and see each other frquently at board meetings.

Formal Structure

Because of their legal standing, boards tend to be structured in formal ways. Their structure is usually formally established in written documents (a constitution and bylaws). A typical structure for a board of directors of a small corporation is shown on the following page.

The chairman of the board is the formal leader. Note that three members of the board are officers of the corporation: the board chairman, the company president, and the company vice-president. Two directors are not employed by the corporation. Finally, there is one staff person, the secretary to the board. The secretary sees to it that minutes of board meetings are taken and distributed, that the agenda for meetings is duplicated and circulated well in advance of each meeting, and that arrangements are made for board meetings. These arrangements may include lodging and meals for the two outside directors if they live out of town.

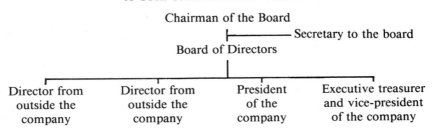

A CORPORATE BOARD STRUCTURE

The membership of a policy or governing board is dictated by two factors: representation and expertise.

Representation

Most boards attempt to include members who represent various constituencies. For elected boards in communities, representation is provided by the voting process. For appointed boards, it is the responsibility of the authority who makes appointments to ensure the representation of necessary interest groups. The board of an agency may include persons who have connections with other agencies or with clients. Some boards include present or former clients because they have a high degree of enthusiasm for the work of the agency. Membership may also be given to influential persons in the community in order to take advantage of their connections.

Expertise

Boards must include members who (1) understand budgets and (2) are familiar with legislative processes. Such expertise is needed in board deliberations. These board members act as consultants to the rest of the board. As a result of these two criteria for selecting board members, meetings tend to be colored by a combination of the political processes of representation and the technical processes of expert consultation. The natural result is both formal and political procedures and group processes.

Formality and Politics

The standard procedures used in board meetings are based upon parliamentary procedure. Since the actions of boards have legal weight, it is necessary to record exactly what was approved or disapproved and who voted in the decision. These decisions must be recorded. The formal processes of making, seconding, discussing, and voting on motions is appropriate under these circumstances. The use of agendas and minutes provides a record of issues that come before a board and the actions taken by the board.

Group processes in boards tend to be political because of the representative nature of board memberships. The members represent interest groups and speak for them in meetings. Sometimes board members form coalitions. Review the board meeting of the Pinedale Church in Chapter 15. Notice the political overtones in that discussion.

The political nature of board processes is encouraged by three factors.

Meetings are held infrequently. Most board meetings occur monthly. Some boards meet as infrequently as twice each year. Consequently, there is little opportunity for members to know each other well. When they are together, members are in a formal meeting. For this reason, the group process is likely to be formal and socially proper.

Board members tend to be geographically dispersed. In large corporations or national associations, members may come from all parts of the United States. Even in local communities, board members represent different neighborhoods. Some boards of international groups may well include members from different parts of the world. The opportunity for people to meet informally and to develop personal relationships is reduced.

Informal meetings are prohibited. In many states, informal meetings of public boards are prohibited by law. These boards may not meet in closed session and they may not hold meetings that have not been announced well in advance. Consequently, members do not have the opportunity to discuss issues and positions before a meeting. However, some members may telephone each other or have lunch together to discuss board business. Rarely do these informal meetings include the total board membership. As is true of the previous two factors, this factor promotes both the formality and the politics that characterize group process in and between board meetings.

Legal and Formal Requirements

All boards that govern or set policy are bound by legal and formal requirements. The membership of the association or organization, the stockholders, or state and federal agencies set the requirements. Rules are established for (1) meetings, (2) agendas, (3) minutes, (4) the election or appointment of members, and (5) leaders.

Meetings

Board meetings often must be at an announced time and place. Public boards must meet in open session. Closed or executive sessions are permitted only to discuss such topics as the hiring or firing of an individual. Real estate purchases may also be negotiated in private. For example, if a school board wants to build a new school and needs to purchase land in a specific location, an enterprising broker could purchase all the available land in the area and then ask the board to pay an excessive price. Consequently, school boards usually discuss such matters in private and make the purchase with very little advance notice.

Agendas

Normally, the agenda for any board is published well ahead of the meeting. It is difficult to add items to the agenda after it has been published. The board members must have notice of the issues to be discussed. They need to prepare for discussion and debate. In addition, persons who may wish to attend public board meetings must be given notice of the specific items to be discussed at each meeting. If the local highway commission is going to discuss the removal of seventeen large oak trees in order to widen an arterial road, the local residents must be given an opportunity to protest. They must be given ample notice of the meeting at which the tree removal will be discussed.

Minutes

The minutes of boards are the only official and legal record of decisions. The minutes should be extremely accurate. In the case of boards which meet in closed session, the minutes are the only public information about the discussion. Outsiders do not have the right to know exactly what was said and what positions were taken by various board members. They do have the right to know what decisions were made. The minutes of board meetings may range from a very minimal recording of the motions, seconds, amendments, and votes, to a very detailed description of the proceedings. Such detailed descriptions may even include appendices that present exhibits or data in support of decisions.

Election or Appointment of Members

Board members are chosen and take office in one of three ways:

1. For some boards, members are elected by citizens, stockholders, or others who have an investment in the association, government, or organization. In effect, these boards are constituted through a process of election by persons who are not members of the board.

2. Board members may be appointed by an authority. This is a common practice in government. Zoning boards are appointed by a mayor or by the city commission. Members of federal boards (the Federal Trade Commission or the Federal Reserve Board, for example) are appointed by the president of the United States. Some presidential appointments require the approval of Congress.

3. There also are self-constituting boards. For example, the board of one human-service agency consists of twelve people. A nominating committee exists within the board. The board members serve for three-year terms with the understanding that no member serves a second term. The nominating committee is responsible for identifying people who will be willing to serve and who have the needed expertise or represent relevant constituencies. The full board votes at the end of each year for the members who will be added to the board as the terms of current board members come to an end. Guidelines are included in written documents so the board has rules for continuously reconstituting itself.

Election or Appointment of Leaders

There are two basic ways in which the leadership of boards is determined:

1. A board may select its own leaders. This is common with public boards and commissions. For example, county commissioners are elected by the public. At their first meeting, the commissioners elect a chairperson for the commission. In addition, they assign members to committees and memberships. Each committee is provided with a leader. Some board members may meet (caucus) in a small group to discuss which members might be effective leaders. Afterwards, the board votes in a meeting open to all members. The majority party in government boards tends to dominate their proceedings. In the Congress of the United States, the majority party selects the Speaker of the House. That person holds a meeting, or party caucus, at which the party members vie for committee memberships and positions as committee chairpersons. Each committee then meets to form subcommittees and select a chairperson. A board or commission structures itself in these ways when there is no higher authority or outside force to do it.

2. Some boards and commissions obtain members through election or through appointment by persons who are not members. The position of chairperson of corporate board of directors is filled by a ballot provided to shareholders. In many cities, there is an election for the mayor and city council members or

commissioners. Professional associations also hold elections for offices such as president, vice-president, and treasurer. These officers become members of the board.

SUMMARY

Businesses, governments, associations, and organizations include a governing board that oversees operations. These boards determine policy and set guidelines which are used by managers to coordinate daily work. In practice, policy and operations overlap and it is difficult to distinguish them.

Boards may be either public or private. Public boards must meet openly and permit comment from citizens and other concerned individuals. Private boards are held responsible by their constituencies.

Boards are structured in formal ways. The leadership usually consists of a chairperson and a vice-chairperson. Chairpersons of different committees may be part of the leadership structure in large "boards" such as the Congress of the United States. Board members are persons who bring special financial or legal expertise to the board, and individuals who are representative of relevant constituencies. By virtue of their relatively infrequent meetings, their dispersed membership, and their interest-group representation, board processes tend to become political.

Meetings are either open or closed. Agendas usually are distributed well in advance of meetings (they must be published for public boards). Minutes are kept and must be made available and kept on file. Membership is most often determined by election or appointment. Some boards select their own new members. The leader of a board may be selected by members. Members may be elected or appointed. Such elections and appointments are by constituencies or authorities who are not members of the boards.

REFLECTING/EXPLORING

1. Attend a city commission meeting, a meeting of the board of elders of a local church, and a meeting of the parent-teacher association in a local school. Compare the structure and the process of these groups. How are they similar and different? In what ways do the decisions made by these groups affect your life? In what ways can you affect their decisions?

2. Obtain information about the board membership of groups in your community. Consult the chamber of commerce or the reference librarian at the public library. What duplication exists either in specific members or in the interest groups or companies represented by members? How does the duplication affect the processes in and among the various boards?

3. Visit a stock brokerage in your community and request copies of the annual reports for various businesses and industries. Compare them in terms of their structure and of the type of information provided to stockholders. What conclusions can you draw about the boards of these groups?

4. Obtain copies of the written documents that contain the policies intended to govern your place of work. To what degree do you believe these policies are put into practice as written? In what ways do managers and supervisors make policy as they coordinate the work of the organization?

5. Determine the procedure you must follow if you wish to influence policy making in an organization of which you are a part. Compare information that exists in writing with the actual practices used to influence the board. To what extent are they consistent?

CHAPTER 26

TELECONFERENCING

Sam Perkins, Judy Elmore, and Dick Dyker sat in a conference room in San Diego. They were conversing with Elizabeth Jones and Al Jackson in New Haven, Connecticut. In two rooms, one on the West Coast and the other on the East Coast, there was an array of equipment. At the front of the room was a large screen displaying a picture of the people on the other side of the continent. Speakers on either side of the screen projected the voices of the participants. In addition, a second screen displayed various charts and graphs in the sequence requested by the participants. There was also a keyboard and a printer in each room.

The meeting started with Sam Perkins introducing Judy and Dick to Elizabeth and Al. Then Sam outlined the purpose of the meeting, which was to review progress on a new personnel assessment form to be used at all corporate division offices. This form has been a "hot topic" in the corporation. Prior editions of the evaluation sheets were heavily criticized by managers as well as by employees. It is important to get a good replacement form out. The latest edition of the form appeared on the auxiliary display screens in both cities. As he talked, Sam was able to move an electronic marker around on the form to correspond with his comments. At one point, Elizabeth Jones interrupted to indicate that she had collected some information on the form and would be sending it over phone lines to the printer. The participants in San Diego could see her move over to the electronic keyboard, punch a few keys, and then resume her seat. Within ten seconds, the printer in San Diego was quickly and quietly putting the data onto paper. Dick stood up, removed the paper from the printer, and put it into a copier. Thus within five minutes all the participants had copies of Elizabeth's data. This occurred while Sam was still reviewing the status of the form.

This was, of course, a teleconference. The half-hour conference cost less than the price of airline tickets, hotel rooms, and meals for two or three people to travel to the other coast. In addition, it saved the corporation the time lost in such travel. A few minutes after the conference was over, all five participants were back at their desks.

Teleconferences are meetings that take advantage of modern technologies. In this chapter, we will explore information that will help teleconference participants. We will explore:

1. Four types of teleconferencing

2. Advantages and disadvantages of teleconferencing

3. The effects of teleconferencing on group tasks and group process

Let's begin by describing the types of teleconferencing that are currently available.

Four Types of Teleconferencing

The types of teleconferences can be categorized by the technology used to transmit and display messages. There are audio, computer, and video conferences, and a version in which audio, video and computer are combined.

Audio teleconferencing. Audio teleconferencing is the oldest and most widely used of the four methods. It was called the *conference call* in the past. Three or more people converse over telephones. Almost all telephone systems in organizations have conference call capability. Many home telephone installations also have the capacity for conference calls. Obviously, messages are restricted to the voice. People cannot see each other nor can they transmit written materials or pictures.

Computer teleconferencing. Computer teleconferencing has potential for people in professions or organizations who must be in touch over long periods of time. Each participant has a computer terminal, a keyboard, a video display, and a printer. The conferences may occur over a period of weeks or even months.

One person will initiate such a conference by posing a problem or situation to which others can respond. Each person involved can sit at a terminal and make suggestions, provide data, or ask questions. This is done by typing the messages, which are first stored in the computer and then transmitted to every other person on demand. Since all of the messages are stored, there is a cumulative record of every item of information generated in the course of the conference. Clearly this is a different kind of conference than the usual face-to-face interaction. That interaction moves quickly and has limited, or no, records.

Video teleconferencing. When pictures of the participants are sent and received, the result is called *videoconferencing.* Voices are also transmitted. Videoconferencing is close to an actual face-to-face conversation between people. The cost is higher than audio or computer conferencing. For technical reasons, it takes much more "space" on a circuit to send both picture and sound.

The most common form of video teleconferencing is described in the conference that opened this chapter. In each meeting location, people sit in a room with a screen at the front. They are able to see the people in the other location. The camera is located at the front of the room and focused on the participants. Ideally, the screen and image size permit the people in the other location to appear roughly life-size. They seem to be seated at the other end of the table or room from the people who are viewing them on the screen. Although not commonly available, it is also technically feasible to use a split-screen technique so that people at three or more locations can participate simultaneously.

Multi-mode teleconferencing. The ultimate in teleconferencing involves the multiple modes described in the conference on page 326. Video pictures show the participants. Their voices also are transmitted. In addition, there are display devices by means of which tables, charts, graphs, and pictures can be transmitted and shown at each location. There are also video display terminals connected through computers and printers to permit the exchange of documents and text.

Advantages and Disadvantages of Teleconferencing

Cost is a major advantage of teleconferencing. The impersonal nature of meeting via media is a significant disadvantage. We will evaluate the use of computer, voice, video, and multiple-mode connections.

The most obvious advantage to all types of teleconferencing is the cost. When people must travel to meetings, time and money is required for travel. In addition, the participants must be housed and fed. When people must travel to another state or country there are high costs involved. A 500-mile business trip for one person using air transportation and reasonable hotel accommodations can cost $300 to $400 for one or two days. Longer distances and longer stays increase the cost considerably. To have three people travel across the country and stay for three days can cost $2500 or more for travel. (Lost work time must be considered a cost also.)

Getting people together by telephone is always less costly than a face-to-face meeting. Even the use of the more costly computer or video channels is less expensive than travel. In some cases, it may be impossible for people to meet face-to-face because of international travel restrictions or job demands.

The most obvious disadvantage is that any electronic medium is less personal than meeting face-to-face in the same room. Being able to shake hands and establish eye contact is important in many situations. Seeing how someone reacts to a suggestion is very helpful. This is difficult if not impossible, even with video.

The use of computer, voice, video, and multiple channels also includes advantages and disadvantages specific to each mode.

Computer links. Computer teleconferencing is the most impersonal of these techniques. Interaction is limited to words printed on a screen or paper. The feelings associated with ideas can be transmitted only in writing. Nonverbal cues do not exist. Instead of being able to say something forcefully, the computer teleconferencer must resort to: "We need to get on with the data analysis. (I feel strongly about this!)" Written dialogue is less immediate and less human than spoken words.

This disadvantage is balanced by the precision that is possible with computer links. Equations, statistics, and exact wording can be transmitted. In addition, all of the information stored is ready to be recalled any time it is needed. Thus, the exact value in the results of an experiment or the precise legal phrase used in a contract can be called up and looked at by any participant. Computer links are more likely to be used in very technical or legalistic settings.

Time is the other big factor in computer links. Responses are slow. It may take a day, even a week, for everyone to access the computer file and respond to a question or message. Fast decisions are difficult or impossible.

Voice links. Talking to someone is faster than typing messages on a keyboard, but still lacks the highly personal features of talking face-to-face. Most of us are accustomed to talking on the telephone to relatives, friends, and business associates. Problems do occur in teleconferencing by voice link alone. One difficulty is in determining who can or should speak next. In a meeting, people look at each other or make movements which indicate they want to talk. The speaker can relinquish the "floor" to the next speaker. This is difficult to ascertain when the other people cannot be seen.

In addition, the inability to see responses and interpret their meaning makes it difficult to assess how a message is received. The voice link is faster than the computer link but still impersonal. Clearly, it is also less accurate, unless the conference members are willing to do a great deal of careful re-reading and comparison of data or information.

Video links. Being able to see someone, even if only on a television or projection screen, is better than not having any image available. The major disadvantages of video links have nothing to do with communication. They are matters of cost and facilities. The transmission lines for video are much more expensive than for voice. Each "conference room" is actually a small TV studio equipped with camera, microphones, monitor, projection equipment, and screen.

Because of the newness of video teleconferencing, people are likely to think that they are part of a television production rather than participants in a meeting. This belief in turn creates a certain self-consciousness. On the other hand, the ability to see the faces and upper bodies of the people in the other location does help make the conference slightly more personal.

Multiple-channel links. By combining audio, video, computer, and display links, the different advantages can be built into a single, more-effective teleconferencing method. (Naturally, the cost also increases.) Video and audio make the conference more human. People are able to see and hear each other, allowing nonverbal cues to be sent and received. Enthusiasm or caution can be communicated. Visual display links allow graphs, charts, pictures, and tables to be viewed simultaneously in both locations just as they would be in a face-to-face conference. The computer connection facilitates the precision and accuracy necessary for technical or legal purposes.

Effects of Teleconferencing

Some research has been done on teleconferencing. The results permit managers and leaders to make better decisions about when to use teleconferencing. The findings also allow meeting participants to understand some of the limitations of teleconferencing. It is also helpful for participants to have some insight into the feelings that may occur in a teleconference setting. Some of the research on teleconferencing is summarized in a recent book entitled *Electronic Meetings*. The authors describe the results of their survey of the research studies. The results can be analyzed according to the effects of teleconferencing on tasks, on interpersonal relations, and on group process. We will explore both areas.

Effects on tasks. Some tasks seem to be more suited to teleconferencing than others. The research has shown that teleconferencing is suited to the exchange of information. Clearly, this kind of task is best facilitated by computer teleconferencing, but audio and video modes are also effective. Giving instructions or orders can also be accomplished by teleconferencing methods. Research has suggested that generating ideas was also done effectively through teleconferencing.

Face-to-face meetings are viewed as more effective for bargaining or negotiating sessions. Also, face-to-face exchanges are much more useful in developing relationships between people. The ability to continue conversations socially after a meeting is over seems to be important in this regard.

According to the research, reaching consensus and voting may be difficult through teleconferencing. The early steps in problem solving—defining the problem and generating solutions—may well be accomplished with teleconferencing. However, the subsequent steps—evaluating solutions and arriving at consensus—could be more difficult. Teleconferencing may be more appropriate to tasks which are highly structured and in which the leader has a high degree of authority. Such tasks lend themselves to the limited time frame and distant, impersonal relationships experienced in the teleconferencing situation.

Effect on process. The research seemed to confirm that meetings conducted through teleconferencing were more orderly than face-to-face discussions. This suggests that some of the spontaneous features of group process in face-to-face meetings are eliminated through the use of voice or video links.

Teleconferences have advantages for goal-oriented decision making. Teleconferences lend focus and objectivity. More sources of information are used in the process of reaching a decision. The teleconference appears more formal than personal meetings because explicit procedures are used.

The teleconference is satisfactory for meetings in which the task is structured and people work well with each other. If goals are not well defined and there are possible disagreements or conflicts, a face-to-face meeting would probably be more successful. Similarly, for motivating a group, and for establishing working relationships among members, face-to-face meetings are beneficial.

Teleconferencing is neither a panacea that will solve the problem of meetings between distant parties, nor an evil that should be avoided at all costs. There are advantages and disadvantages to teleconferences. The same holds true for face-to-face meetings. Some people may be tempted to hold a teleconference simply because it is new and fashionable. Others may see it as a real cost-saving measure in large organizations with far-flung operations.

An intelligent use of teleconferencing will take into account its advantages and disadvantages as a meeting technique. It should be considered in the light of a specific situation. It should not be looked upon simplistically as a technological wonder nor used automatically as a cost-cutting measure.

SUMMARY

There are three basic forms of teleconferencing. The use of computer keyboards, displays, and printers can be effective in long-range technical information exchange and problem solving. The standard conference call, using voice links, allows much more rapid exchanges, but suffers from a lack of ability to use visual, nonverbal messages. By adding video links and showing people how those at the other end are acting and reacting, the teleconference comes closer to the face-to-face meeting.

Overall, teleconferencing tends to make meetings more formal, slower paced, more focused, and more objective. More information sources are used in decision making. Exchanging information, giving instructions, and generating ideas can be done effectively through teleconferencing methods. Development of relationships, conflict management, and bargaining may be better suited to face-to-face meetings.

The teleconference is a new technological method for group meetings. Teleconferencing can save time and money and can be an exciting adventure. The methods need to be used wisely, however.

SECTION EIGHT: READING LIST

Information on groups in particular settings:

Baird, J. E., Jr. *Positive Personnel Practices: Quality Circles.* Prospect Heights, IL: Waveland Press, 1982.

Fisher, R. and W. Ury. *Getting to Yes: Negotiating Agreement without Giving In.* Boston: Houghton Mifflin, 1981.

Johnson, R., J. Vallee, and K. Spangler. *Electronic Meetings: Technical Alternatives and Social Choices.* Reading, MA: Addison-Wesley, 1979.

Payne, R. and C. L. Cooper. *Groups at Work.* New York: Wiley and Sons, 1981.

Raiffa, H. *The Art and Science of Negotiation.* Cambridge, MA: Harvard University Press, 1982.

INDEX

INDEX

NTC COMMUNICATION BOOKS

Speech Communication
Getting Started in Public Speaking, *Prentice and Payne*
Listening by Doing, *Galvin*
Person to Person, *Galvin and Book*
Person to Person Workbook, *Galvin and Book*
Speaking by Doing, *Buys, Sills and Beck*
Self-Awareness, *Ratliffe and Herman*
Literature Alive, *Gamble and Gamble*
Contemporary Speech, *Hopkins and Whitaker*
Creative Speaking, *Buys, et al.*

Business Communication .
Business Communication Today!, *Thomas and Fryar*
Successful Business Writing, *Sitzmann*
Successful Business Speaking, *Fryar and Thomas*
Successful Interviewing, *Sitzmann and Garcia*
Successful Problem Solving, *Fryar and Thomas*
Working in Groups, *Ratliffe and Stech*
Effective Group Communication, *Stech and Ratliffe*

For further information or a current catalog, write:
National Textbook Company
4255 West Touhy Avenue
Lincolnwood, Illinois 60646-1975 U.S.A.